LOVE YOUR WORK, RECLAIM YOUR LIFE

Maggie Hamilton's working life in the public and private sectors has included senior roles in book publishing and broadcasting. She has expertise in self-development, and is a regular media commentator in this area. Maggie gives frequent talks, lectures and workshops; writes for magazines; and is a keen observer of social trends. Her books include *Coming Home: Rediscovering Our Sacred Selves*.

www.maggiehamilton.org

LOVE YOUR WORK,
RECLAIM YOUR LIFE

MAGGIE HAMILTON

VIKING
an imprint of
PENGUIN BOOKS

Viking

Penguin Group (Australia)
250 Camberwell Road, Camberwell, Victoria 3124, Australia
Penguin Books Ltd
80 Strand, London WC2R 0RL, England
Penguin Group (USA) Inc.
375 Hudson Street, New York, New York 10014, USA
Penguin Books, a division of Pearson Canada
10 Alcorn Avenue, Toronto, Ontario, Canada M4V 3B2
Penguin Group (NZ)
cnr Airborne and Rosedale Roads, Albany, Auckland 1310, New Zealand
Penguin Books (South Africa) (Pty) Ltd
24 Sturdee Avenue, Rosebank, Johannesburg 2196, South Africa
Penguin Books India (P) Ltd
11, Community Centre, Panchsheel Park, New Delhi 110 017, India

First published by Penguin Group (Australia),
a division of Pearson Australia Group Pty Ltd, 2004

10 9 8 7 6 5 4 3 2 1

Cover design by Sandy Cull © Penguin Group (Australia)
Text design by Louise Leffler © Penguin Group (Australia)
Typeset in 11.5/16.5pt Fairfield by Post Pre-press Group, Brisbane, Queensland
Printed in Australia by McPherson's Printing Group, Maryborough, Victoria

National Library of Australia
Cataloguing-in-Publication data:

Hamilton, Maggie, 1953–.
Love your work, reclaim your life.

Bibliography.
Includes index.
ISBN 0 670 04186 6.

1. Work environment. 2. Job stress. 3. Work – Psychological aspects. I. Title.

331.256

www.penguin.com.au

When the deepest part of you becomes engaged in what you are doing, when your activities and actions become gratifying and purposeful, when what you do serves both yourself and others, and when you do not tire within but seek the sweet satisfaction of your life and your work . . . then you are doing what you were meant to be doing.

GARY ZUKAV, THE SEAT OF THE SOUL

For my parents, Joan and Douglas,
who inspire me to live each and every moment.

contents

acknowledgements

This book would not have been possible without the time and generous support I have received from so many. My thanks first to Derek, my soulmate of old, who never fails to encourage and support all I do. My appreciation to my parents, Joan and Douglas, for giving me a wider framework for life; and to Pam Sheldrake, who first had the courage to publish me. Thanks to my many friends the world over who continue to love and encourage me in extraordinary ways, and to all who have so generously shared their work experiences, concerns and aspirations. My thanks to Oliver Balch, Corporate Citizenship Company; Jane, Anita and BTG, BTG Studios; Christine Daly, SPC Ardmona; Wendy Canning; Pam Farmer, BT; Andrew Freeman, Freehills; Gary Hirsh, the Enlightened Business Institute; Dyrol Lombard, the Media Trust; Pamela Morgan, the Wellington Women's Loan Fund; Rebecca Murray; Ann-Charlott Paduch; Marit Petersen Pless, the World Diabetes Foundation; and Paul Stevens, Worklife Counselling. I am greatly indebted to my dear friend and agent Selwa Anthony; to my excellent publisher Julie Gibbs, whose confidence and vision mean so much; and to Dan Ruffino, Sally Bateman, Lyn Amy, Bridie Riordan, Anne Rogan, Lindy Leonhardt, Louise Leffler and Sandy Cull for their work and passion. Sincere thanks to my editor, Nicola Young, whose attention to detail has so enriched my work, and to the whole Penguin team for their ongoing commitment and enthusiasm. Most of all, my humble thanks to the Great Spirit – my source, my strength, my inspiration and my constant in this ever-changing world.

introduction

I am certain that after the dust of centuries has passed over our cities, we, too, will be remembered not for victories or defeats in battle or in politics, but for our contribution to the human spirit.
JOHN F. KENNEDY

Why in spite of all we have invested in our work are so many of us so unhappy? At what point did we start sacrificing whole parts of our lives to our work? What has happened to our wider aspirations? And what was the impulse that drove us to put profit before people? Why in spite of our increasing discomfort with work do we continue to perpetuate cultures that crush the human spirit? What act of blindness has caused us to promote those who are morally and creatively bankrupt to positions of leadership? What has caused us to sacrifice so much of what we hold dear for goals that seem nebulous at best?

There have always been challenges around work, but in recent times a dark shadow has fallen across the landscape, and there is much fear and uncertainty abroad. We no longer trust the future. Work has always been linked to survival, but in times past work was also intimately connected with family and community. Now that our work has helped sever these connections, we are left

1

feeling confused, bereft, because in spite of all the focus and energy we devote to our jobs, we seem to achieve little of true worth.

Love Your Work, Reclaim Your Life is not about abandoning work, but about seeing where we are and where, with courage and a renewed sense of vision, we might be. The seeds of this book began almost two decades ago, when in spite of early success in my career in publishing I experienced little joy. The more I achieved, the emptier I became. I knew that something fundamental was wrong with my life, yet what right did I have to be miserable when I seemingly had it all? My work life was rich and full, I enjoyed the support of my peers and the love of many friends, and I shared my life with a beautiful man. Yet somehow this wasn't enough. Increasingly, I experienced a lingering sense of melancholy. I responded by working harder at my job and my relationships, but my freneticism seemed only to fuel my despair. There was a dark space inside that refused to go away. I knew that unless I was able to find a way out, this darkness would consume me utterly. I never told anyone how I was feeling – not my husband, not even close friends – because I felt instinctively that I was the only one who could find the way through what I now recognise as the beginnings of depression.

As I looked at my life more closely, I began to see that while I was successful, I was living by rote – my life had become a never-ending round of activities and responsibilities. I ached to live with more depth and meaning, and with more space. I had always loved being out there and making things happen, yet beneath the constant rush of adrenaline I felt increasingly desperate inside. As I looked more closely at my daily routine, I began to see how my extreme busyness was helping to mask my growing despair. I had become suffocated by the stress and the deadlines and the fatigue. There was never enough time to think, let alone just be. I needed to be able to breathe freely again, to be more spontaneous and more creative, to know myself better, to spend more time with those I loved. I realised that it was time to do something about my despair – and so began an extra-ordinary journey that was to change my life.

Far from leaving work, I remained in publishing, discovering countless ways to enrich the moment for myself and others. My first breakthrough at work came when I learned to meditate. The experience was a profound one, and I knew immediately that this was the space I wanted to inhabit each moment. And so, regardless of how busy my working day was or how much I was travelling, I would meditate each morning. Apart from enjoying a growing sense of peace, clarity and joy at work, I was more energetic – more able to prioritise and to see into the hearts of others, to discern those things needing my attention, and to arrive at the optimum solution with relative ease.

My work continued to open up for me, yet alongside the satisfaction and exhilaration my job brought to my life, I felt compelled to explore life's deeper questions. The more I pursued my quest for knowledge and understanding, the more I met others with equally demanding jobs who were also searching for something more. Then as these individuals began to share with me their stories and their own search for meaning, pieces of life's jigsaw began to fall into place. It was through these friendships forged around work that I became interested in Jung – in the rich world of archetypes and the collective unconscious. It was through work also that I became interested in Siddha Yoga, and in the ancient teachings and impossibly beautiful rituals of Hinduism. From here I began to explore the deep, yet profoundly practical teachings of Buddhism and to familiarise myself with the awesome world-view of the Native Americans, whose respect for the sacredness of all living things was to forever change the way I relate to the natural world. I then discovered the local Theosophical Library down the road from work, and revelled in its extensive collection of spiritual books.

During these years, my work brief and my travel around work continued to grow. I needed a change, and so I left publishing and went to work in broadcasting. There I headed up the public affairs and on-air advertising for fifty-four radio stations and five networks, and was also responsible for a national magazine. Half my team was unionised and the other half was on contract. They had been through a great deal of change, yet together we created a supportive, successful culture, weathering retrenchments, budget cuts and strikes, and developing a cohesive team that was respected by many within and beyond the organisation. When I finally returned to publishing, it was in a climate of retrenchments and takeovers. Yet in the midst of these and other challenges, I enjoyed the deep soul satisfaction of being in the right place at the right time.

I have no doubt that the success I enjoyed during my corporate life was due not only to the honing of my professional expertise, but to the wisdom and insights my studies beyond work afforded me, and to my own sacred practices, because they enabled me to see my working life more intricately and more completely. Inspired, I started to travel to sacred locations in my holidays – from Borobudur, the largest Buddhist temple in the world, in Java; and the great south-western desert of the United States; to the ancient city of Sukhothai in northern Thailand; and the exquisite standing stones of Avebury in England. On each of these and other travels, a new aspect of the sacred possibilities of life was revealed to me. Then when I returned, the insights

I had gained enabled me to continue to finetune whole aspects of my life, including my working life. These journeys contributed immeasurably to my growing sense of serenity and purpose by enabling me to appreciate the possibilities inherent in our work, not just in terms of personal achievement and fulfilment, but in how we might also strive to elevate the human spirit as we work. It was this latter insight that ultimately transformed my experience of work, as I began to sense our potential at work when we realign our vision and values.

As I continued to explore these various spiritual traditions, I began to see the many elements of our current working lives that have taken us away from the celebration of our true selves and the unique gifts we bring to the world, and how by neglecting these life-enhancing qualities we have created a deep-seated unease in the workplace. I also saw how, time and again, we set ourselves up for working lives fraught with difficulty, because of our 'no pain no gain' philosophy, and that by speaking of the work–life balance we have come to believe that our work is something separate from living.

Then as I watched economic rationalism take root, I observed the many ways it crushed initiative and all sense of our true self, leaving a paralysing fear in its wake. The greater the fixation on the bottom line, the harder it became for organisations to achieve consistently good results. Increasingly everyone was operating from a space of profound fear at work, which in turn prevented us from finding new and effective solutions to our problems. Then as our fear infected our thinking and values, we resorted to shrinking the supply of jobs and resources, and to exposing those who remained in the workplace to abusive work practices. As our decency and common sense took a back seat, we allowed gruelling hours and impossible working conditions to become the

norm. This self-limiting way of working not only became acceptable, it became glamorous. As we continued to promote these
ways of working, we ignored their detrimental effects on our
families and community, and on our young and elderly. As
our jobs began to swallow us up, we too began to suffer. The
only way we could survive this life-denying way of operating was
to allow vital parts of our being to shut down. And so the pain
around work has continued to grow. The more tired and stressed
we become, the harder it is for us to see our way out of this
morass. Sadly, many of us now feel we have no other option than
to continue working in this way.

Yet while there is much in the current workplace to depress
us, when we feel the darkness descending, in spite of the way
things seem, we stand on the brink of extraordinary possibilities.
Often it is not until our darkest hour that we glimpse our true
potential, and our many challenges around work are no excep-
tion. Our present discomfort around work is not to be feared;
rather, it is the threshold that can take us beyond the way things
are, to the way they might be. Had it not been for my own
deep dissatisfaction with work, I would not have discovered all
that I have – nor would I have travelled to some of the world's
most awesome locations. It is my *difficulties* at work that have
enriched my life the most, because they challenged my aspirations and values, giving me the courage to stop living someone
else's dream. They left me free to embrace who I am intrinsically,
and to strive to become who I most wanted to be.

I finally realised that a genuinely successful working life is
about much more than doing a great job and being well rewarded.
Our success at work touches the heart of how else we might live,
and the way forward lies in waking up to how much influence
each of us has at work. We can only embrace our full potential at

work, however, when we learn to operate beyond fear – the fear of whether or not we are good enough, whether we will have a job next week. As our fear diminishes we find ourselves less driven and more inspired. We are then more able to use our precious life energy to be genuinely productive, and to build true momentum. When we learn to set our own course, rather than allowing the expectations and responsibilities of work to devour us, our working life will open up for us in ways we cannot now imagine.

In the following pages we will examine the many daily lacerations we face at work, as well as the larger issues, and will discover new ways forward that will not only satisfy our material goals, but will enhance our human spirit. We will learn that it is the *subtle* changes in our attitude and in the way we operate that will have the greatest impact on our working lives. My own journey has taken me through the public and private sectors, through the challenges of working with few resources and blended teams, and through retrenchments and takeovers. While some of these chapters of my working life have been stretching, they have also been extremely valuable, because apart from the priceless experience they delivered, these episodes have made me stronger and wiser, and far more optimistic about life.

When we are able to see our work more expansively, then even the greatest challenges cannot defeat us, because we know that each of us can make a difference at work, and that the more we liberate ourselves from our own fears and uncertainties, the more we help liberate those we work with. Then and only then can we bring about the kinds of work culture we all long for. The challenge of work is ours, and so too is the solution.

Whatever you can do, or dream you can, begin it.
Boldness has genius, power and magic in it.
Begin it now.
JOHANN WOLFGANG VON GOETHE, *FAUST* (TRANS. JOHN ANSTER)

transforming
our work

Life is nothing until it is lived.
JEAN-PAUL SARTRE, 'EXISTENTIALISM IS A HUMANISM'

WHERE ARE WE AT RIGHT NOW?

It has happened again. Another friend has hit the wall. After years of giving her all to work and achieving great success, she has nothing left. Here is someone who has been a role model for many – whose ability to rise to new challenges and turn difficult situations around is exceptional. Now she is fragile and frightened, unable to cope with the stress and fatigue. Her work is her whole life – her relationships and wider passions disappeared some time back. Now she's left wondering what to do next – she can't continue to work like this, but she can't see a way out either.

What is going on at work to make us feel this way? Regardless of the kind of job we have, most of us seem to be under pressure – too much pressure. It's not that we don't want to work; we do, but we want our working lives to be saner – more enjoyable, more fulfilling. We want a life outside of work as well. Most of us don't just work for the salary or the career prospects, we work to give our lives purpose and to enjoy the wider community and stimulation that work can bring. We feel we have something worthwhile to offer, and hope that in turn we might be enriched by our work. We also want an interesting and varied life beyond work. But increasingly work is consuming our whole lives, leaving us stressed out and exhausted most of the time. And no matter how much we apply ourselves at work, we rarely seem to be on top of things.

The more we give, the more is required of us. Yet in spite of our efforts, there seems little joy or satisfaction to be derived from our work. The more demanding work becomes, the more it distances us from those we love – from our friends and family, from the natural world. We have become strangers to those around us and strangers to ourselves. Time out to relax – to do the things we love most – seems almost non-existent. We yearn for lives with more depth and meaning, only to end up feeling empty most of the time. Still we believe that our working lives can get better – a whole lot better – if only we can put the right building blocks in place.

FINDING FULFILMENT

When our work is working for us, we feel like there's nothing we can't do. Each day is as good, if not better, than the last. Work doesn't even feel like work. So motivated are we that we accomplish everything without effort. No longer do we divide our week into weekdays and the weekend. When our work is as it should be, we live each and every day of our lives, experiencing all the exhilaration and stimulation we could hope for. Sadly this is not the experience for most of us at work right now. The workplace has become so complicated that it's hard to keep up. Every time we feel we're getting to grips with our job, more changes occur. And along with all these changes, we're now struggling with increased workloads and a lack of job security as well. Everything feels as if it is only just holding together. Even those in charge of our organisations seem unsure of the way forward. Often their response to these challenges is to tighten control, or to reorganise who reports to whom, leaving an already fragile workplace even more fractured and confused. Still we want to work – we just don't want all the angst that goes with it.

WAKING UP TO THE DYSFUNCTION

Even when work is no longer working for us, we continue to work hard and to give our working lives our all in the hope that tomorrow will be better. Yet as work continues to hijack our lives, many of us no longer have any sense of who we are beyond our job. I was told recently of a CEO battling cancer, who all his adult life had been defined by his work, until it consumed his every moment. Even when he lay dying, he insisted on being hooked up to the markets, so he could watch the performance of his company's stocks. The profound tragedy of this scene overwhelms us. What has happened to us to make us so manic that we can allow life's most significant moments to pass us by?

While our working lives might not have reached these extremes, this story has elements that are true for us all. Time and again, precious moments in our lives have slipped past, because of the demands of work. And it's not just countless moments in our *own* lives that are gone forever, so too are the times we could have shared with those close to us. We have missed out on the many occasions that warm our lives, and for what? As we contemplate the effect work has had on our lives, we begin to realise just how much we have given away. Without meaning

11

to, we have allowed whole chapters of our lives to be swallowed up by another deadline and yet another. We have abandoned the possibility of stable relationships – of having a family, of allowing our lives to be the adventures they were meant to be – for our work. And then we wonder why life seems so lacking much of the time.

We all understand the importance of working hard and the need to do our absolute best, but most of us have given far more to work than this. And the more we give, the more work demands of us, until we find ourselves trapped in a cycle of work and more work – until work becomes all we know. Even when we're successful and well paid we can't quite locate the fulfilment we had hoped for at work. What then is the cause of our dissatisfaction? Is it the overwhelming stress and exhaustion? Is it our inability to be the people we want to be? Is it the lack of a life beyond work? Or is it the tenuous nature of work these days?

CAN WE HAVE IT ALL?

When we first started work we believed the world was our oyster. We embraced the promise that we could have it all. We seized the opportunities that came our way, only to find ourselves trapped in a work culture that demanded everything we had. In spite of our breathtaking technology, our goal-setting and time management, most of us now feel as if we are walking on a razor's edge, as so many of the things that are precious to us have disappeared from sight. Our only solution seems to have been to work harder, until this loveless, joyless way of life is all we now know. Even when we have sufficient money to live well, we convince ourselves it isn't enough. Fearful of exploring the wider possibilities for our lives, we cling to the familiar, promising ourselves that one day we'll have a life. At some level we know that work is not the main reason for living, but in the absence of the time and space to consider what else life might hold, we carry on as if our impossible work lives are all we could hope for.

As in the fairy tales of old, we need to take great care what we aspire to. We can have it all, but we have to be careful of our definition of 'all'. Cities the world over are filled with those who appear to have it all, yet have little of true worth. We see the results of our aspirations in the prevalence of antidepressants, in those addicted to shopping and gambling, to drugs and alcohol. There are many things at work that seem appealing, but often these qualities cannot deliver a deep sense of fulfilment. This does not mean that work cannot offer us a great deal – it can, but only when we can distinguish what is real from what is not. For countless millions around the globe, work has become the grand illusion, and when we become lost in illusion, we experience all the symptoms associated with loss. We become fearful and self-obsessed, weary and confused, and unable to find the way out of our predicament.

Getting on top of work is a challenge, especially when the workplace is evolving daily. This constant change is not only physically, mentally and emotionally exhausting, it also creates a climate of fear and uncertainty. And when we become caught up in this fear, we lose sight of all that is inherently good in our work. Moving beyond the fear and uncertainty takes courage and determination, because work can be daunting – even for the courageous. Yet daring to break free of the constrictions we are currently experiencing at work is not as daunting as living in constant fear, because when we are fearful at work we become vulnerable. That's when we find ourselves agreeing to whatever is asked of us, whether it is reasonable or not, hoping that if we work hard enough we'll survive the staff cuts and the management changes. Then as we are overtaken by our work, we reach the stage where we are no longer living – we are merely surviving, and who wants just to survive?

WHAT IS HAPPENING TO US AT WORK?

The difficulty for most of us is that while we want our working lives to be different, we have little sense of how life might be beyond the stress and fatigue. And as our ability to envisage a better way of living fails us, so too does our ability to make it a reality. What a contrast our stressed-out lives are to the many aspirations we once held for work. How all-encompassing our dreams were back then. One day we wanted to be a dancer or a doctor, and the next we were determined to be a firefighter or an astronaut, and by the time we started our first job we had all the enthusiasm an employer could hope for. If we were lucky, many good things happened at work and, determined to keep up the momentum, we changed jobs now and then, embracing new challenges along the way. But as the pressures and the fatigue continue to escalate, our many aspirations have been transformed into dreams of escape. In times past, employees suffered all kinds of physical abuse. Now the abuse is psychological and far harder to pin down. Yet unless we can recognise the dysfunction at work and do something about it, it will paralyse us, making it almost impossible to realise our potential. A friend recently confessed she had to move on when, within months of joining the company, she saw yet another highly talented member of staff destroyed by work. What had happened to this person proved to be the proverbial canary in the mine. My friend knew if she didn't get out of the company, it was only a matter of time before she'd end up the same way.

14

This growing sense of unease at work not only impacts on our lives, but on our families. As more people are taken out of the workplace, increasing amounts of work are required from those who remain. The very real effect of this additional pressure is felt not only by those attempting to cope with impossible workloads, but by their friends and family, and their community. Similarly, those who long for the dignity of work are crushed; their despair at finding themselves out of work impacts on *their* friends and family and community. The health system is also affected as it attempts to deal with the escalating health problems of the overworked and the unemployed. This is the madness that we have created and which we now perpetuate. It is only when we take a step back that we begin to realise how much our current work practices have diminished our humanity and common sense, creating a system where few prosper and many suffer.

HOW ELSE MIGHT WE LIVE?

Is there another way to work? And is there room for a life beyond work? How can we survive the mergers and the staff cuts? How can we live beyond the all-pervasive fear and uncertainty that poisons so much that is good in our working lives? Few of us would question the fact that the world of work needs a major overhaul, but where do the solutions lie? While we continue to experience constant change around us, few if any improvements in conditions are realised, because more often than not such changes are old ways of dealing with new problems, changes that seek to confine and control, rather than encourage and reward.

Because so many of our decision-makers lack the experience and imagination to step outside the narrow world they have created for themselves, they also fail to realise that we live in a universe that is intricate beyond belief, and that as human beings

15

we reflect this exquisite detail. And so, while the importance of the bottom line and accountability is undeniable, we cannot impose one-dimensional solutions on a multi-dimensional world and hope to gain satisfactory outcomes. If our lives are to deliver all the joy and passion we long for, our approach to work needs to be multifaceted, as does our approach to life beyond work.

We can only create the working lives we dream of when we start seeing ourselves more completely, when we get a much clearer sense of who we are as human beings and all we are capable of. Once we know who we are at a profound level of our being, then we start to discover those things we need to sustain us. And when we know what we need to thrive, it becomes easier to determine what we *don't* need in our lives. When we have this depth of insight, we don't need to wait until we're retrenched or retired or critically ill before we allow ourselves the luxury of getting a life.

UNDERSTANDING WHAT DRIVES US
As we seek to move beyond our present difficulties at work, it is important that we examine our aspirations and values, so we can see how they impact on our day-to-day lives. Then we might just discover that our unhappiness at work comes from living someone else's dream, or from being in our current occupation because we didn't dare follow our hearts. Equally, we might find that while we yearn for simplicity, we too have become consumers par excellence, and that the more we consume, the more we seem to want. As we examine what drives us, we then see how we have allowed our life choices to narrow to the point that we are literally flogging ourselves to death, just so that we can afford whatever it is we believe we need – and how sane is that? More importantly, what is the solution?

HONOURING OUR AUTHENTIC SELVES

I'm not suggesting we abandon work, but that we regain control of our working lives. One of the very real dangers of the contemporary workplace is the temptation to embrace values and behaviours that are not our own. When we trade our unique talents and perceptions to become little more than stereotypes, we cannot help but feel insecure and driven. Trying to live by someone else's rules and expectations is a confusing, soulless way to live. It takes courage to be who we are, but only then will we experience the deep soul satisfaction at work that we long for.

Authenticity is a crucial component in creating the work life we dream of. The more we honour our true selves, the more our stress levels will drop. Our creativity will then be awakened, and new ideas and new ways of working will come to us without effort. We will start to remember all those things that reawaken in us a tangible sense of excitement about work, and we will want to get out of bed in the mornings and embrace a new working day.

GATHERING UP THOSE PARTS OF US WE HAVE GIVEN AWAY

To *live* our dreams we need first to reclaim those parts of ourselves we have given away, so we can remember who we are. In Clarissa Estés's timeless work, *Women Who Run With the Wolves*, she tells the story of the Wolf Woman, who tirelessly scours the desert gathering fragments of wolf bones. Each night this ancient woman then retreats to her cave, where slowly and meticulously she reassembles the wolf bones. When another skeleton is finally complete, a new wolf is born. If we want working lives that fulfil us, then we too need to reclaim those parts of us we have given away. Then and only then can we be the vibrant, successful individuals we have the potential to be at work.

REAWAKENING OUR PASSION AND VISION

As we begin to wake up to the many possibilities that work can bring, we discover new ways of perceiving ourselves and others. We then see that it is through the unique talents and perceptions we bring to our work that we realise our inherent greatness. This is a far more expansive view of work than that which is simply geared to getting to the top of the ladder, even though we may well achieve this goal too. The wider our vision, the more we are motivated to move beyond the stress and the fear, and to experience a whole new level of clarity. The clearer we are about our work, the more we will be aware how best to conduct ourselves at work in even the most challenging situations – how we should deal with the weak and the strong, with those who are altruistic, and with those whose motives seem questionable.

The secret to transforming our work lives is *not* to wait for those running our organisations to come up with the solutions, because these individuals are often as fearful and bewildered as we are. It is up to *us* to create the world we want to inhabit, and that includes the world of work. And so, regardless of how inadequate or distressing our work lives might be right now, we can still create the working environment we long for. Whether we work in white goods or computing, in fashion or fast food, our every comment and gesture has the power to transform or destroy the environment we work in. The choice and responsibility are ours.

MOVING BEYOND OUR FEARS

While there is no longer any such thing as a job for life, we need not be alarmed by this. After all, do we *really* want the same job for life? As we begin to reclaim our lives, our fear and confusion will be replaced by a growing sense of anticipation, as increasingly we are inspired to embrace the adventure of living. As we

18

contemplate these possibilities, we then realise that we are far more than just an accountant, a receptionist or a brain surgeon. We are spiritual beings on the adventure of a lifetime, and how we work, where we work, and what we learn through our work, are essential parts of this extraordinary journey.

The more we awaken to the many gifts that our working life offers, the more we realise that even downsizing and economic rationalism cannot hold us back. We see instead that these and other challenges might be just the gifts we need to enable us to discover who we are and all we can achieve at work and beyond it. *This* moment holds the key to our future. Right now we are being given the chance to expand the possibilities for our lives. We can continue to allow ourselves to be sucked dry by our work, or we can use the pressures we're facing to rekindle our passion and to make our working lives all that we yearn for.

re-enchantment
of work

The real act of discovery consists not in finding new lands,
but in seeing with new eyes.
MARCEL PROUST, 'THE CAPTIVE', REMEMBRANCE OF THINGS PAST

REIGNITING OUR PASSION FOR WORK

Transforming our experience of work is a little bit like falling in love – it's about waking up to all the extraordinary aspects of our working lives that at present have faded from view. We need only remember the excitement we experienced on our first day at work to recall how different our view of working life once was – our every sense was awake to the nuances of our new workplace. How delighted we were to familiarise ourselves with our job and to get to know our workmates. So at one were we with this experience that we absorbed *everything* around us – the unique smell and feel of the place, the textures and colours. We noticed how inviting certain people were, and how distracted others seemed to be. Then as we started to come to terms with the detail of our job, we were elated because we felt we could make a difference.

All these details were a source of great delight, because a new world was opening up. We wanted our job to work out, and so we were attuned to all the things we liked about work. We willingly embraced our many tasks, and so intent were we on learning everything we were able, we didn't mind the additional effort needed to get up to speed. And while there might have been aspects of our new job that were less than desirable, we happily overlooked them because we were determined to make the job work. But then as time passed, all those details that brought us so much joy became *familiar* to us. Slowly but surely the many reasons we loved our job disappeared from sight, until now we are no longer passionate about what we create or what we sell, because we hardly even notice what we are doing any more. How we loved the energy and the vision and the freedom our work brought – but now we are too tired and stressed to think about such things. Even our achievements and our friendships around work don't seem to help, because we are no longer able to locate the joy in our work.

APPRECIATING EVERYTHING OUR WORK BRINGS TO OUR LIVES
The more distanced we become from our *experience* of work, the less we are able to appreciate all that our work can deliver. An important part of enjoying our work is rediscovering our appreciation of all that our work means to us – not just the salary and the kudos, but the daily blessings. Without work, few of us would have the capacity to be generous with family and friends, to afford an impromptu ice-cream or a trip to the movies, to go somewhere we've never been before, to give to charities, to pay medical bills, to call those we care about. And as we work we also provide work for others – for those who grow our food, who make our clothes, who build our homes.

Each human being on this planet is intimately connected to the others, and increasingly our work is a key aspect of this interconnectedness – through our taxes we help build roads and hospitals, we help educate our children and protect the disadvantaged. When we are less than inspired about work, it helps to remind ourselves that our efforts help take care of the sick and the dying, that they help sustain our towns and cities. Even if work isn't perfect right now, it is encouraging to remember that our work enables us to contribute to the greater good.

Let us pause for a moment to consider all that work currently brings to our lives and how it benefits those around us. It often helps to note these things down. Then, as we peruse our list, we are reminded that regardless of what we do, our work is significant. This list is worth keeping for those moments when our vision becomes clouded or our motivation fails.

BALANCING MATERIAL BENEFITS WITH SOULFULNESS

While the material benefits that work brings do warm our lives, these qualities are not enough to sustain our sense of worth. Unless our work elevates the human spirit, it cannot help but be soulless. Our obsession with the material aspects of our jobs will prevent us from experiencing all that work holds for us. This is the root cause of the unease so many are experiencing in the workplace right now.

Chitra has the kind of job many dream of – she enjoys a six-figure salary and many additional benefits – and from the moment she entered the workforce she's been on the fast track. Chitra has always thrived on being out there and making things happen. She loves the adrenaline and her healthy remuneration. Every two or three years she has changed jobs to make sure she remains ahead of the game. Once she was working for a leading multinational she thought she had things made – until the economy started to take a dive. Then work began to get difficult, so difficult that Chitra is now desperate to move on. But she can't move on, because there aren't many jobs that will pay the kind of money she's become accustomed to – at least not in her field.

Now more than ever Chitra needs to maintain her salary, because she recently moved into her waterside home. On the surface, the place is a dream – it is in an excellent location, it has a decor to die for, and state-of-the art appliances. The only problem is that work has become so demanding that Chitra hasn't had time to savour her new home, let alone work out the complicated controls that monitor all the mod cons. Now she is feeling increasingly out of control at work. Home isn't much fun either. It's hard to feel comfortable in a home with appliances you can't fully operate. Chitra admits to feeling as if everything she has worked so hard to create is slipping through her fingers. She feels cheated, because she was only fulfilling the dream that most of us hold for work. She went for the exhilaration and stimulation and remuneration. Now all Chitra dreams of is finding a way out.

WORK AS SACRED PRACTICE

For too long we have divided the physical world from that of the spirit, and now we are struggling to inject some depth and meaning into what has become a life-denying way of working. In many spiritual traditions work is an integral part of sacred expression, because it is through the loving attention we bring to our work that we gain deep fulfilment. Whether we bake bread, tend plants or represent our company overseas is immaterial. What matters is that our work enhances who we are – mind, body and spirit. Then each working day can deliver the deep satisfaction we long for.

Imagine how different work might be, if we weren't just working for a salary or to pay bills, but because our work was a glorious expression of all that is precious in life. What if *each* gesture, *each* task honoured the unique qualities we carry within? What if in making sandwiches or transplanting hearts or selling shoes we were able to reach out to those we met through work genuinely and passionately, and help transform their days? Certainly there would be less need for politics and backbiting, and a whole lot more energy for new ways of working, and for infusing our daily tasks with an extraordinary sense of vibrancy and fulfilment.

In many nations, work is still regarded as an extension of all that is sacred in life. In Hindu countries, work is honoured in many ways, including during Diwali, the festival of lights. At Diwali, literally thousands of oil lamps and candles are lit to honour our divine potential. During this five-day festival, all the tools of one's trade are cleansed and blessed to honour the gift of work and all that it brings to our lives. Some cultures bless their fishing fleets before they return to the seas for another season, others ask for a blessing of the planting of new crops or give thanks for the harvest. While we tend to write off such gestures as unsophisticated, these acts of devotion recognise that our work is deeply significant, that it is an integral part of who we are and what we do each day. How much more meaningful our experience of work is when we can honour and celebrate our daily work.

Why not take a moment now to consider how you might honour your work? What small gestures might you set in place to enrich the moment? How might you behave towards others to enhance their expectations of work? Allow yourself to feel how *different* your working day might be if you introduce these possibilities.

CELEBRATING THE WORK COMMUNITY

As we contemplate the wider opportunities for us at work, let us consider the community that has grown up around our work. Each day our working lives are enriched by the intelligence and kindness of others – by their triumphs and challenges, by their good humour, and by their unique way of observing the world. It is at work that often we share our most meaningful moments – the birth of new relationships, our wider aspirations, our travel plans. It is here too that we often receive support during life's darker moments. Even in the most inhospitable work environments there are those who are there for us on the good days, and on the days that take us to the edge. These are the special people who always seem to know when we need a little kindness or support. Their very presence warms our working lives and helps spur us on. These people have much to teach us about work as sacred practice, because they never succumb to the darkness at work. Always they can be relied on to be consistent and decent and fair, no matter how dark the times.

My last two years in book publishing were blessed by Trish, a beautiful lady who would pick a flower each morning, then place it on my keyboard. I cannot tell you how much those little flowers sustained me – especially on the days that stretched me to the limit. Just to contemplate such gestures fills us with joy and a renewed sense of hope. People like Trish are to be cherished, because they understand the sacred potential of each moment. They are often the true heart and soul of our organisations, yet when did we last tell them how much we appreciate them? Perhaps it is time we did something meaningful for them – to illuminate *their* working lives.

As we look more closely at our work, we begin to realise just how extensive our work community is. We then see that even the person who sells us our morning paper, or makes our breakfast or our first coffee of the day, is an important part of our working lives. The daily rituals we share around work are significant, because they nurture us and help dissolve any sense of isolation. It is no accident that cafés have become an important part of our daily routine, because these womb-like spaces are often a home away from home. Here in the midst of our uncertain world, we can lose ourselves in the comforting hiss of the coffee machine and the pleasant buzz of conversation. These and other rituals *actively* support what we do at work, and so why not take a moment to savour them, to see these interactions for what they are – sacred moments that allow small pockets of peace and contentment to flow into our days? As we contemplate these things, we begin to realise that within even our most ordinary working days lie moments of great beauty and lasting satisfaction.

ENJOYING OUR WORK

Once we get a sense of this beauty, we are inspired to create further sacred moments in our working day. Perhaps such moments are to be had on our way to work – in the carved stonework over a doorway, or in the bunches of fresh fruit or flowers that spill out from shops onto the pavement. We might be drawn to the simplicity of an old iron fence marked and rusted with age, or to a solitary window box that brings a solemn building to life. There are myriad experiences that can add piquancy to our journeys to and from work. I used to pass an elderly lady in her dressing gown and slippers, feeding the birds – just to observe the joy she gained from this activity made my soul sing. When we can embrace these and other possibilities, we feed our spirit. The more we can gather up such experiences and hold them close, the more the positive energy they represent becomes an integral part of who we are.

In her beautiful book, *Romancing the Ordinary*, Sarah Ban Breathnach captures the essence of these possibilities when she encourages us to cultivate our sense of *wonder*. This is a critical message – especially for those of us who have become jaded by our work – because without wonder there is little we can genuinely appreciate in life. When instead of postponing our opportunities for happiness, we can live in the moment, we can begin to see just how many opportunities there are in our working day for joy and stimulation, and also for *celebration*. In recent years we have become so serious at work that many of us have become critical or even contemptuous of our working environment. We work best when we can relax and take ourselves a little less seriously, because then we can enjoy a greater sense of *ease* at work, regardless of how busy we might be. This does not mean we lose focus, but that we allow ourselves playful moments now and then. Why? Because play feeds our spirit. It inspires us to find new solutions to old problems. It motivates us to go the extra mile. And it encourages us to put some of our energy into those around us as well. When our lives abound with joy, we cannot help but approach our work with more passion and imagination, expanding and enriching our contribution to the whole.

COMPARTMENTALISING OUR LIVES

If we are truly passionate about our job, then our working life should flow easily into the rest of our life, creating a rich and varied life experience. Too often we see our lives in terms of the working week and the weekend. When we can instead view our lives as one moment unfolding after the next, we start to see our lives more *completely*, and we are then able to appreciate the possibilities in even the most routine moments at home and at work. We then realise how important it is to apply as much creativity to our leisure time as we do to our work. We also discover how even minor adjustments to our routine can transform our working days. When we make the effort to take up yoga, to enrol for a course on film, or to visit the night markets at the end of the working day, we inject more possibilities into our lives, which in turn transform our view of ourselves and our work.

SEEKING SILENCE AND SPACE

Balance is also an essential part of a successful working life, because no matter how clever or sophisticated we might be, we all need time to be alone – to think, or simply to be. Our whole experience of work will be greatly enhanced when we turn off the mobile phone or the car radio or the Discman. Often we're too scared to allow ourselves some quiet, because we believe the marketers when they tell us we will miss out unless our mobile is always switched on. Yet even while working under great pressure with tight deadlines, this was not my experience. Of course there are times when we have to be on call, but we can also allow ourselves pockets of silence. We do this because we need silence as much as we need food and sleep.

In Sufism, silence is regarded as *bliss*, because it is only when we are silent that we are able to touch the sacred depths of our being. We know when we have accessed this place within, because we will feel a profound sense of relief and joy. Once we start to taste the perfection that silence brings, we are inspired to create quiet moments in the busiest of days, because we know how much more effectively we operate when we are in balance. The more balanced we are, the more we are able to make good decisions and to be more creative. Ovid talked of silence as

28

strength, because through silence we gain insight – we can then see more clearly where our efforts are well spent and where they are being wasted. Over time, we will also find ourselves able to see into the hearts and minds of those around us, discerning those who are supportive and those who are not.

Space is equally important if we are to enjoy balanced working lives. We can only achieve space when we make time before or during the working day to pause and catch our breath. This might mean shutting the office door, or spending a few moments alone in the bathroom, or taking the stairs instead of the lift. It might be a quiet coffee before work, or a few moments in the park at lunchtime. Then at weekends we can extend this search for space by finding a location that feels special, to which we can take ourselves now and then and allow all the stresses of the working week to drop away. Regardless of whether we live in a town or a city, there are places close by that can uplift and inspire us. When we can retreat to such locations for even an hour at the weekend, we will become more vibrant and focused during work and leisure. When we are able to leave behind the endless barrage of thoughts and anxieties around work, we are able to *breathe* again, and to feel more energetic and hopeful. Time out enables us to *lighten* up and to take charge of our lives again. Then as we rediscover our wider passion for living, our working days cannot help but be more satisfying and fun.

SEEING THOSE AROUND US IN A NEW LIGHT

How we regard those we work with will also have a dramatic impact on our experience of work – because whatever we think, we experience. It is tempting to pigeonhole others according to the kinds of jobs they do. Yet when we see someone purely as an accounts clerk or a doctor or a sales executive instead of the unique individual they are, we miss the point. People are rarely as they first appear – Einstein was an average student at best, but that didn't prevent him from becoming one of the greatest scientists of all time. Often there is so much more to those working alongside us than is immediately apparent. But unless we are able to see those we work with more completely and treat them accordingly, our experience of work will be superficial at best.

EVERY DETAIL COUNTS

As we have already observed, ours is an intricate universe, and we too mirror this intricacy. The way we start our working day – the food we eat, the way we dress – will impact on our experience of work. Meditation provides an important start to our day; not only does it give our bodies the peace and quiet needed to operate effectively at work, it clears our mind of chatter, enabling us to see more clearly what is happening inside and around us. Meditation also awakens our powers of intuition and imagination, and helps us sense what is ahead. When we meditate, we somehow seem to know when trouble is brewing, or when a project that seemed fine is being derailed. The more we meditate, the more we are also able to discern the motivations of those around us, to read their emotional states, and to know when someone says yes but they really mean no. Meditation also helps us with specific fears around work such as public speaking or flying, because it gives us a simple process by which we can acknowledge our fears, then move more easily beyond them. When we start the day with meditation, we activate the profound connection we have with the rest of life. We will then find ourselves drawn to the people and places that are right for us, to new ideas and new sources of information without effort. Meditation not only enables us to get to the heart of our issues at work, it boosts our metabolism – and all we need is twenty minutes each morning.

NOURISHING OURSELVES

What we eat and drink is equally important in how we fare at work. If we skip meals, or survive on alcohol, caffeine and fast foods, we damage ourselves body and spirit. The ancients referred to our bodies as temples, because they understood how finely tuned our physical selves are. Even though we might earn a decent salary and dine out in great restaurants, unless we are giving our bodies fresh foods and regular meals, we are likely to be lacking the nutrients needed for our cells to function well and for us to remain healthy. When we're in the middle of a busy day we tend to grab whatever we can find to eat and drink – most of which isn't giving us what our bodies need. It is important to shop for healthy snacks – such as nuts, and dried and fresh fruits – for spring water and for other caffeine-free drinks. There is plenty of information available to assist us with healthy choices. Shopping for food that is nutritious takes no longer than shopping for food that is not. When our bodies are nourished, our spirits soar. We have the stamina and focus needed to be excellent at our work, and have energy for our life outside of work as well.

DRESSING TO INSPIRE

Even our dress can influence our day. Often we dress to be noticed or to outdo those around us, placing a barrier between ourselves and others. To be the object of envy is not the hallmark of success – it is an extremely lonely and depressing space to be in. What most of us need at work is the opportunity to *lighten up*, because at our essence we are beings of light. The English writer Sir Thomas Browne described us as 'a pure flame . . . we live by an invisible Sun within us'. The more enlightened we are, the more Light we have within our being and the lighter we feel. Anything that creates more Light in our lives feeds our spirit. This does not mean we should dress down or inappropriately. We can, however, dress with grace and beauty, seeking always to inspire and uplift. When we choose work clothes that enhance who we are in essence, we will notice the difference. Even the colours we choose are significant, because each colour has its own energy. For too long the working world has been dominated by black, a colour we associate with material power and with mourning. Black is not a life-enhancing colour – it is not helpful for anyone who is angry or depressed – because black always contains whatever energy it encloses, causing negative energies to accumulate around us.

The impact and meaning of colour has been the subject of many books – anyone wishing to learn more about the many benefits of colour might be interested in the Aura-Soma therapies. In brief, red is a vibrant, grounding colour that helps us deal with survival issues such as security and money. Orange relates to our opportunities for bliss – it is connected also to dependency and independence. Yellow denotes our capacity for joy and intellectual fulfilment, while green is connected to our heart and emotions, and to nature. Blue is associated with peace and with our ability to communicate who we are without fear, while royal blue denotes our intuitive selves. Violet is a highly spiritual colour, and is connected with healing and transformation. Once we are aware of the possibilities that colour can bring to our lives, we can allow our intuition to draw to us the colours we need around us to support us at work.

Naomi has worked successfully in corporate life for many years. When she began to discover the healing properties of colour, she got rid of her black wardrobe and chose colours that appealed to her, and to her surprise her experience of work improved dramatically. Just to look at Naomi is an uplifting experience. She is often stopped in the street by strangers who comment on the colours she is wearing. None of the colours she wears is unusual or out of place – most are quite subtle – yet somehow they have an extraordinary impact on those around her. Naomi admits that she consciously dresses to inspire herself and others. 'I just want everyone I work with to feel better, especially as there's so much anxiety at work these days. The colours I now wear not only look good, I can actually feel my body benefiting from them as well.' For men and for those wearing uniforms, the opportunity to wear different colours at work might seem non-existent. However we can still bring colour into the day through our choice of underwear and accessories.

ATTENDING TO OUR WORK SPACE

Basically, life is a dance of energies, and we reflect this movement of energies in our own bodies and in our personal space. When work is getting us down it helps to look around and see where the energy within or around us might have become stagnant, because when the flow of this energy becomes blocked, we feel uncomfortable. As we take a closer look at our work space, we can see certain things that frustrate or depress us, and that interrupt our sense of balance. We then realise that we are feeling down because our in-tray is piled high, or because our plants have died, or because our posters or prints no longer uplift us. We might also realise that we are feeling frustrated because our files need reorganising, or because our expenses have accumulated, or because of all the unread trade magazines piled up on our desk. Or there might have been a lot of tension or exhaustion in the air recently. All of the above signal that it's time to clear our physical and energetic space. If there's no time to do this during the working week, then it's worth staying back one evening or coming in at the weekend to revive the energies of our work space.

As we sort out our files, and clean and tidy our work area, we are able to get rid of all those things we don't need, or that don't inspire us, making way for new experiences and possibilities. Often when people have a serious clear-out at work, something important changes for them. They might end up getting a promotion or changing jobs, because they have literally made some space for the new in their lives. When we can work more consciously with the energies around us, we create the kind of space we want to inhabit at work. If we need to breathe new life into our desk, for example, we might like to buy new desk accessories. They don't have to be expensive; we can take them with us when we depart, or pass them on to a workmate. New or re-potted plants, fresh prints and photos can also inject extra energy into our work space. Once these elements are in place, it is a good idea to bless the space and to visualise it filled with life-enhancing Light. Once we have renewed the energies around our work area, it is important to maintain this space by keeping it tidy and free of conflict.

HONOURING OUR WORK

Too often our work can seem like a never-ending list of things to do, yet our jobs are far more than this. What we do at work not only impacts on our workmates, but on the world at large. Whether we are nursing, assembling cars or flying planes, we provide a service to others, and when we are able to honour our contribution, our relationship with our work will start to change. We can either do our work because it has to be done, or because we respect what we do. If we can honour what we do, then as we serve customers, drive buses or deliver babies we can enjoy taking part in the dance of life. The wider our perspective on work, the greater our capacity for joy and the more we then begin to appreciate the many interesting and unusual people we meet through our work – those who stimulate and challenge us, those who make us feel good, those who teach us more about ourselves and our world. And in recognising these people, we begin to savour their presence and to return their appreciation of us with our own expressions of gratitude. When we allow this warmth into our working day, it will not only feed us, it will give us a greater sense of the possibilities for us at work.

SEEING OURSELVES AS WE ARE

As we start to see our work and those we work with more completely, it is important to look more closely at the *way* we are operating, to ensure we are not sabotaging ourselves by unfortunate attitudes or inferior work. We may then find *we* need to clean up our act. Without meaning to, we might have become someone we hardly recognise at work. We might have become overly ambitious or manic, or we might have lost our confidence or our vision. Would we want our friends to see how we behave towards our staff or our workmates? Would we want them to know we falsify our expenses, that we're lazy or confrontational, or that we get by doing as little as possible? Ours is a universe where each part is intimately connected to the others, and whatever energies we put out are what will return to us many times over. If we want to live and work abundantly, intelligently and joyously, then our actions have to mirror these qualities. And so even if our working lives seem meaningless or questionable right now, this is the perfect time to begin again – to dare to work with more integrity and passion.

REGAINING OUR PASSION FOR OUR WORK

Perhaps it is it time for you to take a more expansive view of work, not just in terms of your career, but in terms of your *experience* of work. Why not take a few moments to contemplate the following questions?

- What were the qualities that inspired you to take your present job?
- Are these qualities still present at work?
- If so, how can you appreciate these qualities more fully – enhance them even?
- If not, how can you reintroduce these qualities into your working day?
- Who is your community at work?
- What does this community bring to your life?
- How best can you nurture this community?
- Where are the opportunities for wonderment within and around your working day?
- How can these special moments become sacred to you?
- What opportunities are there for silence and space, at and beyond work?
- Does your work space need attention?
- If so, what subtle touches can you introduce to it that will inspire you?
- What about the way you operate? Is it time to lift your game? To shift your focus?
- How can you do this?

By putting these possibilities together, you can begin to refine your experience of work, which will enable you to work more effectively and more soulfully.

overcoming a difficult work culture

Though with great difficulty I am got hither, yet now I do not repent me of all the trouble I have been at to arrive where I am.
JOHN BUNYAN, *THE PILGRIM'S PROGRESS*

EVALUATING OUR WORKING ENVIRONMENT

Even when we are able to create a more nurturing space at work, still work will continue to challenge us. How we then respond is crucial. Sometimes we are so involved with work, we haven't even noticed what a draining and dysfunctional environment our workplace has become. Whatever the issues at work right now, they are in our lives for a reason. If instead of becoming lost in our pain or ignoring it altogether, we can look at these issues with an open mind, we will begin to see that beyond our frustration and bewilderment, beyond the backstabbing, the confusion and the fear, new ways of living and being await us.

One of the reasons we struggle at work is that we have a very limited view of what our working lives can deliver. So intent are we on acquiring the requisite skills and experience for progressing in our career, we fail to realise that work can also help us become wiser, more insightful human beings. Wisdom and insight are essential qualities for success. The wiser we are, the less painful our working lives become, because we stop adding to our pain through our confused way of operating. When we are wise, we are able to see the overall picture as well as the detail, to think and act appropriately, to save our energy for the projects and issues that need our attention.

Wisdom is more than just being street smart. It enables us to keep our immediate and long-term goals in sight, to deal with complexity, to be aware of what is peripheral and what is not, and to operate accordingly. We don't talk about wisdom much in the context of work, because it isn't something most of us value. Yet it is the very absence of wisdom from the work agenda that creates so much unhappiness and dissatisfaction at work. Knowledge and expertise we have in abundance, but without wisdom our working lives cannot help but be fraught. We have come to view wisdom as a lack of ambition, yet even when we are wise we continue to aspire – but then our aspiration is to achieve our personal best. When we operate wisely, we no longer feel so fearful or so driven, because we know how to make each moment of our working day a far more productive space.

LOCATING THE GIFTS WITHIN OUR CHALLENGES

We all long for a more straightforward working life, where we can get on with our work and be appreciated for what we do, yet when we become too comfortable at work, often we become complacent. In the absence of challenges, we can lose our vision and our passion and become wedded to our routine, until one day simply dissolves into the next. Our life's purpose is not to hibernate. Life is a series of unfolding opportunities and challenges. To be successful, we need to see clearly what each new situation can bring to our lives, and this includes those work situations we feel we can do without. Unless there is sand in the oyster, we can never attain the pearl of great price. And so when the clouds gather at work, rather than becoming fearful and confused, we can keep going and see where the journey takes us.

Had my working life not continued to challenge me, I would never have become a writer. It was my *difficulties* at work that transformed my values and my outlook, compelling me to find answers to the questions we all pursue. Each answer pointed me forward, showing me how else I might live. Often it is only when life shakes us up that we finally tackle those aspects of our lives that are no longer working. I recently asked a good friend if she would be prepared to relive the painful takeover she had experienced some time ago. 'It was a nightmare,' she admitted, 'but I'm a much better person for it. I wouldn't trade what I know now for anything.' When we are given the chance to gain greater clarity and insight, why would we want to remain confused and frustrated? And so even if you are unhappy or unfulfilled at work right now, instead of feeling desperate or depressed, know that this discomfort may be the threshold beyond which is a far better space in which to work.

TAKING A CLOSER LOOK AT THE WAY WE WORK

The whole purpose of our earthly quest is to lead us towards a greater understanding of ourselves and the world around us. We can only achieve this when we can cultivate a *heightened* awareness of life – of the deeply painful moments, as well as those that bring great joy. Often when things are tough at work we prefer to distract ourselves from the issues that bother us, forgetting that denial only magnifies the pain. It is only when we summon the courage to wake up to our situation and do something positive about it, that we end up where we're meant to be. This was Lisa's experience while holidaying in Florence.

Having spent a great deal of time searching unsuccessfully for the entrance to the Villa Medici gardens, Lisa finally gave up. Then she met another woman, who had also failed to find the doorway to this fifteenth-century garden. 'You'll never find it,' this woman insisted. 'I've been searching for hours.' Then doubly determined to find the gardens, Lisa trudged back to the long stretch of wall she had searched earlier. This time she found the tiny door she had been looking for – and it led her into one of the most exquisite gardens she had ever experienced.

Often when things don't unfold as we'd hoped at work, we allow our sense of self to be diminished and our vision to fade. There will always be people who try to put us down, to compete, to place obstacles in our way. How we cope with these things depends on how we *react*. This in turn is influenced by the vision we hold for ourselves and our commitment to this vision. Had it not been for those discouraging words, Lisa may never have found the Villa Medici gardens. She allowed this negative situation to spur her on, to try again, and we must do the same if our work is to deliver the fulfilment we long for. And so even if we have lost heart, *now* is the time to start to reclaim our vision for our working lives – and to harness our strength and determination to make our vision a reality.

WE ARE PART OF OUR WORK CULTURE
When work fails to satisfy, we are tempted to distance ourselves from those around us, pretending we inhabit a parallel universe. But work is not something that happens outside of us. Our workplace is a *living* entity that reflects the talents and personalities and life energies of each individual within our organisation. If the majority of people we work with are unsupportive and self-seeking, this will be the overall mood of our workplace. If, however, they

are vibrant, positive and outgoing, then our work environment will reflect this dynamism, because we are each connected to the other. This means that *our* presence and conduct, *our* preconceptions and actions are important, because they impact on those around us – sometimes subtly, sometimes dramatically. We might be the kind of person who brings passion and vision and positive values into our workplace, or we might be critical or unhelpful. Either way, those around us are affected by *our* energetic presence.

When we are lucky enough to work around those who are intelligent, vibrant and consistent, each working moment is a profoundly satisfying experience. Their authenticity and inclusiveness inspire us, giving us a greater sense of ourselves. There are so many places in the world that are in need of Light right now, and few more so than the workplace. We need as many people as possible who will stand in a place of truth and goodness – who, regardless of the politics or constant change, will be wise and effective. When we can live each and every moment of our working lives with these kinds of values, we naturally become exceptional at what we do. When we help transform the darker aspects of our working culture so that it becomes one in which people can thrive, we will achieve far more than we first envisaged – and we will also discover the awesome power of one.

LEARNING DETACHMENT

Often we create our own pain at work by taking everything that happens personally. Regardless of how things seem, not everything that takes place at work is about us. Our boss may be difficult because he's dealing with delinquent kids, or because he's battling ill health. If we take his bad temper personally, we not only add to his pain, we allow ourselves to get caught up in *his* issues. Unless we can see clearly in the smoke-and-mirrors environment of work, we will end up taking on *everyone else's* energies – from their failed relationships and demanding family situation, to their broken dreams, and all their work issues. When we react to whatever issue is before us, we end up lurching from one crisis to the next. This is not the best place to be coming from if we want to make progress. When things get tough at work, the most important question to ask ourselves is whether we need someone else's pain in our lives as well as our own.

As we learn to be more detached about the issues we face at work, we start to see the people who hurt and frustrate us in a different light. We then realise that often the unhappiness they create at work is a reflection of a much greater pain they carry within. When we can see their issues with this level of clarity, we then know whether or not the specific issue before us is really about us. We also have a better idea of how to respond. We may still have to challenge certain actions or behaviour or, equally, it might make more sense to cut the person some slack. When we are able to get to the heart of the issue and solve it, we save ourselves and others time and angst. One of the hallmarks of the great spiritual masters is that they never waste an ounce of energy – that is why they are so powerful. If we want to step into our own power at work, then we must also learn not to waste energy.

BEING CLEAR ABOUT WHERE OUR DISSATISFACTION LIES

When our work or our workmates are getting us down, we need to be clear whether we are exhausted or whether there is a *real* problem, because when we are under pressure we can end up projecting our disappointments and frustration onto others. The more tired and stressed we are, the less we are able to take a balanced view. It's only when we step back that we realise it's not a new job or new boss we need so much as a holiday or some other opportunity to regain our vitality, perspective and enthusiasm. When we *do* make the effort to clear our heads or take time out, we have the chance to get back on track – to begin to live each day more fully and creatively – at work and beyond it.

TAKING CARE OF OUR ATTITUDES

Sometimes our unhappiness at work may be due to the ideas we have about how work should unfold for us. If we think like this, then when changes take place at work we are devastated. When we fail to get promoted, we are outraged – not realising that perhaps our time with our present employer is drawing to a close, or that if we had been promoted our lives would no longer have been our own. Life cannot be the adventure we hope for if we try to control everything around us – that's an exhausting, unfulfilling way to live. We might have hoped for the corner office, but why when the office goes to someone else do we allow our lives to be shattered? When we cling to our notions of how work should be, we are more likely to end up in a job we think we should take, rather than in the job that feeds us body and soul. When we cling to our ideas about work we also help create our own unhappiness.

Damian was determined to become sales director of the large stationery company in which he worked. Even though nothing went smoothly with his application, Damian never stopped to think why this might be. So intent was he on making it, he persisted until the job was his. Once he was in his new position, he was shocked to discover that the company was experiencing major financial difficulties – he ended up having to retrench many of his workmates. His whole life was swallowed up as he fought hard to maintain the company's share in a shrinking market. Having committed himself to the job, Damien felt obliged to see his new role through. He admitted to feeling so desperate about work that he even contemplated taking his own life.

When we live without clarity, we make our working lives so much harder than they need to be. When by contrast we have the good sense to follow our inner wisdom, everything will unfold as it should. Sometimes this might mean holding back until the right job comes along, or daring to go with an opportunity that comes out of left field. The important thing to understand is that with insight and patience we can be in the right place at the right time.

RECOGNISING *OUR* IMPACT ON OUR WORK

When we are feeling down, it is far easier to focus on the short-comings of those we work with than to deal with our own inadequacies, and so we end up wasting our energy on petty concerns. Often we add to our unhappiness by becoming lost in certain issues – by getting involved in gossip and criticism. Valuable working time is lost in complaining. Then as we continue to focus on our hurts or annoyances, instead of finding solutions and moving forward, our vitality goes into feeding these negative energies. The bad situations at work cannot affect us unless, like the vampires of old, we invite them in. Once these energies become part of our lives, they will feed off our life energy, draining us. And when we're drained, how can we deal with the challenges that work brings, let alone make our aspirations a reality?

It is not what happens to us at work that creates our happiness or despair, but how *we* respond to what happens. There is little point in creating a sacred space within and around us, through meditation and other practices, if we cannot maintain these energies throughout our working day. Those who have contributed greatly to our planet are those who, in spite of often terrible circumstances, have continued to be courageous and decent and consistent. At work we too need to learn to hold the vision of who we are and what we hope to achieve. We need to learn to live from our inner radiance and wisdom, rather than through comparison and ambition. When we become more aware of the effects of *our* thoughts and actions, we begin to see how *our* grumbling and speculations contribute to an uneasy working environment, and that the more we take part in negativity, the more we contaminate our work space. If we want to be happy and successful at work, then we need to learn to maintain positive, Light-filled attitudes and responses, regardless of the kind of day we are having. This doesn't mean we should ignore the difficulties before us, but that we shouldn't allow them to get us down.

TAKING A CLOSER LOOK AT OURSELVES

To create a life-enhancing space around us at work, we need to be aware of what we are thinking and saying, of how we are reacting, of our insecurities, of our need to be noticed or to be right. Once we wake up to ourselves, we can then see how these responses erode the opportunities for insight and joy in each working day.

Beth realised how destructive her attitude towards work had become while working for a small catering company: 'The hours were long and the pay wasn't brilliant, so everyone got in the habit of mouthing off. Then a new guy started who criticised everything we did. It was only then that I realised how unpleasant it was to be around someone with such a poisonous attitude. Seeing him in action certainly stopped me complaining.'

The Buddhists talk of mindfulness – of continuing to finetune our awareness of each moment, so we can improve our experience of life. When we cultivate our awareness at work we begin to see how things get worse on the days we are negative, and how much better work is when we can be constructive. We also begin to see how we deal fairly with some and dismissively with others, how we make other people's issues our own, and how often we extinguish moments of joy with our determination to swim against the tide. We also see that when we are generous, we strengthen relationships and enhance the possibilities for positive outcomes. Once we are aware of those things we say and do that trip us up, we realise that it is *we* who create much of the conflict around us at work, and that it is *we* who can transform our days.

SEEKING A WAY FORWARD

Even when the tension at work is widespread, we need to look more deeply at the cause of our unhappiness, to determine whether the contentious issues before us are of *genuine* concern. Or are they simply an opportunity for our ego – or little self – to grandstand, or to get back at someone we don't like? Too often we allow our emotional responses to cloud our judgement at work, and draw us into unhelpful positions or attitudes. As we look for a way through our negative feelings about work it also helps to see who is thriving, and what we can learn from them. Are these people prospering because of their uplifting attitudes and values, or because they are an integral part of an increasingly dysfunctional regime? The answers to these questions will help inform our own way forward.

In seeking to improve the climate at work we should always keep a close eye on those around us, so that we don't end up mirroring the behaviour of those we don't respect. How often have we seen perfectly decent workmates change as they rise through the ranks, until they become as autocratic or self-seeking as those they once criticised? When we allow ourselves to be drawn into unworthy behaviour, we diminish our own positive attributes and peace of mind. Often we get involved in unfortunate situations at work because we just don't think.

Jaki told me recently of a number of workmates who organised a party to celebrate the departure of an unpopular manager. 'I didn't like the person who left,' she admitted. 'I didn't respect his values or his decisions, but when I heard about the party I felt sick, because it was a really unpleasant thing to do.' By participating in this event, everyone was drawn into the energies they despised.

The less aware we are, the more destructive our thoughts and actions. Whenever we resort to innuendo or character assassination, or to any other means of destructive behaviour, we don't just create negative vibes, we harm the impossibly fine fabric of our being. We literally cause tears in our Light body, diminishing the flow of the life force through our being. If we were able to see what we were doing to ourselves, we would realise why we feel so ill at ease or depressed by certain things we have thought or done. Sometimes we are so desensitised to our work environment that we have become accustomed to the stress and the pain. When we're not aware of our discomfort at work, we have no idea of the extent to which it is draining our passion and vitality. So used have many of us become to feeling this way that we no longer believe we can have rich and rewarding lives at work. No matter how challenging our work, *we* are responsible for the space we inhabit – it is up to us to ensure our work space is supporting our vitality, our values and our vision. If not, then we need to get rid of the energies that have accumulated there.

We have talked already about ensuring our work space supports our efforts. Again, this is about paying attention to what is going on around us, because while our work space might *appear* ideal, it might not be so in actuality. It is important always to allow our intuition to tell us the way things really are. This was Jan's experience when she went to work for a small design company in newly refurbished premises.

The space was everything Jan had dreamt of, yet there was something about her office that was uninviting. Jan tried to ignore her growing sense of unease, but then she discovered that the previous incumbent had many personal problems and suffered from depression. Once she knew this, Jan cleaned her office thoroughly and burnt dried sage – a herb used to define sacred space and to clear negative energies. She then visualised her work space filled with Light, and asked that it might support feelings of peace and fulfilment. She also brought in some handmade mugs and photos of loved ones to lift the space.

In no time Jan's office was transformed by these simple gestures – everywhere she looked she felt comfortable and uplifted. Jan's workmates also noticed the difference – they would frequently comment on how much they liked being in her office. If we're not feeling comfortable at work right now, then we need to take a closer look at the energetic space we're working in. We might have inherited a work space from someone who was perpetually angry, confused or mischievous, and unless these energies have been cleared, they will still be present. None of us wants to be sitting in someone else's garbage – physical or psychic. When we recognise the negative energies around us and do something about them, we bring hope and joy and a tangible sense of ease to our working day. We also enable everyone around us to thrive.

There are some excellent space-clearing sprays we can use to help raise the energies in and around our work space, without impinging on those around us. Flower essence travel creams can also be useful to have on hand to help us deal with stress, fatigue and disorientation. Many of these contain flower extracts that seal off our aura, allowing us to remain in our own space; these creams will help us re-energise and refocus. All these products can be bought at good health food shops. However, while they will help enhance our personal space, there is little long-term benefit in using them if we continue to contaminate our space with unhelpful actions and emotions.

RECOGNISING WHEN THE ENERGIES AT WORK ARE HARMFUL

We cannot always overcome the energies at work. It is important to be able to distinguish between those workplaces that are difficult, and those that have become toxic. Toxic environments are seriously harmful and should be avoided at all costs. They destroy all who work there, sapping their passion and vitality, and poisoning their outlook. While we may feel we should hang on and try to change things, often all we end up doing is supporting a sick regime. Sometimes organisations have to die before they can be reborn, and so sometimes we need to walk away.

Farida landed her dream marketing job with an independent film company, where she was given plenty of scope to market the films, and was soon making a significant contribution to the company. Yet while Justin, her boss, supported her efforts, he was an extremely volatile individual, and so Farida had to deal with his frequent outbursts. Even though he would apologise for his constant mood swings, his temper proved too much. 'While Justin was technically brilliant, his negativity began to make me feel ill, to the point that I'd spend my days trying to avoid him,'

49

Farida confessed. Once she had moved on, Farida was able to see things differently: 'Now I'm no longer around Justin I feel like myself again. Had I stayed in the job, I know that I'd have become sick. It's sad that Justin's behaviour constantly drives people away.'

DOING THINGS DIFFERENTLY

When work no longer satisfies, often we waste our time waiting for the visionary CEO, or the right systems or equipment to appear. Chances are that everyone else in our organisation is taking the same approach, and so nothing ever improves. Instead of waiting for external events to transform our lives, we can begin to make *subtle* changes to our working day, to help lift the negative vibes at work. One important way to improve our experience of work is to pay more attention to how we start our day. Many of us wake up to the sound of the radio – often to the news – some of which might be good, but a large part of which is often deeply depressing. We shower. We may or may not exercise, then we rush breakfast and dash out the door. If we commute, we join large crushes of people, each with their own issues and anxieties. We grab a newspaper or magazine, and as we flick through we absorb literally dozens of messages – world news, gossip, how to look fabulous, how to find the perfect partner. Or if we walk or drive to work, we listen to the Walkman or the car radio – to hundreds more messages that tug us in a thousand different directions. Then by the time we reach work, our heads are full. Often all it takes is an angry call or unexpected directive, and we feel angry or as if we're not coping. If we're already feeling overloaded by the time we reach work, and those around us are equally stressed, is it any surprise that work is so fraught much of the time?

How else might we start our day? If when we get out of bed we are able to absorb the freshness of a new day, we can begin to feel a sense of *excitement* as we contemplate what this new day might bring. As we shower, we have the opportunity to enhance this feeling of newness by reminding ourselves that today is a fresh slate. Then having showered, our day will be far more satisfactory if we are able to take twenty minutes to meditate. At the end of our meditation we can consciously invite into the day the qualities we would like to experience at work. These qualities might include appreciation, stimulation, joy, peace, fulfilment. Whatever the life-affirming qualities we choose, *this* is the perfect time to invite them into our day. If we choose stimulation, for example, we can then try to imagine what a stimulating work day would feel like. As we isolate the qualities that speak to us, we can then try to *feel* their differing energies in our bodies, so we can start to build up a cellular memory of each quality. Once this memory is implanted within us, we start to recognise these qualities in our daily lives, and to draw them to us. Just before we leave home it also helps to visualise ourselves literally gleaming with Light – that will protect us and draw life-giving energies towards us. When we start our day in this way, it is far easier to have the kind of working day we all hope for.

CLEARING OUR HEADS

In attempting to turn around the climate in which we are working, it is important we give ourselves the chance to clear our head during the day, because we weren't made to sit for six to eight hours straight in air-conditioning under artificial lighting. These conditions, no matter how state-of-the-art, are unnatural. To ground ourselves in the moment, we need to make *regular* contact with the outside world – to feel the rain and the wind, the heat or the chill. When we remain within our work environment all day without any fresh air, it is much harder to stay focused, to see things clearly, to respond wisely. When we can get outside, even for a few minutes, any negative energy we might have picked up at work doesn't have the same chance of accumulating. Then when we get back to our desks, we'll feel energised and will be far more effective at whatever we have to do next. As we have become increasingly busy, we have become chained to our desks – working and eating and working some more – and so we end up taking in all the energies around us as we snack. If we can't get outside for lunch, then it helps to bless our food by visualising it filled with life-giving Light and nourishment. We don't have to say anything out loud – we can perform this blessing quietly but meaningfully with equal effect.

LEAVING WORK BEHIND

Similarly, when we finish work it helps consciously to leave the working day behind, so we don't take the day's tension home. Once we're outside, we can rebalance by breathing in whole lungfuls of fresh air. As we inhale, we can feel ourselves being filled with life-giving energies. After a day of work, often we're living inside our heads, and so as we leave work we need to ground ourselves by bringing our attention back to our body. One of the most effective ways to do this is to bring our attention into our feet – to begin to feel the impact of each step on the pavement. As we do so, we will become more aware of the movement of *different* parts of our feet as we walk. This is a wonderful exercise to anchor us in our bodies. We know when it's working, because our feet feel well and truly planted on the ground.

Often by the end of the day we're tired and stressed, and so we end up taking our work problems home, souring our time with family and friends. If we do need to talk through our day, then it's best to do so outside – to go for a walk in the local park, or out into the garden – so that negative energies don't accumulate in our living space. The less we go on about work, the less life energy we expend, and the less negativity we generate. Again, we should avoid tackling such issues while we eat. When we do get home it's our chance to change pace – to slip into comfortable clothes, to enjoy time to ourselves, and time for pursuits we love. If we're prone to being manic, then we need to think carefully about our out-of-work activities, so that our every waking moment doesn't become a blur of activity. If we are in need of exercise, then it helps to combine physical exercise with activities that clear the mind and uplift the spirit – such as a class in yoga or tai chi. It is important that our time out is spent doing things that genuinely uplift us. It is also extremely beneficial to meditate for twenty minutes in the evening; it is an excellent way to unwind and get rid of any residual stress. And while it is good to keep up with current affairs, this is not necessarily the best diet when we have had a stressful day. It is certainly not a good idea to eat while watching the news, because again we are imbibing the energies of the footage we are witnessing as we ingest our food.

Of course, all these possibilities are about *attention*, about introducing those things into our working day that uplift our spirit. As we become more attentive to our needs, we then realise that even when the climate seems inhospitable at work, we need not become controlling or aggressive, because there are always effective ways forward. Dr Edward Bach, the founder of the healing Bach Flower Remedies, hints at this when describing how his essences work: 'They cure not by attacking the disease, but by . . . Higher Nature, in the presence of which disease melts away as snow in the sunshine.' When our backs are against the wall, we can make life difficult for ourselves and others, or we can allow our wisdom, insight and higher intent to help us move beyond our difficulties. This does not mean that we shouldn't stand up for our rights, but that by relaxing a little we allow our insight and imagination to guide us to a more complete solution for our issues at work. When we can work more constructively, we become an immense force for good.

⊷⊶

A prayer to start the new working day

'O Great Spirit, work seems overwhelming right now. Without meaning to, I have become angry and critical of myself and others. As today is a new day, help me to make a fresh start by inviting into this day those things that are for my highest good. I recognise that everyone in my life has something to teach me, and so help me to see what I can learn from each moment at work, so that my working life can be all that I hope for.'

harnessing the rhythms of life

We lie in the lap of immense intelligence, which makes us receivers of its truth.
RALPH WALDO EMERSON, 'SELF-RELIANCE', *ESSAYS: FIRST SERIES*

UNDERSTANDING THE PATTERNS OF BEING

Everything about work that we are looking at here is about the nuances of life. The more attention we pay to these nuances, the more we can discern the wisdom that is in them for us, and the clearer the way forward will be. The ancients knew the importance of the many patterns in life and studied them closely – not, as some might suppose, for superstitious reasons, but so that they might better understand the nature of human existence. The more familiar we are with the patterns of the natural world, the more we are able to make sense of the rhythms in our own lives. We then begin to realise that our life is a pattern within a pattern within a pattern, and that our work lives have a pattern too. When we fail to take note of these patterns, our lives can seem random or chaotic. That's when we can wear ourselves out trying to make things happen, but never quite succeeding. When we begin to work *with* the rhythms of life,

55

we have a much clearer sense of where we are heading and how best to proceed.

ALLOWING LIFE'S PATTERNS TO ENRICH OUR WORK

Part of being able to appreciate patterns in life is being able to enjoy the gradual unfolding of our working lives – moment by moment, day by day. So goal-oriented have many of us become that we have no sense of these things. Rarely do we take time to acknowledge how much we have achieved, let alone to contemplate what we have learnt on the way. We choose instead to beat ourselves up, or to focus on how far we yet have to travel, and so we lose the many opportunities for more joy and fulfilment at work as we race forward into an uncertain future.

I had an extraordinary dream some years back which, like many of my dreams, was set in a desert. In my dream I wandered around in the desert for a number of years. When finally I emerged, I was shocked to discover I had travelled in a series of spirals. For a long time this dream haunted me. I assumed that it was telling me I'd been going around in never-ending circles, and was greatly disheartened by it. It took me a long time to realise that while there might have been a more direct path through the desert, I was being shown the cycles of my own learning and completion. Each step within the spiral was significant, because it was another step in my understanding of myself and the world. Once I understood this, I was able to honour my successes and failures, and to see them as significant chapters in my life's story.

This dream helped me comprehend life's quest more completely – I now realise that each possibility that comes our way has its own shape and timing. When we become more aware of the cycles of our existence, it becomes obvious to us when to make a move and when to remain where we are. This ability to let go a little doesn't come easily, because many of us are addicted to being in control. We want to shape each moment of our working lives and to decide how best our career should unfold. If we are fortunate, we come to realise that we will travel much further when we can allow the intricate pattern of life to reveal itself to us, and nurture it accordingly. The more conscious we are of the life cycles within and around us, the more our working lives will shift from being a constant battle to being like a free-flowing tide. How often has our destiny been changed, not by a flow chart or a five-year plan, but by a chance meeting or an unexpected situation?

THE PURE JOY OF THE SPRING CYCLE

Each new cycle has its innate qualities – its possibilities and its dangers – and its wisdom. Our work follows this pattern also. One of the cycles that is most familiar is that of the seasons. The more aware we are of the nuances of each season at work, the more we can consciously use this awareness to help navigate our way through times of uncertainty and major change. When we're experiencing a new phase at work, it has all the hallmarks of spring. It's a time of awakening – of warmth and growth. In spring we come alive again, we feel inspired. We are happy to be outside and to be around others. And because the energies around us seem more conducive to action, we often feel restless. We are keen to get things moving – to make things happen. At work we may find ourselves absorbed in new projects or in a new planning phase, where all kinds of fresh possibilities present themselves. This is an exhilarating time, because we feel energised and full of ideas, and more able to hold the vision, as everything we work on seems to burgeon. Best of all, our work no longer feels like work.

During this buoyant time at work, it is important we remain focused and choose our projects wisely. Sometimes we fear that by passing or postponing certain projects we will miss the moment. Yet if we take on too much, our work is likely to be substandard or to fail. We need not be anxious about those projects that are best done later, because they will find their own, more appropriate time. In a spring cycle we also need to pace ourselves with the projects we do undertake, because if we progress too quickly or without sufficient attention, we might jeopardise the opportunities before us.

While our spring phase is an excellent time for new projects, it is also the time of sudden storms, of unexpected frost and cold that can blight the crops and destroy newly born animals. If we proceed with care during our spring phase at work, then we help ensure *all* our projects reach fruition. In our spring phase we must also take care not to alienate those we work with through our impatience to get things happening. We still need to make sure that the basics are taken care of. And even as we seek to advance our own work, we must never lose sight of the goals of our organisation. We must always be clear about how our work contributes to the wider effort.

THE EXPANSIVENESS OF THE SUMMER CYCLE

When we make good progress with our work, we reach the summer phase. Summer is the season most of us live for, because this is the time when all the effort we have put into our projects appears to be paying off. This is the way we believe our work should be. Now more than ever we are inspired to be out in the world – networking, tying up new deals and encouraging customers to raise their level of support. When we are in our summer phase, we enjoy everything we do at work and so we are able to achieve a great deal. As things are working so well, we are more able to be generous with those around us, and we are inclined to take more risks. This is also a time when we feel able to make good use of our many talents.

Yet even when everything is going our way, the summer phase is also the time when we can so easily become burnt out. When our work lives are going well, it is tempting to work even harder, and to forget to rest and to take stock. This is often the time when we tend to neglect our inner lives – when we allow our vision to fade as we become lost in the exhilaration of the moment. No longer do we bother to touch the more profound aspects of life, because we believe we are able to manage our own affairs. Then as our inner life recedes, so too does our insight. Unless we wake up to ourselves, we are in danger of becoming like Icarus. We too can get close to achieving all the goals we have set ourselves, only to fail spectacularly. We sabotage ourselves at work when in our summer phase we overspend, when we fail to attend to the detail, when we ignore the change that is taking place around us. During our summer phase it is important to balance our work with time out – not only for rest, but for review – and to continue to solicit the support and feedback of those around us. Only then will we achieve our goals and deliver all that we have promised.

THE DEEP SATISFACTION OF THE AUTUMN CYCLE

If we manage to stay on course, then we reach autumn – the time when our projects reach completion, when all the effort we have put into our work is most apparent to us and those around us. This is a golden time, because we have achieved what we set out to achieve. We have navigated our way through the uncertainties of spring, through the scorching heat of summer, and now we are able to step back a bit and enjoy the fruits of our labour. At last we can experience the satisfaction of a job well done. Yet even in this golden phase, there is no place for self-satisfaction, because we achieve little in isolation. This is the time for us to honour all those who have helped us accomplish all we have. And in the true spirit of gratitude, it is the time for us to consider how we might share our bounty with others.

Because this is a time of plenty, often we are less concerned about resources. Yet in spite of the abundance of autumn, it is important that we don't take our resources for granted. Even now we need to look to the future – to prepare for those times that might not be as plentiful. As we reflect on our achievements, it is a time also to deepen our awareness – to use all we have learned in this current cycle, so we can step forward with greater confidence. As autumn takes hold and the leaves turn to rust, we are reminded of how willingly the trees part with their leaves – how readily they shed those parts that have sustained and adorned them – to make room for new possibilities. And so, at the end of our own rich harvest cycle at work, we serve ourselves best when we can refocus and re-evaluate the resources we have, and then determine what we are likely to need in the future. If we wish to travel far at work, we need to travel light, and so now is the time to let go of aspects of our current job that no longer serve us, so we can accommodate new opportunities. This might mean reallocating resources, refining systems or re-evaluating the flow of work and information.

Not all harvests are joyous. We can only gain the full benefit of our own harvest cycle if we have tended our projects with care, if we have conducted ourselves appropriately, and if we have been thorough in everything that we have undertaken. But if we have been careless in our work or with our resources, if we have tried to take shortcuts, or if we have disadvantaged or harmed others along the way, then not only will we have to deal with the fallout from such actions, but we will have little support to rely on in the future.

THE OPPORTUNITY FOR REFLECTION IN THE WINTER CYCLE

As autumn gives way to the stark beauty of winter, instead of embracing all that the winter cycle offers us, many of us waste this opportunity for reflection and planning by mourning for what has been or by longing for the next phase of growth. The winter cycle at work can seem uninviting, because our progress is less obvious – whatever we do seems to take a lot more effort for little gain. We may also feel constricted or unsupported at work in this phase, and regard these as bleak times.

Wintertime at work is much easier to cope with when we understand that it is the time to get back to basics – to update our databases, to examine our results, to start thinking about future possibilities. We might have just been through a huge growth phase or have experienced a takeover, and so now is the time to *consolidate*, to attend to the detail of our job, to conserve our energies for the next phase of growth. In ancient times winter was known as the womb time – the time for dreams. In our ignorance we often fight this cycle. Instead of allowing clear plans for the future to emerge, we rush ahead without knowing where we are heading and end up squandering valuable resources and sabotaging perfectly good ideas.

Winter is the also time for the soul, the time when we need to pay closer attention to our *inner* life and our inner resources because, as the days darken, we can no longer rely on our physical sight to get us through at work. In the Chinese world-view, winter is the season of the feminine Yin energy – the time to nurture our life energies in readiness for spring. While we might not be able to see it at the time, winter is a time of huge potential at work, because as we reflect, we allow new ideas and possibilities to begin to take shape. As we allow our *inner* sight to grow, we sense the new possibilities coming to us, and can then work with them and shape them in readiness for another spring. One of the great challenges during our winter phase at work is not to lose heart. This can be especially hard when we are experiencing a winter cycle, and those around us are enjoying a different seasonal cycle altogether. In such times we need the courage and determination to remain focused on where *we* are at. It is important also that we can remain generous, instead of wasting our energy on envy or bitterness. We each have our time in the sun. We can begrudge others their success, or we can allow their achievements to warm our darker moments – to inspire us even.

In spite of any pressures that might be around us during our winter cycle, this is not a time to waste an ounce of energy. It is vital to move forward slowly and with great care. This also means ensuring that our fears and frustration don't drain us. We are masters of our *own* destiny, and when we can hold the faith, we will reach our target. The Roman god Janus, the god of beginnings, had two heads so that he was able to look back as well as forwards. We cannot move successfully into a new cycle at work unless we have fully integrated the lessons from the past. If we fail to build on the experience we have gained, we will end up repeating past mistakes or covering old ground. While we might not always appreciate it, winter can be an extremely fruitful time at work, because it allows us to build up the strength and direction needed for what lies ahead.

ALLOWING THE CYCLES TO POINT THE WAY FORWARD

As we become more aware of our own work cycles, we are able to see the possibilities for us at work and to utilise these insights fully to enhance our working days. As we begin to apply these understandings, we will start to enjoy a more intimate relationship with life – to appreciate nature and its seasons. We might even be inspired to celebrate them in some way: by bringing seasonal flowers or foods to work, or by having posters or prints that mark the seasons in our work space. As we become more attuned to the seasons, we can then start to examine other cycles in our lives and see how our energy levels fluctuate during the day, over a month, and throughout the year. The more aware we are of these fluctuations, the more we are able to capitalise on those times when we are most energetic at work, and to conserve our energy when our vitality is waning. When we can work with our own rhythms we will suffer far less stress and fatigue. I have always been a morning person – that is when I am most productive – and so I attend to the more challenging projects and meetings earlier in the day, saving the more routine aspects of my job for mid- to late afternoon.

At the change of seasons we can often feel exhausted as our bodies adapt. When we realise what is happening, again it gives us the opportunity to carve out a little time for quiet, enabling us to rebuild our strength. We can further boost our vitality by eating foods that are in season, as these foods carry the nutritional qualities needed for the current season and help prepare our bodies for the season to come. Learning to listen to our bodies is essential if we want to make the best of our many unique gifts at work. After being sick, we often rush back to work and immediately start working long hours and socialising after work, giving our bodies little chance to regain their full vitality. This disregard for the healing cycle needed by our bodies often weakens our system and makes us more vulnerable to further health problems, when with a little additional care we could regain full health. The wisdom of nature's cycles is boundless – the more we work with these cycles, the more they will teach us about the challenges and possibilities that are there for us, enabling us to deepen our experience of work and to be far more successful.

CONTEMPLATION OF OUR PRESENT WORK CYCLE

Find somewhere you enjoy being – where you can be alone with your thoughts – and make yourself comfortable. When you feel ready, take three deep breaths, allowing any tension in your body to dissolve. Then, drawing your attention within, gently close your eyes and follow your breath as it moves in and out of your body. As you linger in this peaceful space you might like to consider the following questions and see what inner guidance you receive.

- What phase of work am I in right now?
- What opportunities are there for me in this phase?
- What do I need to take more care over at this time?
- How does my current work phase relate to those of the people around me?
- How might I work with these insights?
- What other rhythms are there in my life that can enrich the moment?
- How best might I work with these wider rhythms?

knowing when we're tired and when we need to move on

When we no longer see through the glass darkly, many things become apparent to us without effort.

DETERMINING WHETHER WE HAVE HAD ENOUGH

There comes a time in any job, no matter how fulfilling, when our passion wanes, or we no longer feel happy and secure. When this happens, we naturally assume it's time to move on – and we may well be right. Equally, the difficulties we are currently facing at work might have presented themselves to enable us to take a quantum leap forward. In that case, if we leave our job prematurely, we will miss out on the opportunities before us. Often we spend our working lives on the run, dreaming of a time when we will have the peace and satisfaction we long for, but because we are in such a hurry to get ahead, we fail to see what the moment offers. Then we wonder why work isn't delivering all we had hoped for!

OPENING UP TO OUR INNER WISDOM

If we are feeling as if we have had enough of our current job, instead of getting out our résumé or contacting a recruitment company, we are better off taking a moment to become still and allow our inner voice to be heard. When we access our inner voice, we become aware of our most profound longings. Our inner voice is the voice of our soul. It is untainted by our wishes and desires, and by the opinions of others. In those cultures, past or present, that honour the sacred, it is natural for people to go deep within when faced with a major dilemma. This is not how most of us approach on-the-job issues, but it is an approach that will never fail us – even at work.

To access our insight, all we need do is find somewhere we love to be, where we can be quiet. It is important we enter this space with reverence, and that we be open to whatever messages we might receive. Then as we settle down and allow all thoughts and distractions to fade, we become more aware of our *inner* space. It helps to close our eyes, to allow the silence of the moment to deepen. Here in this sacred space – beyond the freneticism – we have the opportunity to take a more panoramic view of our working life, rather than seeing just a slice of it. Then as we linger in the silence, we can ask whether we are meant to stay in our current job, or whether it is time to move on. In this moment of contemplation, we might even like to say a short prayer.

⊷⊶

'O Great Spirit I'm feeling low about work right now. Part of me would like to leave, but I realise I might not be seeing the full picture. Help me to see how best I can move forward for my highest good.'

⊷⊶

As we allow our breathing to slow and our attention to move still deeper within, we are reminded that it is in the silence that we align ourselves with the Source of all things. The success of this exercise has nothing to do with whether we have psychic abilities – it's about allowing our inner voice to be heard.

Sometimes we will get an immediate answer to our dilemma around work, and sometimes this contemplation will begin the process of clarification. While most of us want to know what to do *now*, the best outcome will occur if we are able to go with the flow. We might not have instant clarification, because life might be teaching us the strength and wisdom that comes with a little more patience, or perhaps by staying where we are we are being prevented from making a big mistake. When we have the courage to remain at our current workplace until the way ahead becomes clear, we ensure that we end up where we are meant to be.

Nikki had been with her market research company for several years when a rival company approached her, suggesting she might join them. The timing seemed perfect, because this was a prestigious company, and one that Nikki had been watching closely for some time. Nikki had a very productive meeting with the CEO and was ready to accept the position, when she began to feel something wasn't quite right. 'I liked the company – their track record, their culture, their ethics. Yet after the meeting I began to feel apprehensive. There was nothing I could pinpoint, just a feeling that something would go wrong.' In spite of the excellent salary package they offered her, Nikki decided to pass on the opportunity. 'At the time my friends thought I was mad. Part of me thought I was mad as well, but I just couldn't get past how I was feeling.' Less than three months later the company was bought out and most people lost their jobs. 'I can't tell you how relieved I was I hadn't joined them,' Nikki confessed. She went on to explain that this situation had helped her realise it was time to move on – she ended up accepting an even better offer from another company.

BEING SURE IT'S TIME TO MOVE

Just because we're feeling out of sorts doesn't always mean we need to resign. Often our challenges at work can give us the opportunity to overcome the issues that have been holding us back. If we change jobs simply to avoid those aspects of work that cause us discomfort, then all we end up doing is taking our unresolved issues to our next workplace.

Although she was highly capable and hardworking, Pia always seemed to work for managers who took advantage of her. In every job she had, her hours were long, her workload huge and her salary modest. Every two or three years Pia would move on, only to end up in the same situation. 'It wasn't until I looked back that I realised I'd allowed myself to be a doormat all my working life. I was so desperate to be needed that I'd agree to everything anyone asked of me, no matter how impossible it was. Then I'd be devastated when no-one seemed to appreciate all my hard work.'

It was only when Pia realised that her low self-esteem was a major contributor to her unhappiness that her job started to pick up. 'It never occurred to me that *I* might be the problem. Once I realised this, I thought about what *I* wanted from work, and from life outside work. I then realised that I needed to get my life back, so I enrolled in a dance class and booked myself a regular massage. I began to go to more movies and to put serious effort into my holidays and my weekends, and suddenly life was fun again. My tango lessons and massage sessions meant that

I couldn't stay back late at work every night, so those I worked with had to be more organised. The more I stood up for myself, the more I began to look forward to getting out of bed in the morning, and work wasn't such a pain. When I did leave my job, I left for the right reasons. My new position is great, but I'm still careful to guard my own space.'

Howard had a similar experience when working in events management. Although he was good at what he did, Howard constantly got his team-mates offside, because of his inability to finish his projects on time. 'I've never had a problem with coming up with new ideas, or making them work,' Howard explained. 'My problem was being able to see my projects through. I'd get bored and want to get on with the next project, rather than finish the one I was working on. That meant that most projects ended up being a drama as I rushed to get things completed.' Howard had a string of jobs before he realised what he was doing to himself. Until then he'd always felt let down, because although he worked hard and brought in a lot of business, his jobs would end badly. 'I used to get mad at everyone, but it never occurred to me that the cause of the frustration could be me. When I realised, I was so relieved, because I could do something about it.' Howard knew that if he wanted his experience of work to improve he had to be more focused, so he got himself a 'new projects' folder to note down new ideas. 'That folder changed everything,' he admitted. 'I still get a bit bored towards the end of my projects, but I can give myself a lift by taking a look at my new ideas, and thinking about what I might do next.'

Going off and getting another job wasn't the answer for Pia or Howard – or at least not until they had overcome their own difficulties with work. And so before we race off for another round of interviews, we need to be clear about any issues facing

69

us at work right now. Perhaps we are lacking self-esteem, or we might have allowed ourselves to become swamped by our work. Are we taking our stress and frustration out on others, or are we perhaps allowing others to take advantage of us? Before we make a move, it is important we get our act together, so we can make full use of the possibilities that await us.

TAKING A LOOK AT OURSELVES

Even if we can't identify any issues we need to deal with at work at present, before we consider moving on, we need also to take a look at our vitality and at how we are feeling, because when we are unhappy or exhausted, we are hardly in the best position to attract the perfect job. The more tired we feel, the more likely we are to attract difficult and depressing circumstances. We have all experienced moments when we're so tired and stressed we no longer seem to be in control. Nothing seems to go smoothly, and any problems we might be facing seem to go from bad to worse.

Before we make any decisions about whether we should remain at our current workplace, it's a good idea to get away for a bit. Even if we're not able to take a decent holiday, it is a good idea to plan a weekend away, or a weekend where we can relax at home. It also helps to have a few early nights and some decent meals – and to book a shiatsu or aromatherapy session. Acupuncture, Reiki or qigong therapies are also helpful, because they help balance our life energies and enhance the flow of energy through our whole being. As always it is preferable to gain a referral to these services from someone we trust. These opportunities will help bring us back into balance, and enable us to gain some much-needed perspective. They help put us in touch with our inner voice, which prompts us towards actions that are for our highest good. It might become clear that it's time to move on, but then at least we will be moving forward with vitality and clarity.

CONSIDERING OUR TIMING

Once we know with certainty we are to resign, then we need to be clear about whether our move should be immediate, or whether it is something it is best to work towards. Again, when we take note of our inner guidance, we will know which approach is best. Frequently this guidance will come out of left field, or will be like pieces of a jigsaw puzzle that slowly come together to reveal the full picture. One of my major career moves began with a series of dreams that made it clear that it was time to move on. I had no idea where I should go next, so I meditated on this question. To my surprise I started to bump into old publishing workmates. Their joy and passion helped me to realise just how unfulfilling my working life had become. Then one morning a publishing friend produced an unexpected bunch of flowers. As I gazed at her flowers over the days that followed, I realised I wanted to return to publishing. The only problem was there were no jobs going in my area of expertise. Then in a quiet moment, the name of the publishing house came to me. I literally heard it inside my head. This wasn't an obvious choice, but trusting my inner guidance I sent off my résumé. Part of me doubted that there would be a job in the near future, but before I knew it a position had been created for me. Once I was in-house I was able to see just how perfect the job was – not only was I able to work with many spiritual authors, I also had the head space to start writing my own books.

Often when things don't happen immediately we become disheartened. We might then be tempted to rush the process, not realising that even if we end up with a new job, that job will often be less than ideal.

Morgan was very keen to move on from advertising, because he was beginning to stagnate. Then when he came across a good job in TV, it seemed to be the right move. He interviewed well and was sure he had the job, but then discovered it had been awarded to an internal candidate. He was told another position was coming up with the same TV network, so Morgan put his job hunt on hold. Three months later his company offered him a transfer to another city. This proved to be perfect for Morgan – not only were his professional horizons broadened, but his girlfriend, who had been homesick, was happy to be living close to her family again. Because he waited, *all* Morgan's needs were met, allowing him to be in the right place at the right time.

STAYING STUCK

There are times we should move on but we prefer to stay where we are – because it's familiar, because we're feeling fragile, or because we're hoping things will get better. Change can seem threatening, but it is nowhere near as detrimental as remaining somewhere that is no longer working for us. Often we hesitate to make a move, because our outlook on life has narrowed, or because we no longer believe in ourselves. When our belief in ourselves fades, we become like captive animals – we forget what freedom looks and feels like, so we lack the energy and imagination to invite new possibilities into our lives. When we lack the courage even to contemplate new horizons, we start to live and work in limbo, and to feel tired and stressed. Then as we become increasingly frustrated with our lot, everything we have achieved at work starts to disappear – we become critical, less motivated, resentful even. We have all worked around those who have stayed in their jobs too long, and it's not a happy experience.

Gareth was worn out by his role as sales director for a leading paint manufacturer. He liked the company, but his work no longer held the same satisfaction for him. 'It would've been so easy for me to have stayed,' he admitted. 'I had a great package, an industry profile, and no-one my age had ever been appointed to such a senior position. Yet when I took a good look at myself, I saw where I was at. Jobs continued to be cut around me, and my workload kept increasing. The more I gave, the less I got back. I was getting seriously tired. I knew that if I didn't leave, I wouldn't have the energy to get out and find another job.' Luckily Gareth did get out. He went to work for a chain of fitness studios, which enabled him to combine his professional experience with his own passion for fitness.

MOVING BEYOND OUR FEARS

Sometimes we fear change because of our age or personal circumstances. This is natural, but we either believe that life can and will direct us to the job that is perfect for us, or we don't. It is *we* who create our opportunities or block them. Whether we are older, whether there is a recession, whether there are more people than jobs, will have *no* bearing on whether we can find the job we want – unless we *believe* it to be so. Everything in our world begins with a thought, from the Great Wall of China to the latest medical advances. Our lives are also informed by thought – *our* thoughts shape our reality.

Having accepted the importance of our thoughts, it helps to acknowledge any fears we might have around getting a new job, so that we don't sabotage our opportunities for success. When we *feel* our fears instead of trying to push them away, they will quickly begin to shrink down to size. We can assist this process by asking ourselves what would be the worst thing that could happen if we were to make a move. Initially the answers we get might terrify us, but as we sit with this question we will come to realise that the consequences aren't all that devastating. We can instead begin to see how much we have to offer, and how much we need a change or a new challenge. As we stay with these thoughts, we will then reach the stage where we will start to feel *comfortable* with the prospect of moving on.

Once we reach this point, we can consider how best to make our move. We might then realise that it is time to update certain skills, to refresh our image or our outlook. This might be the perfect time to get fit, to join a professional organisation, or to catch up with those we respect in our line of work. Having realised this, it is important we get organised – that we enrol for further study, join a gym, have our hair cut or purchase new work clothes. The very fact that we are open to change will help attract new opportunities to us. If we decide to remain where we are for positive reasons, then we still have the opportunity to recommit ourselves to our work and to take our current job to a whole new level. If it is time to move on, still we must continue to give our best as we wait for our new job to emerge. Either way this is not a life and death choice – it is simply another chapter in the rich tapestry of our lives.

TO STAY OR TO GO?

Why not take yourself off somewhere you feel comfortable and inspired? Then as you take in the peace of this place, allow every part of you to relax. Pay particular attention to any areas of tension in your body – in your shoulders or stomach, or around your shoulders and mouth. Allow these tensions to dissolve as your breathing slows. What a relief it is to let go! Then when the moment feels right, you might like to consider the following questions, and see what inner guidance you receive.

- What are the reasons you are feeling disgruntled at work right now?
- How does your current attitude to work compare with when you first started your job?
- What has changed?
- Are you simply tired and stressed right now, or is there something more going on?
- How much have your actions and expectations contributed to the way you feel?
- Are there any external influences that have contributed to your current feelings?
- Are these positive influences, or are you best to move beyond these influences?
- Is there more your current job can deliver?
- How can you help make this happen?
- If you want to move on, what personal issues need to be addressed before you can move forward?
- Do you have the confidence and vitality to find a new job right now?
- What, if any, are your fears around work?
- Where do these fears come from?
- Are they realistic?
- What practical steps can you take to boost your confidence and vitality?
- List all your achievements at work to date, then as you peruse your achievements, take a moment to acknowledge all you have accomplished. Are there any areas you can improve on?

PLAN OF ACTION

Now it is time to draw up your action plan. Allow your intuition as well as your experience to guide you in the planning process.

1   Write down all you hope to achieve from this plan.
2   Summarise these points in a single sentence.
3   List the actions needed to put your objectives in place.
4   Think about whether there are any additional resources required to meet your objectives.
5   Consider how you might get these resources together.
6   Work out how long it will take to achieve each part of the plan.
7   Decide what the best possible outcome would be.

When you have these details down, you can begin to see the path ahead. Allow yourself to nurture and finetune your plans – then work towards making them a reality.

moving on

Come to the edge, he said. They said: We are afraid.
Come to the edge, he said.
They came. He pushed them . . . and they flew.
GUILLAUME APOLLINAIRE, 'COME TO THE EDGE'

WHERE TO NOW?

Often when we're considering changing jobs, we focus on our skills and achievements and how we can match these to available positions. Yet if we wish to get the most out of our future employment, we need also to determine the *qualities* we would most like in our future workplace, so that we can broaden the scope of what our life can bring. This wider focus also helps us to determine the kind of *environment* and *values* we would like in our new job. That way we don't end up somewhere where we are at odds with the ethics of that workplace, or where the environment does nothing to enhance who we are mentally, emotionally and spiritually. Those who are genuinely successful at work have the edge because they know themselves *intimately*. They know all the qualities they need to feed their passion and to succeed, and so they always ensure that they have what they need to sustain and enhance who they are. When we are aware of the qualities we need to get the most out of our working lives, our experience of work will be greatly enhanced. Naturally, we still need to have certain qualifications for the kind of job we are after, to put the work in on our résumé, and to prepare ourselves thoroughly for our interviews.

DETERMINING EXACTLY WHAT WE NEED FROM OUR WORK

An ideal time to contemplate the three or four qualities we would like in our next job is after morning meditation. Whatever qualities we desire, it is important we give them some thought, and that we write them down. These qualities might include joy, stimulation, genuine fulfilment, ease, integrity, clear purpose, peace, friendship, community, intellect and creativity. Once we have our basic list, we can expand it to include more practical details, such as the location and size of the organisation, the job specifications and the remuneration package. Again, the secret is to be specific, without precluding the wider opportunities that might present themselves; that way we can find the job that is the best for us in *every* way.

Basically this is about ensuring we can enjoy *all* that our new job can offer us, rather than just a part of it. Then as our vision of ourselves expands, so will the opportunities that we draw to us. When considering the location of our next job, for example, instead of choosing specific areas in our town or city where we would like to work, we are best to focus on the *qualities* of the location, such as pleasant/central/busy or within however many minutes from our home. By allowing this level of *flexibility* into our lives, we then attract possibilities to us we hadn't even considered.

SEEING OUR SALARY PACKAGE IN A NEW LIGHT

When thinking about our salary, we will get the optimum result when we ask for a package that will give us an abundant life, rather than setting an absolute value for our remuneration. Often when we're considering a new job, it is hard for us to look beyond our financial commitments. Yet while there are highly attractive salary packages around, unless we are very clear about what we *most* want from our work, we may end up with golden handcuffs. We might joke about selling our souls to the company store, but it's no joke when we're caught in this situation. Each day of our lives is precious, too precious to waste doing something we hate just for the pay. Equally, when we become too prescriptive about our salary, we can end up missing out on the job that is perfect for us, because it comes within a whisker of what we need to live on. If we want our life to be an adventure, then we have to learn to live adventurously. Note that it is the *spirit* of adventure we're talking about here, not recklessness. Through a willingness to be more open, we help locate where we are meant to be.

OPENING OURSELVES UP TO THE ASSISTANCE OF THE UNIVERSE
When we have given our job prospects the time and consideration they deserve, and have done all the additional research and preparation, including our résumé, then and only then are we ready to send off our details. We can add further weight to our application by proclaiming our intent as we despatch it, for example in the following way.

'I now open myself up to all that is for my highest good, knowing that everything I need to flourish will come to me. I ask for the clarity to recognise what is for my benefit, and the wisdom to act upon these things.'

When we have the courage to dream and to believe that our dreams can be realised, we will fly like eagles, because we are putting into action our belief that what we genuinely need in our lives will come to us. Then all we have to do is hold the vision, and move with what life brings our way. This might seem too easy, but divine ease can be ours when we can live and work with this level of openness – we will be *amazed* at what eventuates.

HOW BEST TO MOVE ON

Once we have made the decision to leave, we then have to determine *how* we are going to complete this chapter of our lives. Do we use this opportunity to get back at all those who have given us a hard time, or do we simply ignore everyone? After feeling so disenchanted, suddenly we are in a position of power. This is the kind of circumstance our little self dreams of, because it places us in the spotlight. If we're not careful, we will find ourselves responding to our little self's need to be noticed by doing things that are destructive or that we regret. How we conduct ourselves as we leave is critical; not only will it impact on those we leave behind, but on our future wellbeing. We may have been treated unfairly or thoughtlessly. We may even have doubts about the leadership of our organisation, or about the choice of our successor. We might be in the ideal position to be vindictive, but why would we dishonour ourselves and disappoint others?

If we do feel vindictive, then we can be sure our little self has surfaced. Our little self prompts us to be bitter and ungenerous, to alienate those around us. Often it is hard to let go of our anger and frustration, especially when we have had a tough time, but once we are aware that this is our little self at work, we are in a better position to see how we might progress. When we are in this quandary, it can help to hold a dialogue with our little self, so that we can regain our perspective. We do this by imagining our little self as a small child in need of comfort and by talking to it compassionately. 'I understand how angry you are feeling, little self. A lot of things have happened to disappoint and frustrate you at work, but now you are moving on. The best thing you can do is put all this unhappiness behind you, so you can leave feeling happy and good about yourself.' Any answers we get back from our little self will help isolate the source of our frustration, thus helping us to work through any remaining issues more consciously. When we can continue to respond to any angry outbursts from our little self as we would to a wounded child, we allow our divine self to come to the fore, enabling us to behave with wisdom and grace.

HEALING THE PAST

When we work with our divine self, we can achieve extraordinary things around our departure – old hurts can be mended, injustices rectified and new approaches taken. Then instead of adding insult to injury, we illuminate the way forward for ourselves and others. When we allow our divine self to guide us, not only will it steer us in the direction of *everyone's* highest good, we will help transform the past and create a better future. The choice of how we leave is ours. We can be critical and destructive, adding to the many challenges of those left behind, or we can be generous by only saying and doing those things that will *genuinely* assist those who remain. As we weigh up our options, we are reminded that there is no cause without effect, and that whatever energy we create around our leaving is the energy we take with us into our new job. We can leave with the love and respect of our workmates, or we can leave a trail of bad emotions and dissent that will return to us further down the track.

81

HONOURING WHAT HAS BEEN

As we close this chapter of our working lives, it helps to reflect on all the good things that have come our way in our current job – all of our friendships and achievements, big and small, are significant. We can gather up these precious moments and take them with us into the future. As we recall each of our many uplifting moments at work, we can visualise them as streams of gold surrounding and enfolding us in their warmth. As we re-experience the joy and delight these moments brought, we realise that even when we felt isolated at work, there were people who were there for us, and that good things happened. Knowing this, we are more able to be positive about our future. Once these recollections are complete, we can then take a deep breath and visualise all this energy being absorbed into our every cell, literally en-lightening us as it takes up residence within us. Then as we breathe out, we can visualise all the negative energies from our current job slipping away with our breath and ask that this negativity be turned into light. We may wish to repeat these breaths several times, breathing in all that has been beneficial in our job and letting go of all that was not. We will know when we are done, because we will feel a tangible sense of relief and lightness. This is a powerful exercise, because it enables us to prepare ourselves for a more positive future.

SHARING OUR LIGHT

As we leave, this is the perfect time to thank all those who have worked with us – for their on-the-job advice and support, and for their friendship. When we make the effort to say thank you, we not only bless the lives of others, we give them a wider vision of who they are. How wonderful it is to discover that a tiny gesture or remark of ours has helped someone else. Why would we not tell those we work with how much we appreciate what they have done for us? When we can mirror back to others their kindness and generosity, we light their way. We can also bless them by praying that all the wonderful things these individuals have done may flow back to them many times over. When we take the time for such gestures, we leave a legacy of joy and hopefulness behind.

PUTTING THE PAST BEHIND US
As we prepare to leave there may be unfinished business with some of the people we work with. Perhaps there wasn't the support or the clarity of vision we had hoped for in our job. Perhaps a disagreement has blighted a friendship. Or perhaps we let our focus on work prevent us from listening to others or respecting them. When we can put these old scores to rest, everyone benefits. How we do this depends on the circumstances. Sometimes direct contact with the person concerned makes good sense, while at other times a kind note or some other positive gesture might be more appropriate.

Joanna worked for a mining consortium. It was a tough workplace that was frequently dogged by industrial disputes. Just before she left, there were a couple of female staff she would have liked to support more, had she had the time. 'These women worked in isolated conditions and their jobs were difficult, but because I was up against it, I couldn't give them the support they deserved. Once I'd resigned, I made time to see them individually. I apologised to them, telling them how much I respected them and wishing them well for the future. I left one with a box of her favourite chocolates and the other with a bottle of a perfume I knew she liked. I hope these gestures helped. They certainly helped me to set the record straight.'

The more genuine our desire to heal a situation, the greater our likelihood of success. Still, we need to prepare for such moments. If we plan to speak directly with someone, it helps first to take a moment to become still and ask for the inner guidance to say whatever is most appropriate. Then when we do talk with that person, the focus should be on *healing* the situation and not on returning to old issues. Timing is critical. If the person is stressed or busy, the outcome is unlikely to be positive. Too often we become impatient, and so we rush forward, shattering what might have been an excellent opportunity to put that relationship on a better footing. When we do get together, it is best we do so without any preconceptions. The outcome may be everything we had hoped for, or a level of resentment or fear may still remain. Part of having the courage to honour others is respecting their right to react as they choose. Instead of trying to manipulate someone out of their own negative feelings, we are better to say respectfully and succinctly what needs to be said, then simply thank them for their time and wish them well. By making a *genuine* overture, we help let go of any discord, and are then able to move forward more easily. Whether or not the person responds as we had hoped is not our concern. We will have helped them by letting go of the negativity we held towards them.

The very thought of making these approaches can seem daunting, but they can have a huge impact for good. Again it is important to listen to the promptings of our inner guidance, because sometimes what seems not worth bothering about can have a profound effect on others.

After five harrowing years with a large media organisation, Dana decided to quit. She had worked incredibly hard to turn her department around and improve the company's culture. While she had been successful, she was worn out by the process.

Still she was determined to leave properly, but she had some major regrets. 'I was really disappointed I hadn't been able to do a whole lot more with my job, but the organisation was so dysfunctional every step was hard going. Then one of our senior executives took me aside and thanked me for achieving all I had. He also apologised for the lack of support I'd received, and in a couple of sentences all my regrets about leaving were gone. I'll never forget the fact that he made the time to acknowledge me.' The person who took the time to speak to Dana need not have bothered, but what a difference it made when he did. Why not pause to consider the issues you might need to address around work? Allow your intuition to guide you as to how best you might then go about healing the past, so that everyone can move on. Don't rush this process, because it is an important one.

LEARNING THE GRACE TO LET GO

From the moment we resign, our whole relationship with work changes. Once the euphoria of having resigned settles, we are often left feeling empty or melancholy. We are still looking forward to our new life, but part of us wants to cling to what we know. Now we are forced to face certain realities: no longer will it be appropriate for us to attend some meetings or to have access to certain information. Our workmates will treat us differently – they will start to work around us. When we reach this point, we have two options – we can gently and lovingly begin to let go of our attachment to work and enjoy the resultant sense of release; or we can put ourselves and others in an embarrassing situation by expecting to be treated as if we were remaining in the job.

If we are feeling nervous or down about leaving, the higher path is to replace these feelings with *gracious* behaviour. Grace helps us see our situation as it really is, and not how it feels in a moment when we're feeling shaky. When we can live and work with grace, we can see that our workmates aren't ignoring us so much as starting to adjust to working without us. Once we can see things from *their* perspective, we realise that there is no reason for us to get upset or annoyed. As we empty ourselves of what is rapidly becoming our past, we will find the space in our lives for all the new opportunities that are coming towards us.

MAINTAINING OUR COMMITMENT TO WORK

Just because the dynamics are changing around us doesn't mean we should work any less hard. We have all seen people drop the ball the moment they resign. This is an ungracious response, and one that will lose us whatever kudos we might have gained. When we take this path, we have little respect for ourselves, and we disappoint and de-motivate our workmates. We are still being paid, so we need to act with integrity by giving our work our full attention, and by being judicious about the information we have access to, so that we never take from our workplace those things that are not ours to take. When we can behave ethically and graciously, we can leave with a clear conscience.

THOSE WHO COME AFTER US

We may or may not approve of the person who is to replace us, but again the absolute integrity of our conduct is all – so why would we not be generous with the information we share during our handover? This done, it is important to let go of the outcome. Our successor may take on board the information we have given them, or they might choose to take a different path altogether. Their choices are not our concern. We are here on our earthly quest to follow *our* path, not to be distracted by everything that is going on around us. The important point is that we are able to leave our job with a light heart and a clear conscience.

When the time comes for us to go, the best gift we can give those who remain is to bless their work space by asking that all good things might come to those who work there, including our successor. Our physical work space will also need attention. Often when people pack up, they get rid of a few files and leave the rest for others to clean. This is an ungracious way to depart, and not something we would like to have happen to us. So why not take the time to clean up thoroughly? Having done this, we can then visualise our work space bathed in Light, and can bless it, because this space has enabled us to learn and experience many things. Then we should ask that those who continue to work here will also be blessed by this space. When we can move on in this way, we are able to progress without regret. Once we have left, we must take care not to undo all our good work by careless comments. The best way forward is to maintain a positive outlook and to avoid conversations we will live to regret. All these gestures are about creating a vibrant, light-filled space around us, so that we can continue to attract life-enhancing possibilities to us wherever we are.

<hr />

A prayer on departing

'O Great Spirit, now it's time to move on I feel relieved and anxious. I know the new job is right for me, but part of me is sad to leave behind all that is familiar. Help me to leave well, to bless others with whatever gestures of thanks and reconciliation I can, so that all our futures will be brighter and more fulfilling.'

87

managing our ambitions

It is not titles that honour men, but men that honour titles.
Niccolò Machiavelli, *Discorsi*, XXXVIII

DEFINING WHAT WE MEAN BY SUCCESS

What we do at work shapes our whole lives, and so it is vital to be in the kind of job that shapes us profoundly, that enhances who we are – mind, body and spirit. Sometimes we have difficulty isolating what we most want from our work, and so we take on the aspirations of others. The outside influences on us can be significant, but this does not mean they are beneficial. It is easy to assume that by being as driven as the next person at work we will attain the success we long for. Equally, even though the excessive ambition around us might be unattractive, such values can sneak up on us, robbing us of our humanity and submerging our wider vision for ourselves. We must always be sure that we are managing our ambitions, and that they are not managing us. At the heart of our aspirations is our desire to live more meaningfully. Our work goals might be centred on material considerations, or they might be focused on more altruistic concerns.

Regardless of where the emphasis lies, we still need to be clear about the kind of success we're aiming for at work, and what the trade-off will be to achieve this success.

Too often our goals around work are one-dimensional, which is unfortunate because we as human beings are not. We have the capacity to live in a way that touches many dimensions of being. If we wish our work to be genuinely fulfilling, we need to apply a great deal more care, attention and imagination to our goals, to ensure our life at and beyond work is all we had hoped for. This means being clear about our aspirations and where they might lead us. There is a great deal more to setting clear goals for work than ensuring we have the requisite skills and temperament. We need to be clear about where our boundaries lie – ethically and professionally – and about how much we are prepared to sacrifice to get where we are going. We also need to give some thought to what we plan to do when we reach our desired goal.

When looking ahead, it is important to have a sense of whether we can have the job we aspire to *and* a life beyond work. Will this job satisfy the qualities that are important to us, or are we going to have to compromise in some way? And if there will be compromises, are we happy to make them? Are the qualities we are left with enough to yield a rich and rewarding working life? How do we know this? Who has achieved what we hope to achieve? Do we respect these individuals, or are there aspects about them that make us uncomfortable? If so, can we do things differently? How might we do this? Do we simply want to be the sharpest sales executive in living memory, a high-profile CEO, a multi-award-winning designer, or are there more profound aspirations that we might also incorporate into our work?

At the root of these questions is how we *most* want to live – at work and beyond it – not at some time in the future, but right now. Do we want to work till we drop? Do we want to postpone opportunities for relationships, or to have a family, for our work? Or can we have a rewarding career, a strong relationship *and* a happy family? Buddhist teachings isolate the three causes of suffering that strike at the heart of so many of our aspirations. These are: wanting what we don't have; having what we don't want; and not knowing what we do want. Let us take a closer look at our goals at work. Why do we seek certain things? Is it because we don't like what we currently have at work? Do we want what someone else has? Are we too confused to see the difference? Or are we inspired by a passion that comes from deep within – that has an extraordinary sense of rightness?

WHOSE SUCCESS?

Judy Garland once said the only way to live was to be a first-rate version of yourself, instead of a second-rate version of some-one else – a remark that arose no doubt out of the pain she had experienced. Let us now examine our aspirations around work. *Whose* ambitions do we seek to embrace? Are these *our* ambi-tions, or those of our parents or peers, or of someone we read about in a newspaper or magazine? As we consider our choices, it is important to remind ourselves that it is *we* who must create our own destiny. In *The Mist-Filled Path*, Frank MacEowen also reminds us that often we underestimate our power as shapers of the world, and the power of the world to shape us in ways that are unholy.

Without a genuine connection with our inner life, we can so easily end up living someone else's dream. We must always take great care when setting our course, lest we trade our authentic selves for stereotypes that have been manufactured by advertisers and marketers. To cultivate our inner life takes time, effort,

90

commitment, and a willingness to be *ourselves* and to go *our* own way. It means taking full responsibility for our lives and there's the rub, because it often seems easier to do what others want. And yet the consequences of failing to be the people we long to be can be extremely painful. This is why so many seemingly successful people in the workplace cannot operate without medication, because in spite of their many achievements, they fail to live and work in a way that sustains them body and spirit. So painful is their work space, they can only inhabit it if they numb their feelings and dull their pain.

Sometimes our ambitions are driven by our fears of what others may think of us – fears of whether our current good fortune will last, and fears of not having enough. Our fears around work can also often manifest themselves in an intense neediness – in a desperation to be happy, to feel good, to have more. We all have the right to seek happiness and fulfilment at work, but as we run our eyes down the long list of things we want from our job, it doesn't hurt to ask ourselves *which* part of us will feel good when finally we get the promotion or the new pair of shoes. Is it that part of us that likes to reach out to others, that wants to leave the world a better place? Or is it that part of us that is desperate to be accepted, that fantasises about the attention we will receive when we have achieved this or acquired that?

The problem for many of us is that we are too tired and stressed to think for ourselves, and so we end up accepting what others tell us we should be doing with our lives. But when we do choose to live packaged lives, we no longer give anything much thought. While we flatter ourselves that we remain free thinkers, soon we are following the dictates of fashion and opinion without question. Then our own addictive, non-questioning behaviour rubs off on our kids, turning them into stereotypes. In this way, the never-ending cycle of neediness is perpetuated across the generations.

WHERE HAVE OUR AMBITIONS BROUGHT US?

As we contemplate our aspirations, we also need to ask how our ambitions have shaped our lives to date. How has our current work status impacted on our relationships, on our friends and on our family? Has it made us a better person? Are we more outgoing, more passionate, more vital – or have we become closed-off and self-centred, obsessive or unhappy? How is our mental and physical health? Have we become strangers in our own homes – strangers to ourselves? What essential life-giving qualities have we sacrificed to get where we are going? Are we sure it's been worth it?

Brad recently confessed that while he had enjoyed an extremely privileged upbringing due to his father's excellent job, his childhood home was never a relaxed place to be. 'Dad was rarely there, and when he was he made everyone tense, because he was always so uptight. It's a terrible thing to say, but in the end we all liked it better when he wasn't around. Then Dad was retrenched. You'd think that it would've been a disaster, but it was one of the best things that could've happened for us kids, and for Mum, because we got our father back.'

Being clear about our aspirations means we also need to consider what impact our work might be having on those we love. In a recent article on women in the workplace, journalist Jane Cadzow told the story of a first-time mother and principal legal counsel for a leading global information and technology group, who took part in an international conference call late at night. This might seem unremarkable were it not for the fact that this woman was in the grip of premature labour. By the time the conference call was over an hour and a half later, her contractions were four minutes apart. Her daughter was born a few hours later by emergency caesarean. There are many shocking aspects to this tale. Yet again, we see someone so focused on their career that they were driven to deny one of the most crucial moments of human experience. Would any of us want to be the child of someone so lost, so driven? How does it feel to be so captivated by our job that we daren't even admit to being in labour? And what sort of work culture would permit someone to behave in this way? Too often we have taken on the dysfunctional values of the workplace, damaging ourselves and those we love.

I learned recently of a senior executive who lived and breathed work, who had a heart attack while checking into his hotel. This man was only in his late thirties, and so the attack came as a huge shock. The first call he made was not to his wife and children, but to his secretary asking her to reschedule his appointments. Tragically for this man, his heart attack left him so debilitated he was unable to return to work. His wife and family were then left to deal with his resultant breakdown. Given the choice, what would they have preferred? The house at the beach, or a husband and father who was a genuine part of the family? None of us knows what lies around the corner. We might be lucky. We might have many years of good health ahead of us, yet all we can be certain of is the present moment. Are we doing what we love at work in this moment? Are our ambitions under control, or are we postponing our lives to some future date when we will finally have everything we think we need to be happy?

THERE'S SUCCESS AND SUCCESS

Success can bring as much pain to our lives as failure, if not more. This might seem absurd, because this is not what we are socialised to believe. We are taught early that to succeed we need to take the chances that are available to us, and that if we are lucky doors will start to open. We are gratified when our efforts are acknowledged, and the more our careers bring, the more we often feel compelled to keep going, until winning becomes more important than how we play the game, until we end up trading our friendships and our loved ones for more money and more prestige. Then, naïvely, we are disappointed when our achievements fail to bring us the joy we had hoped for.

If we wish to live wisely, then we need to be clear about what any promotion will bring to our lives. We also need to ask ourselves whether this new opportunity is aligned with our values and our life energy. Perhaps our new job will deliver us more fulfilment than we could dream of. It may even help us on our soul quest to be more loving, more wise. If so, why would we not want to embrace this opportunity? But if what we are being offered at work doesn't enhance who we are intrinsically, by taking the job we are allowing precious years of our life to disappear from sight. Often when faced with the prospect of a promotion, we are so focused on the opportunity before us – on the status and the package – that we fail to look more deeply at what we're being offered. We agree to take a step up, not because we're passionate about what is being presented, but because we like the idea of driving a European car or occupying an office with a million-dollar view, or we embrace what is before us because we fear this opportunity may never come again.

We then begin to live our lives backwards. We convince ourselves that once we've earned a certain amount of money or achieved a level of security, we can have a life. The problem with this outlook is that the goalposts keep on shifting. We begin by convincing ourselves we need a home and some money in the bank before we can live the lives we dream of, but then as time passes we need a bigger home and more assets before we dare to take the plunge, and so our lives pass in what His Holiness the Dalai Lama calls 'practising superficialities'. I had a colleague who went for a promotion he didn't want, simply because his wife decided the house needed to be recarpeted and refurnished. This is a tragic circumstance, but it is far from unique. Millions of people the world over have put their lives on hold for garages and swimming pools and dining room suites. We are far more important than all of these things. No-one is suggesting we be reckless, merely that we dare to be who we are, so we can end up in the workplace that is right for us.

If our aspirations come purely from our ego – from our need to impress or to be better than those around us – then they cannot help but cause ourselves and others pain. That's when we become so desperate to be out there, to be noticed, that we don't even realise we have crossed the line. Life is an intricate process that demands our full attention if we are to achieve something meaningful. We might be the CEO who never fails to deliver the best bottom line, but what is the point if we lack humanity or if we destroy the lives of others on the way? Whatever choices we make, our work will demand a great deal of us, so why would we not choose a path that will enhance who we are, mind, body and spirit?

ASPIRATIONS OR ADDICTIONS?

In his timely book, *Growth Fetish*, Clive Hamilton describes us as 'prisoners of plenty', addicted to consumerism and the elusive promise of happiness contained within the next purchase and the next. When we are consumer addicts, we have to go for the next promotion and the next, just so that we can afford our lifestyle.

That's when we become a slave to our wardrobe or our decor, because we have come to rely on these accessories to feel worth-while. We do so forgetting that everything we possess demands our attention and life energy. All the great teachers warn us to hold whatever we have lightly, because they know how easily possessions can take over our whole lives. Then as our children become consumer addicts, the pressures multiply and our desperation grows.

There is a world of difference between a belief that the universe is here for us to take whatever we want from it, and one that encourages us to live in harmony and respect for all living things. When we begin to appreciate the exquisite intricacy of life, we realise that part of being genuinely successful is our ability to tread the earth with great care, and to be conscious of the resources needed to maintain our way of life. When we understand this principle, we are more mindful of what we choose to possess. So fixated have many of us become on what we earn and what we own, we forget that money is simply energy. If used correctly, our money can enable us to do many good things for ourselves and others. Yet often we get drawn into fear about money. We become scared that unless we play the game we'll end up in poverty or, worse still, on the street. Strangely, the more we have, the more our fears around our assets grow, and so we keep on consuming to try to stay safe.

Rarely when considering our ambitions are we told that our ability to enjoy an abundant life is linked to our ability to love – to enjoy the love we receive and to give love freely in return. Our aspirations are intimately connected to the energy in which we choose to live at each and every moment. When we choose to live in a safe and supportive universe where all our needs are met, we live in a state of love and of endless possibilities. We achieve this more expansive way of working when we dare to do the kind of work we love most. When we have the courage to follow our instinct, we can achieve remarkable things.

STRETCHING OUR IMAGINATIONS

Too often our aspirations are focused in on ourselves, and so we end up ignoring the needs of those around us. If we wish to enhance the life-giving energies within and around us, then our aspirations need to be more inclusive: we need also to consider what we can give back to life through our work. Most of us like the idea of being more generous and open-hearted, but then we get busy and postpone such opportunities. Ambition without contribution is meaningless; we all know this on some level, but often we forget it. In *The Diamond Cutter* we learn the story of diamond trader and Buddhist monk Michael Roach, who after joining the prestigious Andin International Diamond Corporation in New York, went on to create a department that turned over more than US$125 million. During his years with Andin International, Michael continued to live as a monk, keeping only enough money to sustain himself. The rest was used to support monks, and to establish schools, water systems and temples. Michael is now helping to fund the digitisation of all Buddhist texts – some 200 000 works – so they can be accessible to everyone. He has also set up the Enlightened Business Institute (www.info@enlightened business.com), where his methods and other principles for success are taught. Most of us don't necessarily have the imagination or the capacity to generate this level of resources, but we can still use our skills to support causes closer to home by our donations, or with a little of our time.

From here we might also like to think about our role as global citizens. As natural resources become increasingly scarce, we need to be clear about how many pairs of shoes and how many cylinders in our cars we need. And while most of us don't have limitless income, we are still in a position to give to worthy causes, to recycle our possessions, and to help those less fortunate. Often we slave away at work to accumulate whole mountains of things that sit unused in our drawers and cupboards. These are resources that could help the local refuge or halfway house. And so instead of focusing on our next shopping expedition, perhaps we can think about a small donation or a trip to the local refuge, or to wherever our surplus possessions might find a good home. These kinds of gestures are significant, because they help others and bring more heart into our lives.

THE IMPORTANCE OF OUR CONDUCT

Equally, through our kindness, we can ensure that each day we are a blessing to ourselves and others at work. Part of our goals might be to actively enhance the goodness on the planet by the way we work – by our thoughts and actions, by our courage and determination, by our sense of humour. These are not aspirations most of us factor in to our working lives, and yet how else can we ensure we are working meaningfully? Great sales figures and excellent product presentations won't get us there, and nor will achieving a record budget or a reduction in overall costs. If we lose our capacity to relate to ourselves and others, then what do we have of genuine worth?

We must always be careful about what we value, because certain attachments can creep up on us, obscuring so much that is good in our lives. Long ago there lived a king who had a great thirst for spiritual understanding. Then one day a holy man came to his palace. So taken was the king with this man's wisdom that he gave him a home in the palace. Here the holy man lived, owning only the clothes he stood up in and his gourd.

Each afternoon the holy man would give the king instruction in the palace gardens. Then one afternoon, while they were deep in conversation, a servant came running towards them shouting that the palace was on fire and that many priceless objects had been destroyed. The king went to wave his servant away, but on hearing the news the holy man leapt to his feet. 'I must save my gourd,' he cried as he raced towards the palace.

Perhaps without even realising it, our current ambitions around work have caused us to drift away from the place we planned to be. The good news is that there is always a way back to living more completely. There is a beautiful spiritual practice that encourages us to accept everything that comes to us each day as a gift. It suggests that at night before we sleep we take a moment to give back all the bounty we have received – all our friendships and achievements, all our possessions, even our lives – to the Source of all things. This is a profound practice, and one that helps us derive more joy from what we already have in our lives. It also helps free us from attachment, by recognising that all we have, including our brief lives, is transitory. When we can allow a more expansive attitude to inform our every moment, we become free in every aspect of our lives – free of fear and free of unhelpful aspirations and expectations. The more we are able to empty ourselves of all that we have and want, the more our life's journey will be the adventure it was meant to be, and the more we can then enjoy the texture and nuance of our working life.

⊶⊷

A prayer to help us see our way forward
'O Great Spirit, sometimes I get so confused about work.
I do want to make a difference and to be responsible for myself

and for my family, but I have become so caught up in my career and in how much I earn that I have forgotten how to live soulfully. Help me to walk the earth lightly. I want still to be successful, but never at the expense of others. And so as life rewards me, help me always to share this bounty with those who rely on my generosity and compassion. Help me also to make every moment at work count, and not to get lost in some distant goal, so that each working day will deliver all that my soul longs for.'

celebrating family and friends

However self-sufficient we may fancy ourselves,
we exist only in relation.
DERRICK BELL, *ETHICAL AMBITION*

THE IMPACT OF WORK ON OUR PERSONAL LIVES

Work shapes our lives in so many ways. Some ways are subtle, but often they can be dramatic, most of all for our friends and family. Some of the influences work brings make better people of us at home and at work. Equally, our commitment to our jobs can obscure who we are and what is important to us. As we juggle the pressures of work, home and commuting, many of the uplifting aspects of our lives have slipped away – we no longer notice and appreciate those we love, we have become obsessed with our work – and our homes have become little more than places where we keep our clothes and sleep.

THE LOSS OF INTIMACY

Most of us started working life committed to family and friends, and to work, and while we worked hard, our leisure time was equally important to us. Then, almost imperceptibly, the emphasis began to shift, until our family and friends have almost receded from view, until even our most intimate relationships are affected. Our work will take all the time we can give it. When we allow it to dominate our lives, it becomes increasingly difficult for us to enjoy the intimacy we long for, because when we are our overtaken by work there is little imagination or creativity left to warm the life of another. When we get home late, shovel our food down, have distracted conversations, and collapse in front of the TV, we're not living – we're in survival mode.

Our work can affect our opportunities for intimacy in so many ways. Often our conversations with our beloved are more like business meetings than two people who love each other sharing time together. Today even the language of love has largely been subverted by work. Rarely do we refer to those we love in ways that capture the depth of feeling we share – we talk instead of 'our partner', reflecting the emphasis on the material aspects of our relationship. Even the way we handle our money and check our diaries is accomplished with businesslike precision. And when we talk about who brings what to the relationship, rarely do we get beyond who contributes what in terms of income and possessions.

The more distant our relationships, the less meaningful our lives. Finding someone we love is a precious gift, and one that so many long for. Why, if we have found such a relationship, would we not want to nurture it through more life-enhancing behaviour and language? So many of the great works of literature, art and music have been inspired by the miracle of love, and when we experience these works, every part of our being soars. If we genuinely care for each other, then surely we want to balance the challenges of work with the *intimacy* of being with the person we love most. Work is a significant part of our lives, but so too is the opportunity to shut the door on the world and enter into the warmth of our loved one's company.

To create lasting joy and fulfilment in our personal lives, we need to ensure our love is nurtured so that it can flourish. When our love fades and those we love become invisible to us, we start treating them in ways that would once have been unthinkable. A group of bright young women married to high-powered executives talked recently of their despair and intense loneliness, as their roles had become little more than those of servants. 'My husband works really long hours,' one of them explained. 'Then when he gets home I'm not allowed to talk. Sometimes this goes on for hours. We eat most of our meals in silence – just so he can read the paper. Then when he's finished, he's off to do more work, or he sits in front of the TV and falls asleep. And then when there's a company dinner, I'm summoned. I feel more like a servant than a wife.'

What has happened that we would think of treating those we love in this way? Self-abuse and the neglect of those close to us are not uncommon around work, but that doesn't make this behaviour acceptable. Sadly, some even regard neglectful behaviour as being 'switched on'. One couple openly boasted recently about how many birthdays and significant occasions they had missed because of work – they had actually kept a tally. The deep irony is that so many of us work long hours and agree to impossible workloads in the hope that we can gather enough assets to allow us to enjoy family and friendships at some future date. The problem with this approach is that the right moment never seems to come, and so we miss out on all the many opportunities we have for joy. After the intensity of work, we all need replenishment. If we hope to have a healthy balance between work and the rest of our lives, then we need to invest

103

time and energy in our family and friends, and in the sanctuary of our homes.

THE PURPOSE OF FAMILY

Being part of a family is a critical part of our life experience, not just because we are bound by blood, but because we chose our families long before we came into this life. We also selected the circumstances and challenges that being with this group of people would bring, to assist us on our quest to learn the nature of love and to become wise. This was a *mutual* choice, because our families also agreed to be part of our lives. So even if our family background is less than ideal, we can still appreciate all that our parents and siblings have taught us about human nature – about tolerance and intolerance, about how to live our lives, and about how best to conduct ourselves. Our families provide countless opportunities to practise compassion and patience. They also teach us about acceptance, as we learn to take family members as they are, and not how we would like them to be.

Often the most joyful times we share with our families are over informal meals and casual conversations – around tending pets, playing games or relaxing together. These seemingly insignificant moments are the perfect antidote to our many hours spent at work. Our families help us shed the pressures of work by grounding us in the human experience. When we are with the family, we are no longer a brain surgeon or a sales assistant or a pilot. We can instead relax and take our place alongside others. Then as we let go of the distractions of work, we are given the opportunity to be in the present moment. As we collect the kids or shop for groceries or make meals, we also have the honour of helping sustain those we love body and soul.

THE NEGLECT OF OUR CHILDREN

A critical part of our relationship with our families is the bond we enjoy with our children. Countless children the world over suffer from hunger and disease. Our children are also hungry. Theirs is a hunger of spirit, as their needs continue to be pushed aside due to the demands of our work. While we might attempt to compensate for this neglect with holidays and toys, often all we are doing is making our children addicts of consumerism. Possessions are no substitute for parents. We may well have to work long hours to sustain ourselves and our family, but we must be wise about how we compensate for our lack of time and energy.

When work dominates our lives, we lose contact with the natural world and all the inspiration and healing it can bring. We then often pass this way of living onto our children, and so their lives also end up divorced from the beauty and wisdom of nature. The more time our children spend in front of the TV and computer, the less they inhabit their bodies. They are instead lost in a place of unreality, out of touch with themselves and their world. It is no surprise that so many children in the West are suffering from obesity, because they lack fresh air and exercise and prefer foods with little nutritional value. Fast food offers our children a level of comfort for their increasing isolation, but it is no substitute for our attention.

It is ironic that in most affluent countries our children are not only suffering from eating disorders, but from depression. The increased use of medication among teenagers is cause for alarm. What is it about our world that causes so many of our teenagers to feel so joyless that they want to take their own lives? As suicide levels escalate, we need to wake up to the fact that the current climate isn't working for so many of our young. Is it possible that in observing our own driven ways of life, our children assume that this is how life will be for them too? And if our lives lack time and warmth, and a genuine sense of community, then what do our children have to look forward to?

It's not just childhood obesity and teen depression that we're facing right now. Teen violence is also on the increase, both within the home and beyond it. Many of the offenders are children from 'good' homes, but their violence has become so acute that desperate parents have been driven to form support groups to deal with the beatings and the trashing of homes. Journalist Simon Rawles reported recently how in Japan seemingly normal teenagers have become involved in a whole range of serious crimes, from murder to hijackings to planting homemade bombs. Those committing these random acts of terror are often children who live in a virtual world of videos and computer games. In a recent survey conducted by Tokyo's Hakuhodo Institute of Life and Living, one in three Japanese children between the ages of ten and thirteen regarded video games as their friends, and spent most of their free time alone in their rooms. These children also believed that technology and video games were often more satisfying than people. As these games revolve around manipulating a virtual world, these teenagers often believe they can do anything they like. The reasons for this phenomenon are no doubt complex, but it is no coincidence that in a few decades Japan has gone from a rural nation of extended families to a nation of commuters where parents are often working long hours.

TAKING A CLOSE LOOK AT OUR VALUES

All these outcomes are not what we planned for our children. In giving ourselves to our work we hoped that our family would also benefit. We need to take great care about the amount of time and energy we are giving to our work, to ensure our ambitions aren't leading us somewhere we don't want to be.

One young woman, whose father heads up a multinational company, recalled her uneasy childhood, where even holidays were tense. 'We went to plenty of exotic places,' she recalled. 'I'd travel down the back of the plane with Mum and my two brothers. Dad was generally there – just. He'd always travel first-class, because he was so important. Holidays were never very relaxed, because Dad was on the phone a lot of the time, or he was answering faxes and emails. Then when he was free, we'd have to drop what we were doing and do whatever he wanted. Sometimes we wished he wasn't there, because nearly everywhere we went there'd be meetings. Then when we got home he'd rarely be around. If it was lonely for us, it must've been a whole lot worse for Mum.'

STRANGERS IN OUR HOMES

Traditionally men have struggled to balance family and work, but now this is something both parents are struggling with. In the past many men reached retirement only to find the family had left home, or that they had little to talk to their family about.

'It's as if I'm invisible. Everyone talks to each other, but not to me,' one friend complained recently, yet the sad fact is that like so many, this man's work was so all-consuming he was hardly ever home. His wife raised the children, and over those many lonely years his family had learned to live without him. This outcome is tragic for everyone, because no-one wins. In times past, men weren't encouraged to be involved in the day-to-day activities of their family. Their measure of success as a father was what they could provide. These days, fathers have the chance to take a more active role in parenting, and will hopefully help rewrite the scripts by being more involved in the lives of their family. The shortage of time spent at home is now a challenge for women as well. We need to apply all the passion and imagination we have to this issue, if we are to find ways that will deliver the kind of lives we want to lead.

INFECTING OUR CHILDREN WITH OUR MANIC VIEW OF LIFE

No-one is suggesting that parents should stay at home, but far too many of our kids have become casualties of our obsession with work. Even those people who appear to have had it all as kids, later realise that the encouragement they got was often from hired coaches or nannies, and not from those they loved most. As our work pressures grow, so too do our expectations of our children. We willingly shell out money for coaching and tutoring in the hope that our children will succeed, but whose ambitions are we nurturing when we sign our children up for all these activities? And what kind of quality of life do these activities provide? Do our children have sufficient time to savour their childhood, or are their lives becoming as driven as our own?

Childhood is our entry point into this world from the plane of the spirit, and because of this critical transition, our children need a great deal of nurture and space if they are to flourish. They need their parents, and they need community. And so as we attempt to balance work and children, we may need to take another look at our priorities and at how our work may be affecting our children and their experience of the world. No-one is denying our right or need to work, but how much more healthy we would all be, individually and collectively, if our families were given greater priority.

When we have the courage to create a gentler life with more meaning, everyone benefits. There are so many ways we can warm the lives of our children. This might mean ensuring there are times each week for the family to spend together, whether it is Sunday breakfast, a weekly trip to the markets, or enjoying the local park. Encouraging our children to take an interest in nature helps them become more intimate with the world around them. We might like to find simple yet effective ways to celebrate the seasons, or to teach our children the traditions of our ancestors. As we attempt to nurture our children mind, body and spirit, and to give their lives texture and nuance, we reawaken our own capacity for joy. We don't have to do it all ourselves – we can encourage those close to us to be part of our family.

Tara is a busy executive who loves to knit. As she is single and no longer has the time to knit for herself, she knits for all the children in her life. Joseph has a gift shop and every Christmas he makes jobs available to teenagers in the extended family, helping them earn a bit of spending money and gain some valuable work experience. Through these or other gestures we can all enjoy a greater sense of community, enabling us to better balance work and our lives beyond work.

THE NEGLECT OF THE ELDERLY

It isn't just our children who often miss out due to the pressures of work – the elderly are also frequently disadvantaged. When talking with older friends about their grown-up children, their overwhelming response is that these children are doing well, but that they are terribly busy. Often these people don't even hear from their children from one week to the next, and when they do catch up, their children are too distracted to contribute to their time together in a meaningful way. All too rarely do our elderly get listened to, so they have little chance to talk about their aspirations or their anxieties. Today there are few chances for intimacy across the generations, or for precious memories to be handed on. Sometimes we allow work to distance us from our parents, simply to maintain a certain image we have created around work.

Elizabeth is a high-powered executive in a leading law firm, whose parents were poor migrants. She is always terrified when her parents come to visit, fearing that her colleagues might discover her humble origins. When her parents come to stay, Elizabeth ensures that the time they spend with her is kept to a minimum. As her job is so all-consuming, she continues to work late while her parents are staying with her. Ironically, several neighbours have become good friends with her parents and look forward to seeing this elderly couple. No-one is asking Elizabeth to take her parents to lunch with the board, but how sad that she can't find enough room in her heart to honour her parents. We must always have the courage to be genuine and to celebrate who we really are. When our image becomes more important than our authenticity, we have reached a very low ebb. No job is worth losing touch with ourselves.

If work has overtaken us, then how might we turn this situation around and breathe some new life back into our relationship with our parents? If we live close by, then we might like to schedule a regular meal together once a week or fortnight. Di takes her mother for coffee and a movie late on Sunday afternoons, while James takes his Dad to sport or for a walk in the park with the kids most weekends. Other outings might revolve around activities elderly parents enjoy, such as a visit to a show or museum or garden centre, or to see their elderly friends now and then.

Nicole has a busy job and travels a great deal. As her parents live overseas, she keeps a stack of postcards handy, then writes a couple of cards when she has a spare moment, giving her parents a lively update on the week. This, in addition to email and phone calls, enables Nicole to keep in touch with her family. 'I could just phone, but I like writing postcards because it's more personal, and because my parents enjoy getting something in the mail,' she explains. When we invite *intimacy* back into our lives, we are able to balance the cut and thrust of work with the warmth and appreciation of those who are near and dear.

THE GIFT OF FRIENDSHIP

Alongside the opportunities for interaction with our families are those with our friends. Good friendship can do much to enrich our life's path, and if we are wise we will enjoy friendships across the generations – from the freshness and enthusiasm of those who are young, to the nurture and wisdom and delicious humour of those who are older. On the days when we're feeling uninspired or embattled, just to know someone is holding a good space for us can help get us through. Elderly friends can give us a great deal, and we in turn can warm their days. I am fortunate to enjoy the friendship of several women who are older and wiser. These wonderful women have lived through wars and the Great Depression. They have survived their own serious health problems and the loss of loved ones, and yet still they can laugh easily and love unselfishly. Their unwavering kindness and good sense has sustained me through the many turbulent chapters of my corporate years. After a week of meetings and high drama, even a little time spent with such friends is balm to the soul. To share a regular cup of coffee or tea with such friends helps remind us how many more dimensions there are to life beyond budgets and reports, or anything else that has been preoccupying us. To be given a new recipe, to learn how friends and neighbours are faring, to laugh at past mistakes, to make plans to see a film or to share a meal, to discuss ideas for gift-giving, to delight in another's garden – all add light and shade to the day. These shared details are the very fabric of life that point the way forward, that help give us the courage to keep going.

One of the great joys that work brings is the possibility of new friendships – of sharing our lives with those with whom we have something in common. If these friendships are strong, often they can outlast several jobs or decades. Of equal importance are our friendships *beyond* work. There is something comforting about being around those for whom our work holds little or no interest. When we can meet friends in a completely different space, literally and figuratively, we are often energised by this change in focus. Part of the joy of pursuing interests outside of work is meeting new people and making friends with those who are passionate about the same things we are. In my last years of corporate life I began to study alternative healing and was inspired by my fellow students – by their conversation and their ideas, by the books they read, and by the many places they had travelled. A couple of days with these people was like a week's holiday somewhere else, because I was able to relate to them body and spirit.

As we take a closer look at our friendships, we might also like to contemplate how our friendships are formed these days. Are our friendships centred around work? Around mutual interest and the need to be part of a certain group of people? Or do our friendships warm the heart and touch the soul? Do our friendships suffer from lack of time and attention, or can we be relied upon to be there for others when we are needed? Good friends and family have the capacity to warm our lives, to ground us, and to remind us of the many moments of joy that life brings. They balance and enrich our existence, helping us to be successful in all aspects of our lives.

DARING TO DRAW THE LINE

Naturally there are times when work demands a good deal – when there are deadlines or major projects that require more effort. We need to remain clear about how much we are giving to work and why, because each moment is precious.

Ineke is a senior executive with a major bank. Her hours are long, and there is a great deal of socialising around work. 'There are many times I have sat in an expensive restaurant surrounded by people whose values I don't appreciate, wishing I was somewhere else,' she confessed. 'Then one night everything came into focus. We were at yet another restaurant, and although the food was great, those present were too distracted to notice what they were eating. Then someone turned to me and said, "I wonder what the poor people are doing tonight?" They were trying to be funny, but I was so appalled by their comment that I made the decision to cut back the time given to work out of hours.' Ineke didn't drop the ball – she found a way she could share out-of-hours functions with colleagues. From that moment her whole relationship with work improved, as did her life beyond work. 'I used to be desperate to be included in everything that was going on. Then I became desperate to have a life. Now there's nothing I love better than a casual bowl of pasta, or a cup of coffee with good friends. And since I'm clearer about how I spend my time, those I work with are more respectful of it as well.'

As we contemplate how we might balance work, family and friendships, again we need to go back to the qualities we want in our lives. No-one is suggesting we devote our every moment out of work to those we love, simply that we become more creative about how we bring these elements together. To work with the support of family and friends is a far richer experience than going it alone. And the more we can stretch our time and imagination beyond our work, the more energised, focused and fulfilled our working lives will be.

BREATHING NEW LIFE INTO TIME SHARED WITH THOSE WE LOVE

Take time out to be somewhere you haven't been for a while – a favourite café or park – and as you create some space within and around you, why not consider the following?

- What is your relationship with those you care about like right now?
- Have you stopped noticing and appreciating them?
- Has your time with your significant other lost its intimacy?
- What are those things you most love to do together?
- How can you incorporate these possibilities into your day or your week?
- What do those you love do for you?
- How do you acknowledge them for this?
- What else might you bring to this relationship?
- What special attention might your parents and/or children need?
- What can you realistically do to make this happen?
- Who else might be able to assist you with this?
- How are your wider relationships faring at present?
- What simple gestures might you make to enrich the bond you share with friends?

All these questions can open up new possibilities. If time for friends is short then perhaps you might like to organise movie tickets or a shared subscription to the theatre. It might be time to get the extended family together for a casual picnic or barbecue, or to take a romantic weekend or day away with your beloved. As you embrace these possibilities, be open to all that each shared moment offers. Then when you are together, allow yourself to relax, to enjoy the moment. Be sure to participate and to acknowledge those you are with, so that all those parts of you that have fallen asleep can begin to reawaken, enabling you to regain your passion for living.

breathing new life into our homes

The more we invite the sacred to be present, the more each moment, each space becomes sacred.

ENSURING OUR HOME IS A HOME

As we think about how else we might work, we need also to consider the quality of relaxation and inspiration available to us when we leave work behind at the end of the day. Does our home feel like a home, or has it lost its warmth? If our home seems lacking at present, then perhaps it is time for us to take another look at this space, to ensure it does nurture us and assist us to relax. This is not about creating the perfect decor, so much as ensuring our home is our sanctuary.

Our home is a *living* space, and it is we who imbue our homes with their living qualities – through our values, through our own energies, through the interactions we experience there, and through the personal touches we bring. It is we who make our home our castle – who make our space welcoming, tense or hostile. Have you ever noticed how when you return home from an extended stay away, the space often feels neglected or a little melancholy, or that the atmosphere seems unusually heavy? Then as we throw open the windows and begin to move about, our home starts to come to life once more. Regardless of who we are or where we live, our home can be that special place we withdraw to from the busyness of work, where we can wind down, where we feel safe and valued, where we can be ourselves, and where others can also experience these life-enhancing qualities.

Let us close our eyes for a moment and take a virtual tour of our home to get a sense of how it feels right now. What are our first impressions as we stand outside our front door? How do *we* feel about our home at present? Does it feel like a sanctuary, or does it make us feel uneasy, or vaguely depressed? Why might this be? Then as we walk inside, how does our home feel as a whole? Do we open the door and willingly absorb the energies of this space, or do we prefer to be out most of the time? Often there are aspects of our homes that make it difficult for us to relax – there might even be whole areas we actually avoid. When we are at home, do we savour our space or are we too tired and distracted even to notice the energy in which we are living? Are our homes decorated to impress, or are they genuinely inviting spaces where we and others feel welcome?

A RETURN TO INTIMACY

To achieve balance between work and the rest of our life we need to create opportunities for intimacy – intimacy with ourselves, with each other and with our homes. We can only enjoy an intimate relationship with where we live when we have a more *personal* relationship with our homes. Often we place great emphasis on our possessions – on what they say about us, on how tasteful, intellectual or in tune they make us appear. When we are overtaken by these considerations, we lose sight of the many opportunities for comfort and joy in our homes, and go for special effects instead. Or we work night and day to decorate our homes, but have no time to enjoy these things. And then we wonder why there is little that genuinely nurtures us in our lives! In many cultures those entering a home leave their shoes at the door – not just to keep the home clean, but to leave the outside world behind. Similarly, when one enters a Shinto shrine, one goes through the ceremonial Torii gates, which separate the secular world from that of the sacred. With a little time and imagination, we can make our home a sacred space.

When we do make the effort to introduce nourishing qualities into our home, something quite wonderful happens. We discover what we most love about where we live is not so much the new fabric or dining table, but the way the floorboards creak, or the sound of the wind in the chimney. These small details are precious because they bring soulful moments into our busy lives. I love our ancient grapevine, which never fails to burst into life at the first sign of spring, and our elderly Italian neighbours who, for over two decades, have warmed our days – with their rich and colourful lives, with tantalising aromas of garlic and herbs that drift over the fence, and the happy sound of laughter as family and friends gather for a meal. Contained within our living space are memories of the happy times shared with those who are still in our lives, and with those who have departed. These details add texture to our days – they help make our home a true haven, enabling us to replenish and to regain our balance and perspective.

GETTING TO KNOW OUR HOMES ALL OVER AGAIN

As we begin to reacquaint ourselves with our home, we slowly rediscover all those details we had stopped noticing. We start to delight in the way the light spills through a certain window, or in the different textures beneath our feet as we move from room to room. We find ourselves able to appreciate the immediate warmth of a gas fire on a cold winter's night, or the comfort of a favourite chair at the end of a long day at work. When we are able to *relax* in our homes, we are inspired to extend these moments – lingering over a cup of tea or a newspaper, luxuriating in a long bath, reconnecting with the sheer magic of being alive. When our homes are genuine homes, then it is far easier for us to leave the petty frustrations and upsets of work behind. As we reconnect with our own sacred space at home, we help heal those parts of us that are broken or lost, and our exhaustion and near despair are more easily replaced by hopefulness and a renewed sense of vision. As we begin to see ourselves in a new light, we become more grateful for what we already have, and more inspired to operate in the world of work with wisdom and grace.

BEING AWARE OF THOSE THINGS THAT GET US DOWN

Sometimes there are aspects of our homes that need our attention – like the door that always rattles, or the window that won't quite shut. It is important to get these things fixed, because they can so easily take the edge off the joy that awaits us at home. Our pocket handkerchief garden used constantly to get my husband and me down, because the plants either died or seemed to go mad. As we both travelled a lot for work, we became increasingly frustrated with spending our weekends pruning trees and bushes. With advice, we were able to plant trees and bushes that would flourish with the minimum attention, and we chose plants that marked the passage of the seasons. With very little work, our garden is now something we can take pleasure in. Perhaps your home or its environs are in need of a few loving touches right now – if so, why not look for *subtle* ways you can transform your living space or your garden?

MAINTAINING LIGHT-FILLED ENERGIES IN OUR HOMES

It isn't just the physical details of our homes we need to pay attention to – we need also to be attuned to the *energetic* space in our homes. When we're tired and distracted, often we don't notice the negative energies that have accumulated at home. These energies might have come about because we have been sick, because we have been anxious or unhappy, or because our homes are dusty and cluttered. We might even feel depressed, because we are holding on to certain possessions that remind us of an unhappy childhood or a friendship that has gone sour. Collectors of antique furniture need to be especially careful, because the energy in their homes can so easily become stale if they fail to neutralise the accumulated energies imprinted on the antiques they have introduced into their living space. When visiting an antique shop we can often feel the dense energies of the past in the furniture and other objects, because they make the atmosphere feel heavy.

The energies in our homes are real and can have a major impact on our wellbeing, so it is important to take note of them. A good friend had someone examine the energy in her home recently, and was surprised to discover that the energies emanating from her sick brother, who had died years before, still pervaded the bedroom he had occupied. It is always helpful to cleanse our space at least once a year, and to neutralise the energy in any objects we bring home by cleaning them, blessing them, and then visualising them imbued with Light. If we feel upset by the memories behind certain objects, including family heirlooms, we have in our possession, then we are better off getting rid of them.

If they don't enhance who we are, then there is no point keeping them, no matter how valuable they are.

Other energies that might affect the peace and joy we experience in our home might be those of the people we invite into our space. Do we entertain the people we love, or those who might be helpful to us? Has our socialising become too frantic or too formal? And what sort of music do we play at home? Does it create a peaceful atmosphere, or are the lyrics angry and destructive? What videos and TV programs do we watch? What kinds of books do we read? Only now are we beginning to realise that colour is living energy. Do the colours around us uplift us, or do they overstimulate or depress us? Is there enough colour in our homes, or has everything become washed out? What do we clean our homes with? Do we use a cocktail of chemicals, or do we use natural alternatives wherever possible? Whatever we use we will end up eating or drinking one day. Do we walk lightly by using the resources available to us wisely, or do we squander the water and electricity in our homes?

TAKING CARE NOT TO BRING OUR WORK HOME

When we pay attention to the vibes around us, we become far more aware of the energies we are introducing into our homes, including those energies we bring home from work. Do we really want to bring home the negative energies behind office politics or unfortunate decisions? We also need to consider our work clothes; it is important that we not only keep them clean, but that we cleanse them of any negative energy we might have collected at work by hanging them in the sunlight or fresh air. It is also important not to litter our homes with paper or any other items associated with work. As many of us work at home, it is important to put an area aside for this purpose and ensure it doesn't encroach on the rest of our living space. When our work is scattered through our homes, it's likely our work is taking over our lives. As we learn to look more deeply at our home, we begin to see how everything we do impacts on seemingly unrelated parts of our lives, including our working lives.

WASHING OUR WOES AWAY

Whenever we return home exhausted from work, it is a good idea to replenish our energies by taking a brief shower and allowing the stress of the day to be washed away. If we are able to have a bath, then even better, because it provides us with a chance to relax and detoxify. For deeper relaxation and cleansing, we can place 500 grams of sea salt in the bath water to cleanse our aura and remove any negativity, or we can use the same amount of Epsom salts for deeper cleansing. When we use Epsom salts it is important to limit our bath to seven minutes, as the salts are potent. Our relaxation time can be enhanced by a few candles or some nice soap. Or we might like to play soothing music while we bathe. If we don't have a bath, then a footbath can also be restorative. Why not place a whole lemon in a basin, then once the basin is filled with warm water, slice the lemon under the water to help capture its essential energy. That done, we can then place our feet in the basin and cover our legs with a towel, so we can also enjoy the warmth rising from the water. This is a wonderful way to relax. Then when we're done, we can prolong our relaxation by taking some time out to lie quietly on the bed or the sofa.

THE FOODS WE EAT

So often when we come home from work we are too exhausted to make ourselves proper meals, and so we resort to takeaways or to food that does not nourish us. If we must have a take-away, then it is a good idea to bless the food, asking that it be filled with nourishment and Light. If we choose to eat at home, it is important to make the effort to shop for fresh fruit and vegetables – and to have good foods around us to snack on, for those times when we're too tired to cook a more substantial meal. Then no matter how simple or spontaneous our meal, we can still get the nourishment our bodies need. If we are prone to snacking, then it is a good idea to keep a jar of tahini in the fridge, because it is full of goodness.

When we can take time to fully appreciate our food, it will nourish us even more. As we eat we can visualise the rain, wind, sunshine and soil that helped make this meal possible, and feel the joy and energy contained within these various elements. When we can bring this level of attention to our food, we are able to partake in the miracle of life. As we eat, we are reminded also of the blessing of having enough food to eat, and to sustain those we love and to share with friends. Our enjoyment of our food will be enhanced when we can express our gratitude for this abundance.

ENSURING OUR SPACE IS A *LIVING* SPACE

When taking a fresh look at our homes it is also useful to determine how much space we are actually using right now, as often only around twenty per cent of the home is used regularly. As we delve deeper, we might then discover that this is because whole parts of the home are cluttered or dark or neglected, or that we are living with energies that belong to the past – or with the trauma of a burglary or death. Any unwelcome or uncomfortable energies we sense in certain parts of our home might pre-date our time in this space. It is vital to cleanse our home regularly by visualising

123

it suffused with Light, by keeping our living space clean, by blessing it, and by allowing as much Light as possible into it. When we can care for our home in this way, ours will become a genuinely nurturing space. It is also important to ensure there is space at home for energies to move around freely and bring new possibilities into the moment. This means only keeping what we need and getting rid of the rest. As our attention is on work, it is especially important to dispose of material from work that is no longer of any use, because this also weighs us down. All this is about living lightly, about allowing life-enhancing qualities into *every* part of our lives.

ADDING FRESH TOUCHES

Once we have the basics right, we can then attend to the nuances of how we might perk up a certain corner of a room or bring more Light into a hallway. There are many imaginative touches we can bring to our homes to further enhance our *living* space. We might choose to fill a corner with cushions, so we can relax by sitting or lying comfortably on the floor when we get home from work. Some years back, friends bought my husband a hammock, where we read or sleep on lazy afternoons. Wind chimes can bring another level of harmony into our homes, as can sun-catchers – I have a sun-catcher in the kitchen that fills the whole room with prisms of light. Tibetan prayer flags grace our entrance and make our home a welcoming space. Both these treasures were gifts from friends – they have added even more light and beauty to our home.

In many places on the planet, flowers and leaves are carefully gathered and arranged to enhance the entrance to homes and shops, and to honour family shrines. Even though most of us live in towns and cities, we often have access to trees and plants that shed beautiful flowers and leaves onto the pavement. But because we have forgotten the power of beauty to lift the moment, these flowers and leaves frequently get trampled underfoot. When we can recognise beauty in all its forms, we are more able to honour it by making it part of our lives. Why not gather up a few stray flowers, leaves and twigs, or bring shells and stones back from the beach to grace your home? Such beautiful touches heal us, allowing every part of us to relax. When our homes are sanctuaries, they not only help us come back into balance but make us more equal to the demands of our work.

FILLING OUR HOMES WITH THE WARMTH WE LONG FOR
Take a moment now to close your eyes and enter your inner space. Allow yourself to move through your home a room at a time, paying attention to each room as a whole, as well as to different parts of the room. Why not ask yourself these questions?

- How does your home feel right now?
- Which areas feel sad or unwelcoming or neglected?
- Are there any little details you loved about your home that you had forgotten about?
- Why not allow yourself to rediscover those details that brought you so much joy?
- Are there perhaps other aspects of your home that have the capacity to delight you?
- What objects are you better off getting rid of or cleansing?
- What qualities do you most want in your home?
- What resources do you need to invite these qualities to be present there?
- How might you make your home a more sacred space?
- How will you then maintain this space?

Once your home becomes a haven, it will benefit all who enter it.

dealing with burnout

Desire to have things done quickly
prevents their being done thoroughly.
Looking at small advantages prevents great affairs
from being accomplished.
CONFUCIUS

IDENTIFYING WORKPLACE ABUSE

As work continues to challenge us, so too does the way in which we work. It is important that our work not only brings us joy and satisfaction, but that we have the energy and passion to *sustain* us at work. There is no doubt that the workplace puts many pressures on us these days. Equally, we put many pressures on ourselves in our determination to make the grade. But when we push ourselves too hard at work, we become stressed and exhausted, and then we can no longer operate effectively, let alone be the passionate, innovative people we long to be. Regardless of our work culture, ultimately it is *we* who call the shots. We can get drawn into the crash and burn way of working, or we can learn to work beyond these extremes.

Even though burnout is a key issue in the workplace right now, little is being done to encourage employees to move beyond their terminal fatigue. We have come to believe that the more hours we get out of individuals, the more productive they are. Yet when we agree to do more than we should, our vitality is seriously compromised, and sooner or later we will become sick. Work has become a major factor in the breakdown of health. Not only are many more people becoming sick through work-related illnesses, but substance abuse and psychological disorders continue to rise as individuals try to cope with impossible workloads and the many expectations they place on themselves. And while we might attempt to medicate our way out of these problems, the underlying issues remain, and will have to be dealt with at some future date.

Today burnout in the workplace is not always immediately evident, because it has become the norm to be driven and self-obsessed, to work crazy hours, to forgo a life beyond work. We are quick to promote these kinds of lifestyles, but rarely do we talk about the toll they exact.

UNDERSTANDING OUR ROLE IN ABUSE

The basis of any type of abuse is a lack of self-worth and self-knowledge. When we have no sense of who we really are, naturally we are going to be far more vulnerable to the many influences around us.

James was a high-ranking public servant who, although highly respected, lived in fear of the day he would no longer be indispensable. He ended up in hospital undergoing minor surgery, and even though his doctors insisted he rest after his operation, he went back to work the following day. I know, because I found him bent over his desk in a great deal of pain. His shirt was stained with blood, so he kept his jacket on and kept on working.

I heard a story a while back about a man who had become

accustomed to walking around with a rock in his hand. Everywhere this man went he would take his rock him. One day he decided to take a swim in a nearby lake, and as he swam away from the shore the rock started to drag him down. Seeing this, a bystander called out to him to let go of the rock. Even though each stroke became more difficult, still the man held on to his rock. By the time he had reached the middle of the lake he was in serious trouble. 'Let go of the rock,' the bystander yelled, but still the man refused, even though he had started to disappear beneath the water. 'Just drop the rock, won't you?' screamed the desperate bystander. 'No, I can't,' cried the man, as he sank beneath the water for the last time.

These kinds of scenarios appal us – not just because they are senseless, but because they deny some of our most basic rights as human beings. There are times in life when this level of sacrifice might be warranted, but not in our day-to-day work. And yet most of us work as if our lives literally depended on working in this manic way. While we might blame others for our circumstances, often it is our *own* fears and attitudes that drive us into the ground. We become slaves to our need to stay in control, to be perceived in a certain way, to impress, to lead a certain lifestyle. And as long as we promote this kind of behaviour, we will continue to suffer burnout and to give second best.

BEING CLEAR ABOUT OUR TIME

In the brave new world of work we seem almost to be fighting our true selves. We want our jobs to open up for us, but rarely are we able to raise our heads above the balance sheets or the next product presentation. The more stressed and fatigued we are, the more we become lost in the routine aspects of our job. For too long we have been addicted to the 'no pain, no gain' way of living. The more impossible our work schedules, the more invaluable we believe ourselves to be. Yet if we're truthful, often what is demanded of us frightens us. We have become accustomed to agreeing to the impossible, to living on the edge, and we're afraid because we know it will only take a little more pressure to destroy us.

Daily we talk about our time in terms of money, and we have as a result reduced our precious lives to a handful of shekels. Yet our time is *not* money; rather it is a succession of unique moments in our brief lives that once gone cannot be reclaimed. Those who are genuinely successful understand this. They work hard to ensure their lives are not reduced to an endless list of things needing to be done, but are instead a careful interweaving of possibilities that create something worthwhile. The genuinely successful are less concerned about being busy than they are about being fruitful, because they understand that often less is more.

PERMISSION TO BE HUMAN

When one speaks to health professionals it is clear that our ways of working are exacting a heavy penalty, and that our bodies are paying the price. The consequences of this trend are far-reaching – not only do families and communities suffer, but the health care system comes under a massive strain as people become critically ill far younger. The whole question of *how* we work is not just a question of health and wellbeing; there are also wider philosophical and spiritual questions to be considered. We have to start getting creative if we hope to find our way out of this cycle of pain. We can begin by putting people before profit, by having the courage to embrace a life apart from work without feeling inadequate. If there is any hope of us having a life – and a family and community life also – then we have to allow people to start working sensible hours, to stay sane and to enjoy the full spectrum of possibilities that being human means. Every time we ask others, or we agree, to do more than is reasonable, we shatter the possibilities for a healthier workplace and for a better world. We cannot afford to continue living this way.

THE EFFECTS OF EXHAUSTION

All the great spiritual teachings emphasise the importance of rest and contemplation, because without these qualities the impossibly fine fabric of our being cannot function properly. When we are tired, not only does our physical body suffer, but our mind clouds and we become emotionally more vulnerable. Our light body becomes distended, so that life-enhancing energies can no longer flow smoothly through our whole being. It doesn't matter how brilliant our résumé or how exceptional our experience, if this incredible body of ours starts to fail, then our life's quest is severely impaired. When we're living in a cycle of exhaustion, we're in no position to deal with the challenges of work, let alone dream the big dreams. When we have to drag ourselves out of bed in the morning, when we spend our weeks longing for the weekend, we're in trouble.

While a certain bravado has developed around those who work late and who fail to take their holidays, often these individuals are far from efficient. They frequently lack clarity and a sense of proportion. Far too many organisations today are run by those living in a fog of exhaustion. This is why we are experiencing so many changes and irrational decisions, autocratic management styles and punitive behaviour. There is nothing smart about failing to give our bodies the rest they desperately need, because once our health is gone there is no turning back. How quickly our lives change when we discover we have a serious, if not terminal, illness. Suddenly we want to eat the right foods, to exercise, to rest. The question is, how sick or tired do we have to be before we will do the right thing by ourselves and those we love?

IS THIS ALL THERE IS?

If we were to see our manic lives before we were born, how would we react? Would this inspire us to journey here? Would it give us the impetus to struggle through childhood and adolescence, to take our education seriously? When will we allow our terminal exhaustion to end? When we get sick, when we retire, or when we get lucky? While we might consider ourselves fortunate to lead bold, sophisticated lives, when we holiday far from home and observe peoples who lead simpler lives, often we are surprised at how fulfilled these people seem. Something inside us stirs and we long to taste another way of living. Then when it is time for us to go back home, there is often a lingering sadness that we have to return to the frenetic lives we have created for ourselves. We can't all go and live on a desert island, but we can bring some more balance into our working lives – by being a little less available out of work, by turning off the mobile from time to time, by shutting down the computer, and by getting a life. While the very thought of this might terrify us, once we begin to reclaim our own space, we won't look back.

LEARNING TO LET GO

So dogged have many of us become by the detail and volume of our work that when things aren't coming together in the way we had hoped, we respond by putting in even more effort, hoping to get past the post by sheer grit and willpower, and causing an even greater drain on our life energy. When we work this way, we're operating from our little self, from that part of us that likes to assume we are God. Our divine self knows differently. It

131

understands the need to step back, to take a break and refresh ourselves. When we're not getting anywhere with our projects, we are far better off taking a little time out, or leaving work at a reasonable hour, then coming into work early the following day. The practice of letting go is an invaluable one in such situations, because it teaches us how to tap into the wider resources of life. When we let go, we clear our heads and access our inner wisdom, which will then show us the best way forward. One excellent way to practise letting go is at traffic lights. Instead of getting wound up when the lights are red and willing them to change, we can let go our grip on the wheel and allow ourselves to relax. The more we relax, the more we will find everything, including our time, will flow more easily. The practice of letting go is also invaluable when we are trying to find a car park, or when we are late for a meeting. By loosening up, our journey will become more fluid, and often we will arrive where we need to be in record time.

TIME TO BREATHE

Part of our journey back to balance is in imagining how else we might live. This does not necessarily mean we have to make radical changes to our daily lives, so much as embrace the *subtle* changes that are within reach. As Lao Tzu, the father of Taoism, reminds us, a successful life involves 'respect for all small and subtle things'. Part of this process is about allowing ourselves time to take stock and to give ourselves credit for what we have already achieved. How tragic it is that so many people at work expend all their life's energy on their achievements, but allow no time to savour the fruits of their labour. When we take time to celebrate the moment, we bring delight into our days. This infusion of joy then stimulates our vitality and creativity, illuminating the way forward. In agrarian societies, time was always set aside for reflection and celebration. People made the effort to welcome spring, to mark the summer or winter solstices, to bless the land, because they understood the sacredness of the moment. These kinds of rituals enabled people to reflect on what had been and to contemplate the possibilities ahead.

DEVELOPING A NEW RELATIONSHIP WITH TIME

Our time might be limited, but we can learn to *stretch* time. Have you noticed how our activities always seem to fill the space available? When we're going away we get through massive amounts of work in a short space of time, because that's all the time we have. Time is elastic. We have the ability to interact with time more creatively by relaxing a little and holding a clear intent that everything that needs to get done will get done, well and on time. The process of relaxing enables us to enter into a different relationship with time, to experience its elasticity. Once we start to work with this principle and to benefit from it, then it is much easier for us to make time for moments of reflection – for a sacred coffee, for silence, for a breath of fresh air, for fun and laughter. Then as we start to clear our heads, we can incorporate little rituals into our working day that will enable us to continue to savour each moment, such as enjoying a special lunch at work now and then, catching up with those we love and respect at work, or attending a course that will inspire us at the end of the day. When we honour ourselves in this way, we are giving ourselves the chance to refocus and reclaim our energy, so we can then work with less effort and angst.

LIGHTENING UP

One of our difficulties with work is that our working life has become more like a list of things to do than a glorious adventure.

Yet when we dare to take a more expansive view of our work, new worlds will begin to open up, allowing us to travel further than would otherwise have been possible. Those whose jobs work for them are those who are not afraid to be human, to enjoy what they do. Their enjoyment is communicated to those around them, enabling everyone to feel more positive about their work.

Samantha's team had been under a lot of pressure, so she brought a life-sized toy monkey to work. The next time a member of staff was feeling overwhelmed, she placed the monkey at their desk, reminding them to lighten up. Monkey became such a popular figure that he eventually became the department's mascot.

Doug acquired an automatic decision-maker, a small gadget that would give one of half a dozen answers at random. Whenever Doug's team was in a quandary, he would use this simple device to help break the tension. Everyone would have a laugh and relax, and the solution that was needed would come with relative ease.

Such well-timed gestures help raise the collective energies, enabling everyone to become more motivated and focused.

Organisations that understand the need to lighten up enable a far healthier work culture to develop. Some companies are now beginning to understand the need for rest and relaxation, and have put in place policies that ban work at the weekend. In 1998, France passed legislation in support of a 35-hour week, which came into effect for companies with more than one hundred employees at the beginning of 2000. Workers have retained their levels of pay, and employers who fail to comply with these new rulings are penalised. These are significant moves because they allow us to begin to reclaim our lives. We can't wait for those running our organisations to wake up to this possibility, however. It is up to *us* to start changing our ways of working so that our work will deliver all the joy and fulfilment we have the right to expect.

MOVING BEYOND THE STRESS AND EXHAUSTION

Why not take yourself off somewhere you can be alone with your thoughts? Then as you relax, you can contemplate where you are at the moment, and where you'd like to be, as you consider the following questions.

- How stressed and exhausted are you right now?
- How does your body feel – as a whole, and the different parts of your body?
- What are your current anxieties around work?
- How do these anxieties feed your stress and exhaustion?
- How different would your work be if you weren't so tired and tense?
- What qualities do you most need at work to move you beyond the fatigue and the tension? Write them down.
- What else can you do today to help overcome your stress and exhaustion?
- What practical steps can you take in the coming weeks to move beyond your stress and exhaustion?
- How do you want to be feeling about yourself and your work in six months' time?
- What reward will you give yourself for achieving this goal?

getting into better work habits

Those who do not attempt everything accomplish something.
MENCIUS (MENG TZU)

HONOURING OUR WORK AGREEMENT

When we accept a new job we enter into an agreement to perform a specific set of tasks to the best of our ability. Like any undertaking, we should consider this agreement sacred, so that our word is always our bond. When we commence work there is also an understanding that we will be productive and attentive, loyal and thorough. This sounds great, but how do we remain focused and passionate about our job week after week? We achieve this in part by giving our best, but when we have issues around work this can be hard. We're tempted to put in the minimum effort, but this is not the path that enhances the human spirit. Our life's quest is about courage, vision and consistency, and about living in the moment, which means embracing the difficult chapters at work, as well those that are bursting with potential.

136

SETTING THE MOOD FOR THE DAY

We have talked already about the importance of meditation and about giving ourselves sufficient silence and space before we begin work. It is also important to set the pace each day by having a clear sense of what we hope to achieve. Writing a list of tasks before we leave work in the evening helps us remember what we have to do the following day, and to switch off. The following morning we can then evaluate and prioritise these tasks. When we begin our day with a clear sense of what is to be done, we gain a sense of the shape of our day, as well as the specifics. Getting to work early also helps, because we are able to start our day with a more positive relationship with time. Often we can get through two or three times as much work as usual before everyone arrives. *How* we start our day is also important. Lengthy conversations are unprofessional and unproductive. Once we get into the day it helps to cluster such activities as phone calls and emails, to enable us to get through a great deal in a relatively short space of time.

There are no shortcuts to excellence – to be good at what we do and to build a satisfying career we must always pay attention to the detail while keeping an eye on the larger picture. When we understand this, we are less discouraged by those who take shortcuts or who put in minimal effort. There are always going to be difficult or less interesting aspects to our work. Often we prefer to put these tasks to one side, yet they need to be done with the same thoroughness as those things we enjoy. When instead we can tackle whatever is before us cheerfully, we frequently discover that those aspects of our job that we dislike are often nowhere near as difficult or as tedious as we had suspected – only our postponement of them makes them so.

GENEROSITY OF SPIRIT

Not everything we do will have the desired outcome. Sometimes others will surpass us through fair means or foul. When others around us shine, it is easy to become embittered or want to compete. Or if someone has been dishonest we might want to retaliate. If something underhand has taken place, it is best for us to speak truthfully, harmlessly and succinctly about the situation, then let it go. Equally, we might have been overtaken because someone else's work is better than ours. While this is disappointing, there is much we can learn from this situation. It is always best to seek to move beyond any negative feelings, so that we can be generous and genuine towards the person who has done well. By treating others as we would wish to be treated, we allow ourselves to move on and to share their joy. Then we can concentrate on refining our skills or refocusing our efforts.

HANDLING MISTAKES

It is always disappointing when, after working hard, we let ourselves down. We must always attempt to achieve the highest possible standards, while accepting we are not infallible. When we have made a mistake it is best to accept full responsibility, then rectify the situation quickly and effectively. It takes character to admit we have made a mess of things, but the sooner we do so, the sooner we are able to concentrate on finding a solution. By acting responsibly, we also assist those around us to focus on the solution. And then, having solved the problem, we can all move on. Often we are haunted by past mistakes, yet when we beat ourselves up about them, we lower our life energy and destroy our focus. Nothing that comes to us need ever be wasted; the only value in such situations is to *learn* from them, so that we can work more effectively in the future.

INFORMATION AND HOW WE USE IT

Just as we hope others will cut us some slack when we have taken a wrong turn, we must be willing to do the same for them. Information is power, yet we must always take great care about how we use the information to which we have access. Sometimes we come across potentially explosive information – about someone we work with, or about our organisation – but before we speak out, we need to think very carefully about the impact our actions will have. If what we have to say will cause hurt or dissent then why, apart from being foolish or spiteful, would we speak up? It is how we choose to conduct ourselves in these moments that adds or detracts from our inner radiance. We elevate the human spirit when we bring peace where there is strife, hope where there is despair. This possibility is just as true for the way we deal with the minutiae that come up at work as it is for the big issues.

Sometimes we compromise ourselves by passing on information in confidence to a close friend. This is foolish, because such knowledge is a burden on them, and in spite of our insistence that this information remain confidential, all but the most wise cannot resist passing on what they have been told. Again we have to distinguish between information that has serious ethical implications, and information that is more likely to fuel rumour and innuendo. Naturally, if the information we come across raises moral issues, then we have some serious decisions to make. We will then need all the discernment we possess to reach the right decision on how best to proceed. Then if we do speak out, we must always speak truthfully and stick to the facts.

TELLING THE TRUTH

This brings us to the question of right speech. All the great spiritual traditions emphasise the importance of being truthful, but equally we must be mindful of our every word, because truthfulness without wisdom can be destructive. It is easy to harm others by being opinionated, or by careless talk. It can be difficult when, for example, we are asked to give a reference for someone whose work or attitude is less than ideal. In such cases, it is especially important for our appraisal to be balanced and fair. While it is essential to be truthful about the person's short-comings, we must steer clear of gossip and speculation and stick to the facts. We must also make full mention of the person's strengths and achievements. When we can conduct ourselves truthfully and *harmlessly*, there are no regrets. But when we become obsessed by gossip, it is a sure sign our lives have lost their lustre, because we only resort to gossip when we're fearful or needy. We might try to justify our actions as an attempt to bond with those around us at work, but this is not how we achieve genuine closeness. The little self loves gossip, because it gives us the illusion of being in control, but gossip simply reinforces our feelings of powerlessness, and drains and distracts us as well.

DEALING WISELY WITH THE SOCIAL DEMANDS OF WORK

Often there are expectations that we will be available for social events outside of work. If these events are attached to our work, then it is wise to participate, but we must ensure that we don't allow our lives to be swallowed up by such things. Often we turn up because we fear there will be repercussions if we don't, or we attend out of neediness, fearing we will miss out unless we attend everything we are invited to. How we deal with such demands comes back to the question of *balance*. There are times when it is appropriate to attend work functions, and times when other aspects of our lives must come first. It is important to know the difference. If we're smart, we'll share social responsibilities so that everyone is able to have a life beyond work.

Often when we do attend functions, we go straight from work and are exhausted. We rarely have enough time to go home to shower and change, but we can still spend a few moments outside to clear the energies of the day. Then before we enter the function it also helps to re-establish our personal space by relaxing, visualising ourselves suffused with Light, and asking that this Light sustain and protect us throughout the evening. This little exercise enables us to conserve our energy and to maintain our own sacred space, so that we don't end up taking on everyone else's stress and fatigue, and so that we can be suitably vibrant for the occasion.

NETWORKING

Much emphasis has been placed on being seen at appropriate forums and social gatherings. This is important, but again, unless we are judicious with our time, these activities can make us even more driven. We have all met those who pride themselves on meeting as many people at functions as they can. It is exhausting to watch these individuals spraying their business cards around a room. When we are living in the flow, we are able to operate in a way that is more relaxed and insightful. By setting our intent for what we hope to achieve then letting go, we enable life to *help* us. We will then meet the people we need to meet without effort. Often we will encounter these individuals the moment we enter the room, or we might even strike up a conversation with them on the way in. The more in tune we are, the more we will meet those we are meant to meet in the most unexpected places – in parks and in supermarkets, or standing in line at the movies. Again, this is about experiencing the *effortlessness* that comes when we are attuned to our *divine* selves. My whole career was contingent upon my contacts who, while extensive, would more often than not find me.

When we work *with* life, we will begin to develop a *soul* network through work. Our soul network or family will often comprise people with whom we feel a distinct sense of intimacy and understanding. When we meet someone who is to become part of our soul network we will sense an instant rapport and often a profound sense of recognition as well. Our soul network is to be nurtured, because it helps us stay strong at work. Even though we might not see each other often, we can exchange ideas and information, and encourage each other. The presence of our soul network in our lives is significant, because when those of like energies connect, they each amplify the energies they share – that is why times together are so precious. When you meet those who are to become part of your soul network, be sure to cherish them.

CREATING THE WORKPLACE WE LONG FOR

We would all love to work exclusively with those with whom we have a soul connection, but generally this is not our path at work, and so frequently we become discouraged. Yet often it is our ability to find ways to work with those who are different from us that helps awaken us to our potential. We then realise that if we want to work in a climate that is imbued with joy and passion, with integrity, loyalty and diligence, then we must start by spreading these qualities around. This means being big enough to encourage and mentor those around us, to treat others as we long to be treated, to share our knowledge and experience. Then as we promote the qualities that enhance the human spirit at work, those around us are inspired to do likewise.

142

CHOOSING A ROLE MODEL

Not only do we need experience, goals and sacred practices to focus and motivate us at work, we also need worthy role models. It is the *innate* qualities of good role models that matter, not their material success. The best way to find a worthwhile role model is to study the lives of those we know to be genuinely great, until we find someone with whom we feel we can resonate. Our role models may or may not be from the world of work. They might be from childhood, or they might be a world figure such as Nelson Mandela, or they might be a great spiritual being, such as Jesus or Buddha. Once we have settled on our role model, we can begin to sense their energy by focusing on them, or on how we imagine them to be in quiet moments, and then see what insights come to us. Then whenever we are in a dilemma, we can ask ourselves how this person might react. Would they embroil themselves in office politics? Would they hire and fire without thought? Would they take credit for other people's work? Would they conceal their mistakes? Or would they work that bit harder, support those around them, come up with workable solutions to the most difficult problems? Would they share their ideas and resources and cut those who have made a mistake some slack? Would they hold their achievements lightly, find joy in even the most mundane tasks? By examining their likely responses we begin to see the most appropriate way forward. The more we can use our creativity to help us work with our role model, the more we will be inspired to find new and effective ways forward.

When we anchor ourselves in clear values, not only will we know where we are heading at work, but the universe will help to get us there. The more authentic our daily interactions, the more we will inspire others. Then we are able not only to contribute to the overall work effort, but also to benefit the lives of those we work with. While we must always hold on to the vision of what we are attempting in our working lives, it is also important not to get so fixated on our goals that we fail to enjoy the moment-by-moment experience of work.

REFINING THE WAY YOU WORK

In a quiet moment, why not consider how you can get more focus and enjoyment from work by answering these questions?

- How do you commence your working day?
- What subtle adjustments might you make to this start to give you greater impetus?
- How else might you handle those tasks that least excite you?
- Are you satisfied with the way you handle mistakes?
- How might you deal with difficulties in the future?
- How do you handle sensitive information?
- Are the social demands around work proving onerous?
- If so, how can you bring this part of your life into balance?
- Who are your soul contacts at work?
- How might you nurture these relationships?
- Do you need to take a fresh look at your role models?
- If so, who might be more suitable?
- How best might you work with them?

Again, it is by attending to the *subtleties* of the way you work that you will make the most difference to your working life.

being clear about where we stand

If you look at the spectacular corporate collapses, you'll find there was always a moral collapse before there was an economic collapse.
JOHN ELKINGTON, *CANNIBALS WITH FORKS*

KNOWING WHERE WE STAND

If we want our working life to be all that we hope for, then we must be meticulous about our conduct, and about those who seek to influence our values. Knowing where we stand and what we stand for is essential at work, because the impact of our attitudes and actions can be far-reaching. The more dependent we are on the approval of others, the more vulnerable we are. Then as the darkness of dysfunction creeps into the way we work, it obscures our better judgement, drawing us into questionable behaviour. The status quo at work can seem overwhelming, but only when we don't know our true selves.

SEEING CLEARLY WHAT IS GOING ON AROUND US

Being clear about who we are does not mean making every issue at work one for the soapbox. Rather, it is about looking more deeply at the people and interactions around us, so that we can then see the mischief behind a seemingly innocuous suggestion, or the lack of compassion or direction behind the latest organisational change. When we can see things as they are, and not how they are sold to us at work, we are more conscious of the choices we are making moment by moment. We then discover that it's not the huge ethical issues that trip us up, so much as the seemingly small issues we let pass, believing no harm is done.

Questionable actions are often sold as the most pragmatic way forward, which deliberately masks the fact that they are fundamentally wrong. How much healthier our working life would be if we were to ask the questions that need asking, and to *name* what is being suggested as it really is. When we name something, we define its essential nature. How different the outcomes at work would be if we were to name our actions and take full responsibility for our decisions. In recent years, we have become adept at concealing the truth. We have dressed up unethical behaviour and actions by making them seem the most obvious or most attractive thing to do. It is tempting to fall in behind our colleagues when the numbers are against us, or when working life is full-on, but the price of ignoring what we know to be true can be high. Expediency has destroyed many who had the potential for greatness. Every time we choose the easy way out or we compromise, we contribute to the dubious decisions and actions being made around us.

What then are we to do? It isn't appropriate to turn every issue at work into a battle, nor to beat others over the head with our point of view. We expend so much of our effort on *doing* in life that we fail to understand the importance of *being*. When we are clear about where we stand at work, our very presence gives those around us cause to think again, because they know we are bound to speak our mind when certain issues arise. We won't win every point, but often all it takes is one person who is prepared to take a wider view, to start to change the status quo. When we can summon the strength to be our *true* self, we encourage others to take a more authentic approach to their work. Whenever we are feeling faint-hearted, it helps to remember that the many spectacular corporate collapses were brought about because those who were in a position to oppose inappropriate actions and decisions failed to do so.

DEALING WITH DIFFERING POINTS OF VIEW

One of the most difficult challenges at work is handling conflict. Yet when we can apply the Light of humanity and reason to seeking a solution, we invite all life's resources to be present. Then as we prepare to talk with those who have an opposing point of view, it helps to pray that our meeting be peaceful and safe, and to visualise the meeting space being filled with Light. That way we can create a space of goodness and truth for the meeting to help everyone arrive at the best possible solution. When we invite Light to be present, we are more able to access our inner wisdom, and to reach out to the inner wisdom of those with whom we are to meet. Then as we get together, instead of fighting over the situation, we should allow the higher energies of life to help *dissolve* the differences around the situation. When we hold a good space for others, our Light helps reassure them, enabling them to feel safe and to see their way forward.

Then as the meeting gets under way it is important we make our case simply and firmly, allowing our inner wisdom to give us the appropriate words. If we fail to make immediate progress, then we must still be gracious, so that the Light we have invited into the situation remains undiminished. I have used this technique on countless occasions and have been amazed at the outcomes.

At one stage I was in negotiations with a group of corporate heavies notorious for their hardline tactics. The aggression at the beginning of our meeting would have been totally off-putting had I not prepared thoroughly for the meeting professionally and spiritually. As the meeting progressed, I continued to visualise everyone being surrounded by Light, and to hold the intent that the outcome would be for everyone's highest good. About five minutes into the meeting the most aggressive person in the room began to calm down, then her colleagues followed suit. By the end of the meeting it was as if we had worked together harmoniously for years. Not only did we come up with creative solutions to the issues that challenged us, we arrived at a whole list of possibilities for future joint ventures.

This approach is a far more profound way of operating than seeking a win–win outcome. By taking this higher approach we are able to relate to the divine connection we all share. We can only access this profound space when we move beyond the need to succeed at all costs, and choose instead to reach an outcome that will be of the greatest benefit to everyone concerned. The joy that comes with this *inclusive* way of working is immense. Not only does it help us succeed, it empowers others, inspiring them to work more positively. Sometimes we might appear to have made little or no impact, and when this happens it is easy to become disheartened. But regardless of how we feel, we must always conduct ourselves *lightly*, thus ensuring we continue to bring Light into our every moment, and illuminate the way forward for ourselves and others. This ability to remain solid under pressure is significant, because when we can be relied upon to be fair and consistent regardless of what is going down at work, we do ourselves and others a great service, as we are someone others can trust.

WORKING TO CONSUME

As we seek to transform our experience of work, it is critical to pay attention to our neediness and to the values we have come to espouse. Without meaning to, many of us have helped take materialism to a whole new level. We joke about indulging in retail therapy, not realising how empty our lives become when we flog ourselves to death just so that we can afford the new car accessory or sound system. This compulsive way of living has taken over so many at work, causing them to lose all perspective. As our attention turns inwards, we become more and more self-centred and obsessive, until we end up with little or no respect for those who are on a fraction of the money we might be earning. Our excess becomes their distress.

Some time ago, Abbie, who worked in the arts, approached her boss about a salary increase. The amount she requested was modest, given her experience and contribution to the organisation. Her request was refused on the grounds that money was tight. A few weeks later her boss invited her to join him for dinner with overseas guests. Abbie was enjoying the evening until the bill came and she realised that the price of the meal was more than the amount she had requested to help keep her afloat through the coming year. In that moment, all the goodwill she had for work was shattered.

The point of this story is not that we should avoid eating in good restaurants, or that we should leave our staff behind when we do so – it's about being *consistent* and *transparent* in our behaviour. When our excess causes our decency and humanity to fade, our discernment tends to go out of the window as well. We begin to feel hollow, because we are *becoming* hollow. We cannot always meet the salary expectations of those we work with, but there are other ways to honour those around us. When we can stretch

149

our attention beyond ourselves and allow everyone to share more equitably in the passion and profit of our organisation, we create a culture in which *everyone* can thrive.

JOINING THE CLUB

As work continues to make major demands on us, it is easy to be seduced by the heady egos and the powerbrokers, and to find ourselves wanting to imitate those who have 'made it', or to join their club. Yet as appealing as this path might appear, this is a soulless way of life that thrives on exclusion. Those who gather others around them in this way are never strong – they need these other people to help them overcome their fears and inadequacies. When we join forces with people of this ilk we do not become wise or genuinely great, we end up indulging our own anxieties and weaknesses. We also learn that our fears don't diminish once we have 'arrived', because we then have to spend our time ensuring we remain in the club. When we are able to stand in our own space, and be excellent, consistent and authentic in the way we work, we become an asset our organisation won't want to be without.

LEARNING TO BE COMFORTABLE IN OUR OWN SPACE

While we might not to want to join forces with the powerbrokers, still we might be tempted to create our own clan. In every workplace there are those with whom we feel more chemistry than others, yet when we include some and exclude others we start to fracture the possibilities for happiness, because whenever clans are created, sooner or later a political element emerges. Then before we know it we have different interest groups competing for control. How quickly a gathering of those of like mind can become a collection of people whose behaviour is dysfunctional.

As appealing as factions might be, they offer us a false sense of security. Today they rule the world and tomorrow they are out of favour. If we want our working lives to yield all the fulfilment possible, we don't need this roller-coaster way of working. It takes courage to operate outside the clan. Yet when we can be our own person, we are more able to form deeper relationships with others. That way we avoid the intense emotions within the cliques, and are instead free to be on good terms with *all* those we work with. Then when we need help, we are able to get assistance from more than just one quarter.

CREATING A GENUINE COMMUNITY AT WORK

When we are more comfortable with our own space at work, it is no difficulty for us to encourage others. It then becomes natural for us to want to reach out to all those with whom we come into contact – like Janet, who always had a stash of chocolate hearts for anyone who seemed down; or Gina, who would bring in leftovers from her children's parties, reminding everyone of the joy of their childhood years; or Andrew, who would frequently turn up to long meetings with something sweet for everyone to enjoy. None of these gestures cost a fortune, but time and again they lifted the moment. They are about creating a greater sense of belonging at work, about building a meaningful community with shared values.

There are few of us who do not long for these things at work, but often other concerns seem to get in the way. In the heady rhetoric of staff meetings or sales conferences, we often refer to our organisations as families, forgetting that real families are a group of people committed to each other through the good times and the bad. Real families are about nurture and shared experiences and values. If we are going to describe our workplace in this way, then we have to be committed to this level of cohesion and loyalty. No amount of talk will get us there. We cannot treat people well in the good times, then exploit them and fill them with fear when times are tough. How quick companies are to remove those benefits that warm the lives of their staff when things are tight, while at the same time demanding more effort without additional compensation. Where is the foresight and respect in this way of operating? We need instead to be courageous, and to take everyone with us as we continue to work towards our many goals.

THE DARK FACE OF CAREERISM

The whole nature of our organisations is influenced by those who run them. Today, strong leadership informed by a wider vision seems to be in short supply. Instead of promoting those who are able to empower work cultures through their own strong ethics, professionalism and commitment to the greater good, we hire careerists, who are often unstable and lacking in genuine commitment, and who only add to the instability and dysfunction of the workplace. We elevate those who are not only determined to get where they're going, but who have little or no moral fibre. We have made these individuals our role models, and even when they fail spectacularly we reward them, often cutting staff and services to help pay for this extravagance. Time and again we have hired or promoted those whose ambition far outweighs their abilities, and in their determination to succeed, these misguided individuals have often destroyed much of the good that has been achieved personally and professionally within the company. Frequently, when careerists join an organisation, rather than building on the past, they destroy it, creating even greater confusion and fragmentation. They hire and fire staff without compassion or conscience, then leave before the consequences of their changes become apparent.

How could we have allowed charisma and spin to get in the way of genuine experience and integrity? As we contemplate this question, we must ponder our *own* values, because it is our growing dependence on materialism that has enabled these kinds of people to have this much influence. In our desire to have more, we have aided and abetted regimes lacking in decency and experience. We can only turn this trend around by getting clear about our own values.

James was pleased to be approached about an attractive position with a new marketing concern. When he met with the owner, he was impressed by her confidence and entrepreneurialism, until it became increasingly clear she had no real interest in her new company, other than to build up the business and then sell it. Disappointed, James turned down the job. 'I was offered a great package, but I just couldn't work with someone that soulless,' he confessed.

UNDERSTANDING OUR WORK CRISIS

This lack of soul is at the core of many of our dilemmas around work. When we lose our connection with who we really are, we become obsessive and narcissistic. So great is our neediness that we have little conscience and even less regard for others. In our hunger for meaning and recognition, we behave like any other hungry person – we steal whatever we can from those around us, to try to assuage our hunger. We steal their ideas and life energy, their passion and commitment, giving them little if anything in return. We all have the right to succeed, but when we lose all proportion, when we allow expediency to get in the way of what is right, when we agree to decisions that hurt others just so we can

153

look good or so we can survive, we're in trouble. How often have we sold our souls to pay for the school fees or the home refurbishment? We can make a thousand and one excuses for what we have done, but this does not alter the fact that it is wrong. And while we may prosper materially, sooner or later we will experience the pain we have created. This is a great and immutable law of life, based not on punishment, but on the principle of cause and effect.

GETTING CREATIVE ABOUT OUR RESOURCES

The way we operate at work and the resources we use impact on the many living things with which we share the planet. When we're busy, it's easy to see our work just as a set of tasks. Yet as resources are precious, we need to use our imagination, passion and experience to come up with better and more profound ways of getting the job done. Good resource decisions can be anything from using environmentally friendly stationery to choosing appropriate corporate gifts.

In Rita's company they buy clients toiletries that have natural ingredients and have not been tested on animals. The response to these gifts has more than confirmed their choice – not only do recipients love the toiletries, they feel good about supporting brands with high ethical standards and a strong environmental commitment.

Kelly's company decided to go green and support non-exploitative practices, which influenced everything from the toilet paper used in bathrooms to the coffee available for staff. The company informs staff of their choice of resources, and so the staff have become more aware of their own decisions as consumers.

Let us think about the resources within our own organisation. What is the best way to manage them? What new possibilities might there be that we haven't yet thought of? How might these innovations contribute to our material goals and inspire those we work with?

BENEFITING THE PLANET

The implications of our actions are far-reaching. How we market our products is also critical. All too frequently, we are happy to exploit the beauty and diversity of the natural world – to use it to sell everything from shampoo to mobile phones – but how often do we honour this relationship? How often do we give something back? In ancient times, shamans and healers were most respectful of nature, because they knew that they too were part of the sacred web of life. When digging up a plant or picking berries, they would ask permission and it would then be made clear what it was appropriate to take and what to leave. Similarly, hunters would give thanks for the lives of the animals they killed, because they understood that life in all forms was precious. They also honoured the fact that by forfeiting its life, this animal enabled many to thrive. These seemingly primitive peoples would never have dreamt of appropriating anything from the natural world without giving something of themselves in return. And so if we do choose to exploit nature in some way, then perhaps it is time to consider meaningful ways to give something back.

THE PATH TO PROFITABILITY

Often so much of what we hope for at work gets lost in the race for profitability. When we are overly fixated on the bottom line, we neglect those things that can make our organisations great. Profitability is important, but of equal importance is how we make our profits. Is it through genuine growth, or through the exploitation of those who are paid little? Is it through pollution and abuse of the earth's resources, or is it through ethical business practices? Are the products and services we sell for the betterment or exploitation of others? Do we genuinely respect our customers?

Troy was in a meeting for children's licensed products some time ago and was devastated to observe that in talking of the many new products about to be launched onto the market, they only ever mentioned children in the context of money. 'It made me realise just how low we'd sunk when everything, including childhood, has a price,' he confessed.

In our race for profitability, it seems we are willing to exploit whatever market can bring in the money. Researchers have now discovered the 'tween' market, which targets girls aged between eight and twelve. Manufacturers are now offering tweens everything from glittery tops to baby bras. They are delighted with this new demographic, because these kids are anxious to please and highly impressionable. As there's serious money to be made, few seem concerned about exploitation or about the erosion of a child's self-esteem. It is a great pity that more countries can't take Sweden's lead and ban advertising targeted at children under twelve. As we consider how best to operate at work, Gary Zukav hints at the way forward in his *Seat of the Soul*, when he comments that without the perception of the holiness of all things, the world becomes cold and barren, mechanical and random.

❦

A *prayer to help us get back on track*

'O Great Spirit, things seem a little dark at work right now. It is hard to be the person I want to be, because there are so many powerful forces around me. I know that I can only succeed when I can harness the Light within. Help me to reach

out to that Light, so that it can illuminate the way forward and can positively touch the hearts of those around me. Help me to honour my true self, and to embrace all the authenticity I can bring to my job, so that each day of my working life is worthwhile, not only for myself but for all living things.'

moving beyond our fears and emotions

You are not what you seem to be in these moments of sadness.
You are better than that.
PAULO COELHO, *THE MANUAL OF THE WARRIOR OF LIGHT*

UNDERSTANDING OUR EMOTIONS

One of the most trying aspects of life at work is the way certain people and situations can overwhelm us. One minute we are feeling on top of the world, and the next we are speechless with rage or cut to the core. The more pressured our jobs, the more we often find ourselves on an emotional roller-coaster, which leaves us feeling upset, distracted and out of control. We hate to work like this, but often we're too busy to consider how else we might work, and so we struggle on through the seemingly endless highs and lows.

Our emotions are literally our life energy in motion. Of themselves, our emotions are neither good nor harmful – it is how we use our emotions that makes the difference. Whether we acknowledge it or not, all the emotions we experience arise from within us, and so whether our emotions are out in the open or buried deep within, they are still *our* emotions. Positive emotions

158

uplift and sustain us, enabling us to achieve many things, and to relate to others in ways we hadn't thought possible. When we are around those who are positive, our whole being expands. We feel safe and inspired, able to embrace new possibilities, willing to put in additional effort and also able to assist others. When we are around those who are emotionally unstable, we often feel the full force of their emotions, directly experiencing their anger, their jealousy, their despair.

WHEN EMOTIONS ARE HARMFUL

Our emotions enable us to taste the many textures of life. They give our days nuance, and are the means by which we can express our humanity. Even our negative emotions can help us to be wiser and more compassionate. Often we cut ourselves off from our emotions at work, because we have been conditioned to believe that emotions can't serve us there. We elevate those who are adept at suppressing their emotions, admiring those who can hire and fire, who put figures before people, who put their job before their own needs. Yet when we behave in this way, we separate ourselves from all that is soulful within and around us.

The more we then cut ourselves off from our emotions, the less we are able to feel. Then the only way we can feel alive is by living a life of extremes – by being manically busy or happy or pushing ourselves harder. So deadened have many of us become, that we no longer believe we're alive unless we can live with this level of intensity. Such extreme emotions fragment our lives, because they not only drain and distract us, they distort our vision of reality, making it harder for us to see the way through. Then if we can't access such intensity ourselves, we rely on medication, or on our addictions, to help keep us up or down. In *Light Emerging*, renowned healer and teacher Barbara Ann Brennan explains that when we deny our pain, anger or fear we block the positive aspects of that same experience. Barbara describes these suppressed emotions as 'frozen psychic time blocks' that then cluster together in our bodies, 'literally walling off the deeper part of ourselves from our conscious awareness and our exterior life'. We are then left to navigate our way through with only a fraction of our mental, physical, emotional and spiritual resources.

WHEN EMOTIONS CONTAMINATE OUR SPACE

While some suppress their emotions at work, others feel they have the right to vent their emotions whenever they like. We are all human, and part of the experience of being human is to feel anger or hurt or despair, but it is our ability to deal positively with these spontaneous emotions that is central to how effective or otherwise we are at work. The inappropriate expression of negative emotions harms us, and is also a form of energetic pollution, because negative emotions contaminate our personal space, destroying the clarity and positivity around us.

Ruth worked with a colleague who had a serious temper. After each major outburst, this woman would rush out and buy Ruth a big bunch of flowers. 'She blamed the way she behaved on her upbringing. Apparently, everyone used to scream at each other when she was growing up. All I can say is that *I* felt as if she'd vomited all over me. The flowers were her way of apologising, but I'd have preferred it if she'd got a grip on herself in the first place,' Ruth confessed.

In spiritual teachings, our emotions are often characterised as wild beasts that are both magnificent and dangerous. This image illustrates how our emotions have the potential to expand the moment or to harm us. When negative energies remain unchecked, they tear at the fine fabric of our being, literally wounding us. After an emotional outburst, we will often feel as if we have no energy, or as if we have been hit in the solar plexus (our power centre), because this is what has happened energetically. Similarly, when we are around those with inflated egos, or those who are monumentally ambitious, we can often feel stifled. Again, what we are experiencing is *real*, because this person is overwhelming us energetically. Their overblown energies often affect our throat chakra, the energy centre in our body that enables us to speak our truth and to be who we are without fear. The detrimental effects of being around others at work who are overly emotional might not always be so obvious, yet still their emotions can harm us. But because we're already tired, we scarcely give them any thought. All emotion is fuelled by life energy, and when we buy into other people's negative energy, we allow *our* life energy to fuel their emotions. Once we understand the energetic interchange around negative emotions, we then realise the importance of dealing wisely with *all* emotions, whether they are our own energies or those of others.

FACING OUR FEARS

We get an even greater insight into negative emotions when we realise that ultimately all unhelpful energies are fuelled by fear. We often fear our emotions because we don't like to feel angry or hurt or depressed. Once we understand our fear, it can teach us as much about ourselves as it can about others. In *Light Emerging*, Barbara Ann Brennan's spiritual guide, Heyoan, describes fear as 'the opposite of love . . . Most fear is not of what is happening now but of what might be. If you are able to stay in the moment, fear will not find you'. We cannot always prevent negative emotions from surfacing, but Heyoan points the way forward by encouraging us to feel our fear the moment it arises, then let it go. This technique is also emphasised in Buddhist teachings.

We can feel our fear by giving it a name or phrase as it emerges. Our fear might be about the loss of work, loss of income, or even a loss of credibility. By *naming* our fear, we start to pinpoint it, and can then begin to move beyond it. If our fear is more than a momentary anxiety, we can help shrink it down to size by imagining what this specific fear might *look* like. What is its substance? Is it like concrete, like a sponge, like treacle? And what *shape* is our fear? Is it round or square or spiky? How big is our fear? What colour is it? As we go through this exercise, we are allowing ourselves to embrace and define our fear. Normally, we are taught to ignore fear, but ignoring our fear doesn't make it go away – we simply park it, causing it to block the energy and possibilities within and around us. When we can name our fear, we take the sting out of its tail, and can then move beyond it. As we do this exercise, we will observe that the energy around our fear will start to change. We will then be able to watch our fear begin to shrink or to break up, until it no longer holds any resonance for us.

RECOGNISING OUR FEARS

When we can recognise the fears within ourselves and those around us, we begin to sense how best we can overcome them. It is important to face our fears, because fear is contagious. It can blight our days and our relationship with others, causing them to be more fearful too. So many organisations are currently ruled by fear. It is *fear* that has made many people so controlling, so fixated on the bottom line. They are too afraid to relax and enjoy their work, fearing that if they do so everything will fall to pieces. It is fear that prompts us to agree to abusive situations at work, because we're afraid that if we don't we'll get fired, or we'll lose our credibility or our chance to progress. Yet if we were able to step back a bit, we could use our intelligence and imagination to find the way through our fears – not only for ourselves but for everyone involved.

Many working women are driven by the fear not only of failure, but also of poverty. Regardless of their assets, they remain petrified that unless they continue to work impossibly hard, they will end up on the street. The irony is that at a profound level of our being we already know what is good for us, and when we see others daring to live and work beyond fear we are inspired. Yet too often our anxieties prevent us from living to this same level of fulfilment, so our fear rules the day. Whether our fear is of being inadequate, of being rejected by our peers, of making a mistake, even of being surpassed, doesn't matter, because these fears are equally debilitating. We must always remember that it is *we* who make a moment-by-moment choice about how we work. We can allow our fears to distract and disempower us, or we can use them to become stronger and wiser, and to help us find powerful and effective ways to move forward.

PAST, PRESENT AND FUTURE ARE CONNECTED

When we can admit to ourselves that we are feeling fearful at work, we can start to pin down the nature of our fear. Then we will often find that our specific anxiety is part of a much greater fear that relates back to earlier chapters in our lives. We might then see that we are intimidated by our CEO, because he or she represents our fear of all the authority figures that have dominated or disempowered us in the past. Once we recognise these *resonances* we can begin to unravel our old fears by looking more deeply at the intimidating situation before us. We might then

LOVE YOUR WORK, RECLAIM YOUR LIFE

realise that it is our little self that is fearful of our CEO, because it craves acceptance or because it is paralysed by anger.

Recognising this, we can then deal with this fear in a much more balanced way. As we attempt to sort out our problem with our CEO, we can then reassure our little self through a simple exchange: 'I know, little self, that your boss is powerful, and that they can be intimidating. But they can only intimidate you if you allow them to. If you look at the situation more closely, you'll notice something very interesting. You will see that beneath their anger, they are often as frightened as you are. And so instead of getting hurt or becoming terrified next time they get mad, why not talk to that part of them that is confused or frightened, and help reassure them? Then as they calm down, you'll feel better, and can start to build a more positive relationship with them.'

We will get the most out of this interchange when we can then listen closely, from a space of wisdom and compassion, to any responses we get from our little self. Then we will start to see the issues that are holding us back, and how *our* own emotional responses to our CEO, whether articulated or not, might have helped distort the relationship between us. As we bring *positive* attention to our fear, we begin the healing process. This time and effort will pay dividends, as Barbara Ann Brennan notes: 'Through healing work, one of the small frozen psychic time blocks is released. The increased energy released into the auric field then, in turn, automatically starts releasing the other small segments of time conglomerate (related pains and fears), because they are of like energy.' And so in healing *one* aspect of ourselves, we also enable healing around *related* issues to begin.

Having worked through the issues around our CEO doesn't mean this person will suddenly become reasonable or open. They might still be volatile or overbearing, but the difference is that they won't have the same effect on us, because we no longer choose to take their energies on board. This does not mean that we put up with abusive situations, or that we deny our feelings – we simply choose not to waste an ounce of our energy. Then if we feel the need to speak out or to make some other gesture, we are able to be far more positive and even-handed.

OWNING OUR EMOTIONS

As we look at each emotional situation we face at work, we can begin to acknowledge that regardless of the scenario, it is *we* who have chosen to get angry or to be upset. As our emotions occur, we can further understand them by consciously *feeling* their effects in our bodies – in our stomachs, around our necks and shoulders, or wherever it might be. Then as we start to experience the tension we have created or taken on board, we start to be more conscious of the effects our negative emotions are having. The more we *refine* our understanding and use of our emotions, the sooner we reach the point where we can simply acknowledge the emotion we are feeling and move on. The more we stop fuelling our negative emotions, the more our life energy will be available for more positive work situations.

If during the working day certain emotions arise that are hard to deal with, it helps to find somewhere quiet. Then we can close our eyes, focus on our breath, breathe in, filling our lungs to capacity, and visualise our whole being filled with Light that cleanses us of our negativity. As we breathe out, emptying the lungs, we can consciously expel all the negative energy from our bodies with force, using the sound 'haaaggghhh' to ensure that our lungs are fully emptied. Our breath is life-giving on so many levels, and when we use it in this way we are also healing ourselves. We might want to do this exercise a few times until we have shifted all the negative energy out of our bodies. Once we're done, it helps to sit quietly for a minute to ground ourselves, and to have a glass of water or a warm drink. The more we can allow our negative emotions simply to flow through us, the more effective we will be, because we will be carrying far less baggage.

ALLOWING OUR FEAR TO BE OUR FRIEND

Sometimes our fear is reasonable, because it is warning us we are about to step into unfamiliar territory. We might have been asked to do work that is new to us, or to undertake a project for which we feel ill equipped. We can allow our fear to paralyse us, or we can use it as a catalyst to take us even further. Even after years of extraordinary success, many of the world's leading performers are terrified every time they walk out on stage. However, they have learned to use their fear to give breathtaking performances, and we can do the same. Even though we're feeling apprehensive, this might be the perfect time to use our fear to move beyond old ways of working or of presenting ourselves at work. If we are fearful about a new project or new responsibilities, instead of depleting our energy with worry, we are far better off *using* our fear to help focus us, so that we can do our homework and garner the assistance we need to do an excellent job. If we didn't feel this fear about the new assignment, we might well end up producing a mediocre result.

We can help transform our fear by closing our eyes for a moment and focusing on the outcome we are seeking. Once the outcome is firmly fixed in our mind, we can focus on the fear we have around the issue, and visualise the energy around it as arrows of Light speeding towards our goal, energising it and causing it to glow. When we have completed this exercise, we can pause for a moment to note how we feel right now. We may have to do this exercise several times before our fear is under control. That done, it is time to do our homework and solicit all the help and resources we need to succeed. In *The Seat of the Soul*, Gary Zukav reminds us that when we choose to live unconsciously, we evolve unconsciously. When we live consciously, our evolution is a *conscious* process and when we can handle our emotions positively at work, instead of crippling us, they can help us transform even the most difficult situation into a fruitful outcome.

MOVING FORWARD

Still there will be those around us at work who are out of control. The important thing is that we don't end up taking on their issues. The more we protect ourselves, the less they can affect us. We have talked already of the importance of surrounding and suffusing ourselves with Light before we leave for work in the morning, to shield ourselves from unwanted energy. This process provides us with an early warning system that helps us to recognise the harmful energies at work and deal with them before they get the chance to affect us. Energy, positive and negative, can so easily be transmitted from one person to the next. When we fail to take note of the emotional environment in which we are working, we not only make ourselves vulnerable, but we also often contribute to the negative energies through our own displays of anger or through our grumbling or politicking. Then we end up as depressed and angry as those around us.

It is important to realise that our emotions are still valuable, because they help us to read others much more easily – to see where they are coming from, to understand what motivates them and what fills them with fear. When we are able to use this level of understanding in our interactions with others, we can become extremely effective, because rarely will we miss the mark. This is especially helpful when working under pressure, because we are able to reach positive and long-lasting solutions with far greater ease. The more we understand emotions, the more we are able to be a force for good at work. It is no difficulty for us then to respect the feelings and aspirations of others, to be a team player and to enjoy working towards a wider goal.

SACRED ALCHEMY

All emotions need to be treated with care, and none more so than anger, because while some regard displays of anger as heroic, all anger is in fact harmful. There is often plenty to get annoyed about at work, yet the only worthwhile response when feeling angry is to transform our frustrations into positive outcomes. Those who are ambassadors for peace are highly skilled professionals, not only because of their ability to navigate their way through extremely complex situations, but because they can be relied upon to remain calm and collected at all times. If there has been an injustice at work, we are far better off applying our energy to finding a solution than exploding and causing others to lose their cool.

Once we understand how to transform our negative responses into something worthwhile, extraordinary things can happen. This was the case for the Venerable Robina Courtin, a former radical lesbian feminist, who is now a California-based Buddhist nun. When talking to author Vicki Mackenzie for the book *Why Buddhism?*, she commented, 'It was as though I'd exhausted all other possibilities. I'd been a hippy, a communist. I'd been into black politics. I'd blamed straight people, white people, rich people. Then I'd blamed male people. There was no one left.' Once Robina realised the answers to her own anger and frustration about life weren't outside herself, she embraced Buddhism and now works with prisoners, including those on death row, through the Liberation Prison Project (www.liberation prisonproject.org).

MANAGING OUR RESPONSES

As always, we have choices about how to operate at work. We can wear ourselves out fighting everyone and everything around us, or we can be more judicious about how we use our life energy. We must always ask ourselves what is *really* happening when we or others are feeling anxious, upset or out of control. Often we react needlessly, when with a little diplomacy or honesty, we could have achieved the preferred outcome. If we allow our little self to inform our working life, then we will respond inappropriately to difficult situations. The irony is that frequently the situations that bother us at work aren't nearly as big a deal as we had imagined. As Sigmund Freud is said to have pointed out, 'Sometimes a cigar is just a cigar.' And so when next someone else makes a mistake or unfortunate comment, we can cut everyone some slack by responding intelligently and generously. There is great wisdom in treating others the way we would like to be treated. When, like Robina, we can gather up all our unhelpful emotions, we can use our positive intent to transform them into something of great worth. We become like alchemists, creating pure gold out of base metals.

⊷

A *prayer for assistance with our emotions*

'O Great Spirit, sometimes I find it hard to keep my cool at work. I get so angry and upset at everything I see around me. Teach me patience. Help me also to be wiser and more compassionate, so that I can use my life energy far more productively and enjoyably at work.'

being part of
the team

You can survive on your own; you can grow strong on your own; you can prevail on your own; but you cannot become human on your own. FREDERICK BUECHNER, *THE SACRED JOURNEY*

MAKING THE DREAM A REALITY

We all love the idea of being part of a team, in theory at least. We yearn for the camaraderie and stimulation of working with those who share our passion and values, because we know intuitively that we are part of something greater than our individual selves. Anyone who plays a musical instrument will know the joy of playing with others; not only is the sound richer and fuller, but there is also more energy and momentum to the music. The same is true of a good team. When a team is working well, we capitalise on each other's strengths and compensate for each other's weaknesses. We look out for each other. We take pleasure in each other's achievements, and comfort each other when things don't work out as we'd hoped. Being part of a good team enables us to express our ideas, and to benefit from the experience of those around us. It also helps us to be less self-absorbed, as we come to appreciate the joy of shared goals and a shared history.

DARING TO INCLUDE OTHERS

This is what we dream of, yet often we become frustrated when working with others, because their approach differs from ours, or because they don't always behave as we would hope. It can be de-motivating to be with those who contribute less, who try to take charge, who discount our contributions, or who take credit that isn't theirs. However, being part of a team not only means working together, it demands a willingness to try to work things out. Often when imbalances occur within a team situation, we fail to deal with them. We hope instead that these problems will go away. Then over time our inaction creates even bigger challenges. When we can face the issues before us truthfully and harmlessly, we can often resolve them with the minimum of angst, saving our energies for more demanding situations. There will be times when workmates could have contributed more. There are also times when the team members, while producing less, are giving all they have got. Instead of losing it, we should try to see the situation more clearly. We might then discover that someone's output is lower than expected because they are overworked or under-resourced, or because they might not have received the full training or briefing to perform as we would hope. Similarly, when someone takes charge within the team, while this might irk us, if no-one else is providing direction, then sitting on the sidelines and sniping will achieve little.

DEALING WITH THOSE WHO OPERATE OUTSIDE THE TEAM

Perhaps the hardest individuals to deal with in a team are those who have little team spirit. Often such individuals are desperate for credit. Their behaviour is fuelled by extreme neediness and fear. More than anything, they long to be acknowledged and accepted. We tend to respond to their lack of team spirit by

171

distancing ourselves, thus making them feel even more needy. When, however, we can be honest with them about their difficulties and can actively encourage and assist them to be part of the team, everyone benefits. Once these individuals start to experience a level of acceptance within the team, it will often help to transform the way they operate – they will then start to relax and to share ideas and information. If they have a relapse, it is nothing to be alarmed about – they are learning new behaviour and none of us gets everything right first up. Again, this is about giving others a chance. If they persist in their unwillingness to be part of the team, more stringent measures might be called for. By continuing to encourage them we are helping heal their unease with the Light of goodness and wisdom.

STRETCHING OUR ATTENTION BEYOND OURSELVES

Sometimes *we* might not be the ideal team player. We might have become so distracted by our responsibilities at work that we have started to ignore those around us and to focus in on ourselves. Or in our determination to get ahead, we might have become overly competitive, manipulating people and events to try to succeed. When we become fixated on our own performance to the exclusion of all else, we have forgotten to put back into our work. This is an exhausting and unproductive way to operate and takes a lot of effort. When we can balance giving and receiving, we are in *surplus*. We then have plenty of ideas and energy and can find time in the day to say or do something for someone else. This doesn't mean we do other people's work, or that we spend copious amounts of time interacting with others, but when we are in surplus we naturally want to give out – to transform the moment. What a wonderful thing it is when someone touches our working life with a momentary kindness, when they recognise something within us we might not have seen, or when they selflessly mentor us or promote our cause. Years ago I got my big break in publishing when a friend encouraged me to go for a promotion. While I had the skills, I lacked the confidence to pursue this possibility. In response to my friend's advice, I applied for the position and got it without difficulty. This move literally changed the whole course of my working life.

There's a lot of talk about mentoring at work, but here we are considering the profound connection we all share. In *Dogs That Know When Their Owners Are Coming Home*, scientist Dr Rupert Sheldrake examines the social bonds that exist within species, which he describes as morphic fields. Each morphic field contains a collective inherited memory that individual members of that group can tap into. It is the *elasticity* of this morphic field that enables telepathic communication within the species to take place. Dr Sheldrake considers communication within herds, flocks of birds and schools of fish, which enables large numbers of animals to change direction suddenly, often at high speeds within a fraction of a second. This high level of communication enables animals not only to survive, but to take advantage of whatever possibilities present themselves. Imagine how much more fulfilling our experience of work would be if we were able to interact with this level of awareness and cohesion – just think of the energy we might save and the momentum we might achieve! First we must become aware that we are part of a team and respect wider needs – only then can we benefit from the connections we share with others at work, enabling us all to be more effective.

SHARING THE VISION

All these principles are about learning to work beyond fear by being genuinely *inclusive*. When we're inclusive, we allow everyone to be part of the vision, and to enlarge their personal vision also. Today our working lives are awash with mission statements and detailed goals. Yet often these initiatives fail to inspire, because they are imposed. The impetus to succeed can only come from *within*. When the vision we hold for ourselves and those we work with acknowledges the connection we share, we enter a more *intimate* relationship with those around us. This does not mean that our working relationships lack independence, but that we consciously support and respect each other – that we work together with a whole new level of cohesion. With this intimacy comes a far greater willingness to understand each other, to share ideas and information. When we can work with this level of openness, we can experience the exhilaration of being part of something greater than our selves.

SUPPORTING OTHERS

When we support each other, we gain strength, and far more possibilities present themselves. This is helpful, because none of us is brilliant at everything we do. We have only reached our present level of expertise because others have been willing to guide and support us. To be a genuine team member we need to stretch our focus beyond what work can deliver, by assisting and encouraging those who work alongside us. In ancient cultures, the opportunity to help those less able was seen as a sacred possibility, because the gods were believed to walk among us disguised as everyday people. At work we have the opportunity to touch the sacred within each other by working together authentically and unselfconsciously for the wider good.

SEEING THE BIGGER PICTURE

It is relatively easy to work well with others when everything is going our way, yet not all our efforts will be successful, and

174

sometimes our suggestions will be passed over. When this happens it is tempting to drop the ball, but to do so will let ourselves and others down. The best way to respond to such disappointments is to ensure that regardless of our views and feelings, we are not destructive in any way. If our current contribution is not appreciated, we need to find out why. We might discover that there are better ways forward, or that the time is not right to bring our suggestion to fruition. By carefully analysing our situation we move beyond self-interest and find a way through that is for the *greater* good. This does not mean we lack ambition, or that we don't challenge certain decisions, but that we don't allow personal interests to jeopardise the overall effort. The great benefit in working with others is in learning not only to resolve our differences, but to embrace and celebrate them. When we can take off our blinkers, there is much we can learn from those we work with, including those who might not be as experienced as we are.

WORKING WELL WITH EVERYONE

Frequently conflict arises in a team because of the notions we form about our workmates. When we move jobs it doesn't take long for us to work out those who are our kind of people, and those who are not. While these observations are a natural part of settling in to a new workplace, when we cling to these attitudes, we fracture the possibilities of working well with everyone. When instead we can give those with whom we have little in common a chance, often they too can prove stimulating to be around.

Sometimes the pressure to exclude certain people will come from the team itself. In our desire to fit in, we might be tempted to take sides. Yet to live and work more authentically, we must tread our *own* path and stand up for those in need of our support. The less partisan we are, the more freedom we will enjoy. If we want to benefit from working in a team, then we need to widen our focus so we can better understand our workmates and respect their concerns. We can get to know what they love and what motivates them, as well as those things that cause them unhappiness and distress. Then when someone is having a bad day, we are more able to understand what is going on, and to help them, rather than criticise or ignore them.

TIME OUT

One of the biggest pressures in a team situation can be around social activities outside of work. While it is good to share time out with workmates, it is equally important to develop a full and interesting life *beyond* work. Frequently, informal social gatherings after work are for a select few, and can be divisive. These gatherings are generally held over a few drinks, where the combination of alcohol and exhaustion can be problematic. Exhaustion dulls our perception, and alcohol magnifies whatever emotions are predominant at that time. If we are feeling angry or upset before we go for drinks after work, it is likely our negative emotions will come to the fore over drinks. This is why so many seemingly innocuous gatherings end in character assassination or in petty squabbles, shattering the strong working relationships everyone has worked so hard to build. Our life's journey has the potential to yield us a whole range of friendships and experiences; we must take care to cherish our work relationships without becoming too dependent on them or allowing them to become destructive.

BEING THERE FOR THE GOOD TIMES AND THE BAD

Success is always sweetest when it is shared. When we can operate more inclusively, we honour those we work with, and enable them to honour us too. Being part of a team will stretch our capacity to be loyal and courageous, and our determination. It is easy to give our best when we're flying high, but true greatness comes when we can continue to be a committed and productive member of the team when the odds seem stacked against us. Often it is not until we are in a tough work situation that we begin to realise our potential or have the pleasure of seeing others thrive.

◦—◦

A prayer for the difficult moments

'O Great Spirit, sometimes work can be so frustrating that I wish I could go it alone. Help me to appreciate all that working with others can bring, so that I can then embrace these possibilities. Then as the opportunities at work expand for me, help me to encourage those around me, because when others benefit, I benefit too.'

◦—◦

EMBRACING THE OPPORTUNITIES AT WORK

There are so many more opportunities for you at work. Why not take time out to contemplate what additional possibilities there might be for you? Consider the following questions.

- How do you feel about your team at work right now?
- What more would you like to get out of working with this team?
- How might you achieve this?
- How can you begin to support those around you actively?
- Are there individuals within the team you might have underestimated or ignored?

177

- How might you help make them feel more a part of the team?
- What have been some of the best moments?
- What are the great moments you can share in the future?

Allow these many possibilities to inspire you, so that each working day your interactions are more productive and meaningful.

managing our managers

Wisdom denotes the pursuing of the best ends by the best means.
FRANCIS HUTCHESON, *INQUIRY INTO THE ORIGINAL OF OUR IDEAS OF BEAUTY AND VIRTUE*

RECLAIMING OUR POWER

So much of our happiness at work revolves around those who supervise us. This is great if we have a good boss, but what do we do when we work for someone who is thoughtless or confrontational? Frequently we imbue those above us in the workplace with a god-like status, and in so doing we hand over our personal power. The more autocratic our organisation, the more prevalent this way of working. When we are reliant on our boss for our happiness, we are only able to have a good day when they are having a good day. Often we replicate this pattern in other areas of our lives, becoming dependent on our children and friends for our wellbeing. It is tempting to look to externals – to people and situations – for our happiness, yet when we walk the path of spirit we learn to take charge of our own destiny, to create the circumstances in our lives that we need to thrive.

UNDERSTANDING THEIR LIMITATIONS

Ultimately, our superiors are simply fellow journeyers on life's quest. They may give impressive presentations or put together great strategic documents, but often they have minimal training in how best to support and enhance the working lives of their staff. This doesn't mean our boss doesn't care, or that they can't learn how to be good people managers, but that they may need a little help. When we can take responsibility for our relationship with our boss, we are more able to create the circumstances we long for. And so the next time our boss behaves thoughtlessly, instead of getting angry or upset, first we need to take a clear look at the situation. We may then discover our boss is angry or uncommunicative because they are under pressure. We can help by getting on with our job, and by providing back-up. The last thing a stressed boss needs is an employee who is high-maintenance.

Alternatively, we might discover that we are the problem. We might have failed to deliver in some aspect of our work, or our conduct might be problematic. Once we are aware of this, we need to talk with our boss, so we can find out how best to rectify the situation. The more open-minded we are, the more honest our boss can be with us. If we can then demonstrate a willingness to set things right, and focus our energies on getting ourselves back on track, we have a good chance of turning the whole situation around. If we are concerned that talking with our boss will inflame the situation, then we can find someone else to give us reliable feedback. With this wider perspective, we can be clear about our shortcomings and begin to work them out.

If our boss is mistaken about our performance or behaviour, then it is important to clarify this with them. We are best to prepare for our meeting by assembling the facts and by surrounding ourselves and the situation with Light. By calling on the Light we are more able to access our inner wisdom, rather than our ego, during the meeting. We might also want to ask that we be given the words needed to speak truthfully yet harmlessly, so that we can reach a solution for everyone's highest good. Should our boss refuse to accept our point of view, then at least we know where the flashpoints are and can work towards demonstrating the true nature of our output or behaviour. If our differences seem irretrievable, then we need to determine whether we can continue to work well in these circumstances. As we sit with this question we might realise this is not possible. Equally, we might see a positive way through the difficulty.

Most of us hate dealing with these kinds of issues. The only way through is to face them and solve them. The path of the spirit teaches us to look beyond the way things are to how they might be, so that we can form a clear vision for the future and get a sense of where we're heading. Then by holding on to our vision and by working to make it a daily reality, we help create a better outcome. This path takes courage. It means finding the strength to work through the difficult situation until it is sorted out. Our creativity is also important here, because it will help us find new ways to integrate our vision into our every waking moment. When we have the courage to tackle such issues, we move from being a victim to taking charge of our working lives. This is how our dreams are realised too.

GAINING RECOGNITION

We tend to assume our boss always knows what we are up to, yet as workloads increase, often this is not the case. Most executives can barely get through their working day, let alone know what those around them have achieved in detail. The only way through the mounting pressures is for our boss to focus on the staff and

181

issues that are problematic, leaving those who are capable to get on with it. While this isn't ideal, it makes sense. The way out of such a frustrating situation is to give our boss regular updates that are pertinent and brief. If our boss is hard to pin down, then a succinct email or short report might be what is needed. When we make the effort to provide this level of feedback, we not only create a more meaningful working relationship, we help inform the decisions our boss makes.

HANDLING THE RESOURCE ISSUE

Similarly when we are under-resourced or needing some other kind of support, instead of waiting for our boss to raise this issue, it is far better if we are open and discuss our requirements with them. Often we fail to do this, because we don't want to waste their time, or we assume they will say no. Or we present our boss with a list of demands, leaving little room for negotiation, so they *do* say no. It is only by being straightforward and sensible that we can enjoy a productive relationship with our boss. When we fail to have these kinds of discussions, our frustration grows, which then reflects on our work and our relationship with our boss. Eventually we lose our cool, jeopardising any possibility we had of getting whatever it was we were hoping for.

Before we talk with our boss, we need to clarify the resources we are seeking, to be sure that our request is realistic in the current work climate. It helps also to take a look around to see if the resource issue in question is widespread throughout our organisation. This helps ensure that our expectations are realistic. To ask for resources that are not obtainable wastes everyone's time and erodes our credibility. If when we talk with our boss, we learn that the resources aren't readily available, there are other avenues we can explore. There might be aspects of our job we can put to one side, or interim resources we can have access to. If there is no immediate answer, we can still review the issue further down the track. When we explore the situation with our boss, they are more able to appreciate our requirements, and to work towards getting us the resources we need.

If we have been turned down, how we conduct ourselves from here on in is critical. While none of us should put up with abuse, there is little point in being destructive. It is *our* choice to remain at work or to leave. It is important to continue to work and to remain gracious regardless, because when we bring grace into our working days, its Light-filled energies will continue to work on our behalf. By keeping the vision of what we hope for before us, we may then see how we can redistribute our current resources – or resources may come to us from an unexpected quarter. This might seem a pipe dream, but it works. Most of my working life has been in organisations with less than ideal resources, yet I have always ended up with the resources I needed and some to spare.

CUTTING OUR BOSS SOME SLACK

We all want to hold on to the vision at work, but so often we kill this possibility with our impatience and frustration. The more pressured our work, the more needy we can become. As we become lost in our own agendas, we forget that our boss might also need a boost now and then. When instead of making their lives miserable, we are authentic and dignified in our interactions with them, positive outcomes are more likely to follow. Dignity is particularly important, because if we want a healthy relation-ship with our boss, ours must be a *mature* working relationship, and not one where dependency creeps in. There is nothing more destructive in a team or organisation than a boss who gathers a select few around them to prop them up and shuts everyone else out, or when staff become dependent on their boss. And so the next time our boss does something worthwhile, why not encourage and support them? Sometimes we might feel uncomfortable about doing this, because we don't want our gestures to be misconstrued, but when we are supportive of *everyone* we work with, it will be natural for us to make such gestures.

GIVING NEGATIVE FEEDBACK

We can also support our boss by being honest enough to give them feedback on unfortunate situations taking place at work. Before we speak out we need to be clear about what is to be said, and why we want to give this feedback. Timing is also critical. If our boss has a major deadline or crisis, then unless what we have to say is pertinent to their current concerns, it is best to wait for a more appropriate moment. If our feedback ranges beyond our own issues, then it is important to have read the landscape correctly, so that we don't get caught up in issues that are petty or mischievous. When we do speak out, no matter how incensed we might be, we must speak harmlessly and truthfully, and never resort to blackmail. Our feedback must be motivated by a genuine desire to improve the situation, and we must always stick to the facts. We should never reveal our sources, except in the most exceptional circumstances, or if we have permission to do so. When we can be honest and trustworthy in giving such feedback, we can often help improve the work situation for everyone. Our boss also benefits, because they are more fully aware of the issues facing our department or organisation.

FINDING SOLUTIONS

Problem-solving is always required at work, and often we have an expectation that our boss can or should come up with all the answers. The more we take this approach, the less we use our initiative. And if we fail to show any initiative to solve the problem ourselves, why would our boss suddenly rely on us to come up with the right solution? When we encounter problems in our job, unless we are in an emergency situation, it is best to think through the issue ourselves and to attempt to come up with a positive solution. We won't always arrive at the best answer, but we will be across the issues and more able to discuss them coherently. When we use our initiative, we start to take greater responsibility for ourselves and our work. This doesn't mean we then go ahead and implement a solution without consultation, but that we take a more active role in our work. Then, instead of rushing into our boss's office with yet another drama, we can take our boss through the issues and suggest a solution. This approach not only saves everyone's time, it often helps us move more speedily towards a successful outcome. Our boss may or may not agree with our suggestions, but the greater our initiative, the more responsibility we are likely to be given over time.

REMEMBERING TO SAY THANK YOU

Often we forget that our boss has feelings, and so we treat them differently, causing our relationship to be awkward and unfulfilling. The more we allow our *humanity* to guide us, the better our relationship will be. When our boss makes a positive gesture, whether it be granting us a promotion or days in lieu, it is appropriate to thank them. Sometimes we neglect these courtesies, because we are too proud or just plain forgetful. When we fail to thank our boss, we fail to acknowledge that even if our bonus or pay rise is well-deserved, still our boss would have had to mount a case and to persuade colleagues we are worthy of this gesture. For far too long, inhumanity has characterised relationships at work. The more humanity we can exercise, the more we enhance our own humanity and the humanity of those around us.

STANDING ON OUR OWN TWO FEET

Not all managers will encourage us or thank us for a job well done. This is disappointing, but the more we focus on our *inner* resources, the less dependent we will be on our managers' emotional support. This does not mean we put up with abusive situations, but that we don't allow our experience of work to be tainted by a boss who is thoughtless or dysfunctional.

Caroline was a talented designer who went to work for an innovative packaging company. While her boss had been very positive about her joining the company, once she was part of the team he seemed oblivious to her excellent work. 'It was such a shock,' she admitted. 'I didn't want to be the centre of attention, but a little acknowledgement would've been great. My work brought in a lot of new business, yet I was treated as if I didn't exist.' For some time this behaviour distressed Caroline. The more she tried to please her boss, the more withdrawn he became. 'I loved the job, but didn't know what to do,' she admitted. 'Eventually I realised that what mattered was that I still enjoyed what I did, and the people I worked with. The moment I stopped waiting to be acknowledged, my boss settled down, or perhaps I just didn't notice his behaviour any more.' Subsequently Caroline discovered that her CEO was a profoundly shy man. She also found out he had major problems with a severely handicapped child. 'It was only then I realised he was probably giving me as much as he could, so that was okay.'

On seeing her situation as it was Caroline was able to direct her life energies accordingly. On a soul level she learned that the more frustrating the climate at work, the more she had been able to draw on her own inner reserves to gain the nurture and satisfaction she longed for. Through this, Caroline became more self-reliant. She learned to let go of the aspects of her job she couldn't change, and to embrace the many aspects she did enjoy. So often when we're faced with frustration at work, we spend our time and energy trying to fix the bits that don't quite work, believing that with more effort and determination we will win through. Sometimes this approach will work, but sometimes we are better off letting go and focusing on everything that does work for us in our job. Again, this gets back to our notions of fulfilment. If we convince ourselves we can only be happy if our boss loves and appreciates our every move, then most of us will be doomed to disappointment. If, however, we learn to take a more comprehensive view of our work, then joy and fulfilment can be ours.

STANDING UP FOR OURSELVES

This doesn't mean we won't ever have to stand up for ourselves, but that when we do assert ourselves, we will do so in a way that is intelligent, harmless and dignified.

Nick had a boss who would regularly lose his cool. Then one day when Nick was in his office, he started sounding off yet again. 'Suddenly the light went on,' Nick confessed. 'I realised I didn't have to put up with this. I didn't want to be disrespectful, but I was tired of his outbursts. I found myself saying that this wasn't a good time for our discussion, and that I'd be happy to talk later. Then I excused myself.' This was a bold move, because like most of us, Nick hated confrontation and he needed his job. 'I didn't want to make trouble, but I wasn't going to be treated like this any more,' Nick explained. When he took a closer look at his relationship with his boss, Nick could see his boss was confrontational because he was always worried about how the business was tracking. 'Once I finally understood him, the way he behaved made sense. I didn't want to embarrass him – I just wanted to be treated with more respect, and I think because I didn't confront him, he got that.' Nick's actions might have made his boss more aggressive, but they didn't because he acted with respect. After this, whenever his boss began to lose his temper, Nick would pull himself back, enabling them to have a far more productive working relationship.

We all have the right to be taken seriously at work and to be treated with respect. When we allow others to treat us badly, frustration builds until all the negative energy we have been accumulating explodes, or it remains inside us, making us sick. It is natural for us to want nurturing relationships at work, but often it is those who make life challenging who do us the biggest favours, because they nudge us out of our comfort zone, forcing us to find new ways of living and being. When we are able to take a more respectful and compassionate approach to our difficulties at work, these positive energies create a different dynamic around us. Then even though others might not always agree with us, they will feel safe around us, and through this they will learn to trust us as well. And where there is trust, even seemingly impossible situations can be remedied.

ENHANCING YOUR RELATIONSHIP WITH YOUR BOSS

When you have some quiet time, think back to your first moments with your boss and your present job, and all the hopefulness they contained. Even though your experience of work might not be like this right now, how might you improve on the way you work together?

- What characteristics of your boss do you most appreciate?
- What do they appreciate about you?

- What can your boss teach you about work?
- What has your boss taught you about yourself?
- What is it you most want to be appreciated for?
- How might you gain this appreciation?
- How can you work with your boss to help create a relationship that will benefit you both?

Like all relationships, your relationship with your boss will continue to evolve. If you allow your creativity, intelligence and pure intent to guide you, then you will help create a rich and rewarding relationship.

handling conflict

*The biggest contribution to end the world's suffering
is to end your own suffering.*
THE GYUTO MONKS OF TIBET

RECOGNISING THAT CONFLICT ARISES OUT OF FEAR

As the world continues to change around us, it can appear as if
there are few people and even fewer institutions we can trust.
Then as we read about acts of terrorism, domestic violence and
road rage, we can end up feeling as if we have little or no control over what is happening around us. These fears are often
magnified by the ever-changing world of work, leaving us with
a sense that everything in life, including work, is too hard. When
we feel like we are barely coping, then not only is conflict more
likely to arise, we are less able to handle it well. Life brings us
together with our colleagues through a shared passion for work.
The rewards we gain from our time together far outweigh the
benefits of a salary and career, because *everyone* we work with
has the potential to teach us something – even those who drive
us to distraction.

In the hothouse of deadlines and ambitions, there are bound

to be disagreements over priorities and approaches. When we are equal to these challenges, we are exhilarated by new ideas and new ways of working and we also broaden our experience. When work is difficult, every problem we face can seem like yet another battle, or we can make it an opportunity for learning and healing. Often we blame disharmony at work on the politics of the workplace, or on those we work with, yet if we want peace at work it is important to be aware of how often we contribute to the tensions around us through our thoughts and actions, and through our unwillingness to work things out. Conflict at work is no different from that between warring nations, except by degree. There is no point in saying we won't treat those around us fairly unless they lose their attitude and learn some respect. Nor do we enhance the atmosphere at work when we refuse to let go of past differences. It is up to *us* to deal swiftly and effectively with conflict in our working lives – then and only then can we demonstrate a genuine commitment to peace.

MAKING PEACE AT WORK A REALITY

Taking the peaceful path might not seem an option when those around us are being volatile or destructive, yet peace at work is essential if we're hoping for long-term success. It takes strength and insight to behave decently and sensibly when everyone else is going to pieces. This does not mean we should allow others to walk all over us, or that we should tolerate unacceptable behaviour, but that we should be clear about finding a positive way through our current difficulties. One of the key factors in dealing effectively with conflict is the ability to separate the issue or unhelpful behaviour from the person concerned. We may not respect a person's confrontational approach or poor work, but this does not mean we have to hate or actively dislike that person.

When we do hate or dislike others, we are living in fear. And when we are fearful, all our energy goes into fuelling our anger and frustration. These unhelpful emotions then obscure the issues, making it harder for us to arrive at a positive outcome.

We can only handle disharmony effectively when we can take the time to look at the way things are in *this* moment. By concentrating on the present, we don't get lost in past issues or in speculation about the future. How we deal with conflict also depends on our state of mind. If we are happy and focused, then even major conflicts can have relatively little effect on us. We have all experienced how different work is when we return after a decent break. Even though everyone around us might be stressed out, we're fine because we have everything in perspective. But then as we get busy our equanimity fades, and often we are drawn back into all the old issues.

TAKING RESPONSIBILITY FOR OUR WELLBEING

While we yearn for more balanced lives at work, often we fail to put in place those mechanisms that make this possible. One of the best ways to achieve balance at work is through meditation, because its benefits are far-reaching, as Daniel Goleman demonstrates in *Destructive Emotions*. In March 2000, His Holiness the Dalai Lama gathered together some of the world's leading scientists who, with Daniel, examined emotions from a scientific perspective. Tests were performed with state-of-the-art equipment on long-term meditator and Tibetan monk Lama Oser. In one test Oser was shown footage of a variety of subjects experiencing subtle changes in mood. The micro-emotions on screen appeared as fleeting facial expressions lasting just one-fifth of a second in one case, and one-thirtieth of a second in another. Out of literally thousands of participants, including police, psychiatrists and secret service agents, Oser and another experienced meditator read the emotions of those on screen more acutely than anyone else tested. The implications of this test are profound, because when we see people as they truly are, our whole relationship with them is changed. Oser also had two separate conversations with scientists who took an opposing rationalist view of life – one scientist was easygoing, while the other had a reputation for being confrontational. The latter scientist admitted to finding it *impossible* to be aggressive with Oser, sensing something 'like a shadow or an aura' emanating from the monk. 'I was always met with reason and smiles; it's overwhelming,' he confessed. When we can hold a good space for another as powerfully as Lama Oser, then we allow others to enter a Light-filled space, and to experience all the positive effects of this Light. As we absorb this understanding, it provides us with a powerful clue as to how we might operate productively in the emotionally charged atmosphere of work.

PEACE WITHIN CREATES PEACE AROUND US

We can only deal wisely with those who are difficult when we come from a space of genuine peace. Often we have learnt to handle ourselves at work so that we seem calm at all times, while inside we are like a raging inferno. We cannot create peace when we don't know the shape and feel of peace in our bodies and lives. The more peaceful we are, the more we reside in a Light-filled space, and so we know how to lighten up. Still there will be dramas at work, but these will affect us less. Again, meditation is central here, because the more we meditate, the more intimate is our relationship with peace. We can then carry the peace experienced during meditation into our working day. Then when conflict arises, instead of fighting back or avoiding those who are problematic, we learn to shift our focus, so that we can look deeply at the people and issues before us. We will then often realise that it isn't this person's problem with the finance department or the sales results that bothers them, so much as their profound sense of unworthiness, or their fear of being out of control. When we can see into the *heart* of someone's outburst, then instead of reacting as if it were a personal attack, we move quickly towards finding a solution, because we also realise that when someone is angry or upset, what they most want is to be put back in control.

When we can operate *beyond* the many emotions at work, we occupy a far more productive space. We are then able to use our energy to be vibrant, creative and forward-thinking. When we use our energy and ingenuity to help us find new solutions to the perennial conflicts at work, doing our job becomes a deeply satisfying experience.

Tracy had a boss who humiliated her. No matter how well she performed, still he was confrontational. Then a healer friend encouraged her to take a good look at this man not as she usually saw him, but as he was deep inside. When Tracy did so, she got a very different picture of her boss. 'I was shocked to see how unhappy he was, in spite of his designer suits and all the things he made a big deal about,' she confessed. 'I also realised that every time I got frustrated, I only added to the negative vibes between us. My friend suggested that every time he got me going I should let go of my anger and frustration by visualising him in a large swimming pool and loving every moment. She also explained that the free-flowing energy of water would help lighten him up, so that's what I did and it really helped. Every time my boss started to get uptight, I'd visualise him in water enjoying himself and he'd calm right down. After a while I'd just send him good vibes and that worked as well – it was a kind of a blessing, I guess.'

ADDING RESPECT TO THE EQUATION

What we want most when we are facing conflict is to be listened to and to be taken seriously. Often when we feel threatened we fail to listen to the other party. We jump to conclusions, not realising that often what people are most upset about is not what they appear to be concerned about. A customer might be angry because their goods haven't been delivered on time, but if we *really* listen, we might find they are *most* upset because they feel our organisation has stopped taking them seriously, or because they have lost faith in our ability to deliver goods in a way that is satisfactory to them. When we can listen carefully to what others are saying – not just to their words, but to the energy *behind* their words – we will learn a great deal. When we can then act on this insight, our response will often spark a huge sense of relief for that person, because they are being respected and understood more completely. We have all experienced the relief at our complaint being attended to, or when we receive an unprompted apology for an error. We work smartest when we can tackle the apparent issue before us, as well as the one that underpins it. We are then able to reach a far more satisfying solution.

Being respectful does not mean we compromise our ethics or agree to whatever others put before us, but that we avoid being aggressive, so that the energy between us becomes lighter and more inviting. Not everyone we come into contact with will react as we had hoped. There will be some who are mischievous or destructive. Sometimes people have become so accustomed to behaving badly, they have forgotten how else to resolve issues. I was saddened to come across a former workmate recently, who

I hadn't seen for some time. As we talked, his every sentence was laced with poisonous remarks about those he had worked with a decade earlier. Ten years is a long time to keep feeding a dead issue, especially when we're using our precious life energy to do so.

When we can be an oasis of calm and good sense in the midst of all the chaos and confusion at work, others are touched by our inner radiance, and slowly but surely those parts of them that were angry and wounded will begin to heal. This deeper path takes us far beyond win–win techniques, because it acknowledges the Light within each of us that binds us together. And when instead of trying only to satisfy our own needs, we can hold onto the vision of a successful outcome for *everyone*, we allow our divine self to draw us into sacred alignment with the divine self of the person with whom we have issues, thus enabling us both to be more accommodating. When we can resolve our problems with those we find trying, often the whole chemistry between us will change. Not only will a mutual respect develop, but frequently we will discover the person is nothing like we had previously imagined. As they become more amenable, they often become someone we enjoy working with. There are times when we might have to agree to disagree, but it is still important to remain respectful and gracious. Once the issue is settled, it should not be discussed again, lest we end up destroying whatever goodwill we have gained, by revisiting those things that should be left alone.

BEING AWARE OF SUBTERFUGE

Even as we attempt to reach peaceful solutions to conflict at work, we must always act wisely, because not all the issues we face will be immediately obvious to us. There are those at work whose problematic behaviour is hard to recognise. These are the people who change their minds about the brief when a project is almost complete – who spend hours in our office when we are screamingly busy, or who expect our undying support for their latest catastrophe. Whether this is a workmate or our boss makes little difference – the effect can be equally harmful if we don't wise up.

Gemma was personal assistant to a high-powered magazine executive. Her boss was so disorganised that he would only start to focus on his work at the end of the day. No matter how organised Gemma was, her boss continually threw her days into chaos. Gemma's boss travelled a great deal and was constantly changing his schedule and losing personal items along the way. He would then return to the office with receipts for his expenses, which were little more than a chaotic collection of pieces of paper that Gemma had to try and make sense of. This man was so disorganised he would frequently double-book appointments, leaving Gemma to deal with the fallout. Because her boss was so charming, Gemma would willingly give up nights and weekends to put everything back together, yet whenever anything went wrong it was always Gemma's fault. Over time, Gemma's confidence was severely eroded. She began to believe she was incompetent – until she met her boss's former assistant. Then Gemma realised what kind of boss she was dealing with and moved on.

Even though such individuals appear to be team players, often their dysfunction will undermine the efforts of those around them.

Mark worked in a tight-knit sales team that took months to wake up to the fact they were losing valuable time and momentum supporting someone who, while charismatic, was lazy and disorganised. Mark almost missed out on a well-deserved promotion because he was spending so much time helping this man through his every crisis. Those who are extremely needy at work often create conflict because they are blinded by fear, but that doesn't make their hidden agendas any less painful for those around them.

It can also be devastating to have our confidences betrayed and ideas stolen. This was Justin's experience with Jayne, when she ended up with one of his best clients, because she followed up a lead that was his to pursue. By the time Justin found out about it, the deal was done.

These situations can test our ability to reach a peaceful solution. They also provide painful, but powerful lessons in insight. While we might be tempted to lash out, or to withdraw from the person concerned, the wisest course is to be harmless and up-front about the problems that have arisen, and to ensure this person has no further opportunity to appropriate what is not theirs. This done, it is vital we continue to inhabit a life-enhancing space, so that we can release ourselves from the grip of potentially destructive emotions. This more profound way of dealing with conflict recognises that even the most painful situations at work have the capacity to make better people of us.

A CONTEMPLATION ON HOW WE MIGHT MOVE FORWARD
Why not try the following meditation, which Jack Kornfield describes so beautifully, and see where it takes you?

❦

'Picture or imagine that this earth is filled with Buddhas, that every single being you encounter is enlightened, except one – yourself! Imagine that they are all here to teach you.

All those you encounter are acting as they do solely for your benefit, to provide just the teachings and difficulties you need to awaken. Sense what lessons they offer to you. Inwardly thank them for this. Throughout a day or a week continue to develop the image of enlightened teachers all around you. Notice how it changes your whole perspective on life.'

leadership with a difference

To know what is going on takes sense,
To know what to do about it takes wisdom.
CHINESE PROVERB

TAKING THE JOB SERIOUSLY

What motivates us to be a leader? The package? The kudos? The power? Is our aim purely to get where we are going, or to achieve something more? Our motives and style of leadership will have a massive impact on our lives – not just on our career and salary, but on our soul's quest. With leadership comes responsibility – lots of it. Leadership has karmic responsibilities as well, because how we lead will affect the lives of those around us. Leadership is not for the faint-hearted. The job can be exhilarating and fulfilling, but it can also be tough. With each advancement up the ladder comes more competition and pressure, and in spite of our good intentions there will be decisions and directions we regret. Sometimes our courage will fail us and our vision will become clouded.

Good leadership is about results, but it's also about tenacity, about the need to stay focused and to see things through. It can be hard to be strong and wise, and to hold onto the vision when everyone else seems to have lost theirs. Yet when we can learn from our mistakes and summon the courage to keep going, even when those around us are ready to give up, each challenge will make us smarter and more effective. Leadership will test our skills and endurance and it will also test our compassion. It is a privilege to be a leader, and so we must always respect those who work alongside us, honouring their individual gifts and their dignity. If we accept a promotion simply because we are desperate to succeed, then sooner or later our intentions will become obvious, and we will lose respect and credibility. When, however, we can be authentic, courageous and consistent, can attend to the detail and watch the direction we are going in, we have the building blocks for success.

HANDLING POWER

One of the greatest challenges we will face as leaders is in handling the power bestowed upon us, because the more successful we become, the more we are in a position to influence outcomes. While we flatter ourselves we are able to handle the most elevated positions with ease, rarely does this prove to be the case. In ancient times, advancement in the temples from one level of prominence and understanding to the next was by initiation. The ability to progress was not only based on one's knowledge, but on one's ability to handle the responsibility ahead. In our brave new world we rarely pay attention to such intricacies, but then we wonder why we come unstuck. Perhaps this is a good time to ask ourselves how we are exercising our power right now. Are we using our influence judiciously, or do we resort to manipulation or to throwing our weight around to get what we want? Does our presence as a leader contribute physically, mentally, emotionally and spiritually to our work-place, or are there areas we are neglecting at present? If so, how might we remedy this?

CREATING SUCCESS

All these questions point towards what we hope to achieve in our current role. Naturally we want to be successful – to bring in good sales results, to produce quality products or services on time – but is there more we can aim for? Often we become so fixated on the material goals of our department or organisation that we forget to determine the *qualities* needed to underpin our endeavours. Excellence in leadership is about forming a workable vision for the future, then creating the appropriate *climate* to support this vision. We arrive at the qualities needed to underpin our vision when we can move beyond the ways things are to consider how they might be, and then work to make this wider perspective a reality. Healer Lilla Bek also suggests we look at everything 'with a deeper level of awareness, trying to sense [on] how many levels we can meet.' If we accept this observation, then on how many levels can we meet our team? Are we choosing simply to pull in the results, or can we achieve outcomes that are not only excellent, but meaningful and worthwhile?

Our team is far more than a collection of people with the requisite skills – it is a coming together of imagination, passion and life experience – and everyone we work with has chosen, consciously or otherwise, to have us in their lives. With these many possibilities before us, how then might we shape this human potential to achieve something extraordinary? What qualities do we need to transform the vision our team has of itself and the way it works? We don't need a treatise or complicated flow chart to envisage the culture we want. We simply need to determine the qualities that will support our material goals and shared human needs. We need also to consider the kind of space we are prepared to hold for those around us, regardless of how demanding our work might be. Are we going to succeed *with* our team and touch their lives profoundly, or are they simply a means to our end?

We can create a competitive, ego-driven group of people who will achieve the results, but when our work culture is one-dimensional, so too are the outcomes. When instead we can promote such life-enhancing qualities as authenticity, creativity, passion, honesty, respect, cooperation, commitment and discernment, we can not only achieve material success, but we can also nurture the human spirit. What then are the qualities we want for our team? And how do these qualities support our organisation's material goals? Some qualities are more achievable than others, and so it is important to have a clear idea of how we can best bring each of these qualities into the group. What resistance might we face to these qualities within and beyond our team? How can we overcome this resistance without jeopardising all we seek to achieve?

The best way to introduce these life-enhancing qualities is to embody them. Then as those around us observe the practical benefits of these qualities at work, they are inspired to embrace them too. As we consider each of the qualities we plan to introduce, how might we exemplify them? How can we best demonstrate *respect* in our interactions with our staff? Do we need to spend a little more time with them, to appreciate their contributions more fully, or to solicit their opinions more frequently? Do we treat them courteously, acknowledging them when they arrive in the mornings and when they depart at night? Do we take into account their wider pressures and talents? Are we even aware of what these might be? Similarly, how might we convey *authenticity* and *creativity* in our day-to-day work?

Every moment of our working day, our colleagues and our team are taking their cues from how we operate and react. They need to see the qualities we are passionate about in action before they can make them their own. It is up to us to create the culture we want, and to have the commitment and imagination to foster this culture. The changes we're aiming for will be threatening for some, and there will be times when we will need to defend our fledgling culture from those who seek to subvert it. There will also be times when some team members or the whole team will fail to support this new culture. While this can be disappointing, it is *our* strength of purpose and ability to steer a steady course that will be central to keeping things on track. Then as those around us begin to make this new culture their own, they too will be motivated to defend and nurture it.

The more beneficial the new culture is for our team, the more they will be inspired to shape it actively. It is exhilarating when we see the culture we have worked so hard to create continuing to grow and flourish. If we're lucky we may see it being transformed into something that is even more wonderful and successful than we had imagined. Creating a life-enhancing culture is central to achieving lasting success, because when our life energies are joined together in a positive manner, the collective energy is far greater than the sum of the individual energies. This then enables all who work in such an environment to realise their potential more easily. And as a whole, a team of this ilk cannot help but inspire many within and beyond our organisation.

LEADERSHIP IS SERVICE

As we contemplate the texture and nuances of leadership, we begin to see that the possibilities for the role are immense, and that while our brief is about directing, resourcing, and coaching, it is also about *serving* those who work with us. The greater the number of staff who report to us, the greater our duty of care. If we are so caught up in managing our careers that we have little or no relationship with our workmates, then we have missed the point. When we take our leadership seriously, we cannot help but ask how we can serve those who work with us. We support our staff best when we are focused and committed – when we can manage the resources and the workflow, and can attend to the detail as well as the big picture. Workloads and stress levels must also be carefully monitored, and close attention must be paid to our systems to ensure that everyone's work is streamlined and effective. When we are able to bring this level of attention to what we do, our staff can not only do their jobs well, they also enjoy them.

THE IMPORTANCE OF JOY

Joy is often a missing ingredient at work these days, because we tend to regard it as frivolous and unbusinesslike. Yet joy is our natural state. Joy not only helps sustain us, it stretches our vision and stimulates our creativity. Where there is enjoyment at work, it becomes infectious, touching workmates and clients, and creating a far more positive experience for everyone. Joy is, however, an internal and spontaneous state; it cannot be enforced, but it can be nurtured. Often we mistake the presence of joy for more superficial emotions or occasions, mistakenly assuming we can create joy by staging social events with staff, or by making occasional gestures of goodwill. It is in providing an environment where our team can thrive and succeed that we can create lasting joy. As workloads grow and resources become scarce, increasingly, whole organisations have become stressed and exhausted. If we want a tangible sense of joy in our team, then we need to guard against stress and exhaustion. We need to know if the members of our team are feeling alive and motivated right now, or whether they have become fearful or lack the vitality to do their jobs well.

ACKNOWLEDGING THOSE WHO WORK WITH US

Joy comes in nurturing the human spirit and from acknowledgement. Even though most people need to work, it helps to remember they don't have to work with *us*. How then might we articulate our respect for those who honour us with their loyalty? What are each team member's needs within and beyond the job? Our focus should always be on what is best for our staff, not what we assume they might want or what makes us look or feel good. When we get these gestures wrong, we dishonour those we work with.

Clare worked with a manager who enjoyed dispensing extravagant gifts to deserving members of staff. 'The only problem was that most of us were working with hardly any resources, and we were struggling to pay the rent. Something more practical would have been a whole lot more use,' she confessed.

Sasha worked in advertising and each year her boss would give her an expensive bottle of perfume. 'It was great he went to the trouble to get me a present, but when I found out he claimed it on his expenses I wished he hadn't bothered. When I got him a present it didn't cost as much, but at least it came out of my pocket.' If we want to honour those we work with, then we should always seek to touch the deep places within them. When we can remain authentic and alive to the possibilities contained within each moment, we will transform our working days.

We can only achieve all we are capable of as a leader when we are able to take *everyone* with us, not just those we like or admire. For too long we have promoted a handful of people at the expense of everyone else. There is a fine line between rewarding top performers and disempowering those who still have some way to go. When we become elitist and focus our efforts on a few key players, we fail to realise that any department or organisation is only as good as its weakest link. The more inclusive we are, the more we encourage weaker players to become strong, and the more our entire team will flourish. This principle honours the inter-connection of all living things and the possibilities that are there for us when we can promote and celebrate this connection. How then might we acknowledge our team? Are we currently focusing on a few at the expense of everyone else? If so, what strategies can we put in place to ensure our whole team feels valued and is operating at its full potential?

MAKING HASTE SLOWLY

Frequently, it is the *subtle* details that radically affect our performance. When taking over a new brief it is tempting to want to make major changes to prove we're the best person for the job. One of the hallmarks of those who are unsure of themselves is the need for constant change in policy or direction. When we take this approach, we not only prevent those we work with from taking initiative and giving their best, we fragment their work lives and undermine their loyalty. When taking on a new position a wise leader proceeds more judiciously. They understand the value of building on past achievements and experience, and so they carefully observe the systems as well as the chemistry between staff. They make themselves thoroughly aware of the goals of their department, so they can see how the flow of work does or does not reflect these goals. They also pay close attention to their team's interactions with other departments and organisations, so they can determine how best the efforts of their department might serve their wider goals. Having gathered this information, they will know the strengths and weaknesses of each individual and of their department as a whole, and the opportunities and difficulties they face.

With a more complete picture, they are then able to progress with greater effect. No amount of flourish can replace true insight and informed decisions. No-one knew this better than Augustus Caesar, whose advice was to hasten slowly. Again, this is about having the courage to lead with clarity and consistency, so our team can remain cohesive, focused and motivated during any finetuning we might undertake. Now might be the perfect time to take another look at our team and its output, and to contemplate the material and human potential before us. What are the opportunities and challenges ahead? How best might we deal with them? Where might this take us? As we consider these questions, it will become more apparent how best we might build on what has been, so that we can reach our material goals and foster the spirit of those who work with us.

BREAKING THE CYCLE OF UNACCEPTABLE BEHAVIOUR
Whenever we take over a new brief there are always areas in need of immediate attention, and none more so than dysfunctional behaviour. No-one can thrive in a low-energy environment, because it kills creativity and cooperation. If we have unacceptable behaviour within our new team, then it must be dealt with at once. Our actions might not be welcomed, but they are necessary. Before we respond, again we need to be clear about the causes of the behaviour, to ensure we fully understand what is going on.

When Will went to work for a large media organisation, he was appalled at the frequent outbursts from certain staff that would often culminate in their leaving the office. Previous managers had been bemused and intimidated by this behaviour, and so the cycle of dysfunction had grown to the point that the department had a bad reputation. The first thing Will did was talk to his staff to determine how work was for them and how they would like it to be. During the course of his one-on-one discussions, he discovered that the main issue was a lack of resources. He could then see that this was the root cause of the confrontational behaviour within the team.

Resources weren't going to appear magically, so Will developed a plan of action, involving everyone in the process. He also made it clear that, while there were issues to be worked through, anyone leaving the building would not be welcome back. He then began to work towards getting his staff additional resources. While the resourcing issue took time, they began visibly to relax. They felt validated to have been listened to, and while there were lapses in behaviour, no-one stormed out; everyone's energy began to go into their work. Will also set up regular morning meetings that brought the team together over coffee and muffins. This was a deliberate attempt to feed the minds and spirit of his team. In these meetings they would discuss issues, problem-solve and celebrate their wins. For the first couple of meetings, the team was cautious, but then they began to look forward to the meetings, and to contribute ideas and food. 'Suddenly I realised we'd become a team,' Will confessed. Some managers might question the need for coffee and muffins, but for Will it was an important part of demonstrating his respect for his team. 'People tend to assume things like food are unbusinesslike or time-consuming, but how long does it take to collect something before work? For me it was a vital part of bringing my people together and motivating them.'

The new environment didn't work for everyone. Those who couldn't cope with the more up-beat atmosphere left, enabling more positive individuals to take their place. Productivity increased and absenteeism dropped, because work was now a place the team *wanted* to be. Within eighteen months, even though Will hadn't acquired all the resources he was after, he had most of them. He did have a first-class team, and as the new culture took shape, Will also benefited. 'The more cohesive the team became, the less effort I had to put into keeping up the momentum. By that stage the team had developed an energy of its own that supported everyone. My role was then a whole lot easier.'

STEPPING BACK

When we are able to pool our strengths and hold the vision, we create a winning environment that stimulates all kinds of opportunities for individuals, and for the team as a whole. Yet no matter how experienced or inspiring we might be as leaders, we cannot sustain a successful environment on our own. We have to take others with us. Sometimes in our passion for work and those we work with, we take on more than we should. Leadership can be gratifying or draining, depending on how we choose to operate. When we take on too much, we exhaust ourselves and we don't perform well. As we become wiser, we learn to step back and take stock. Then it becomes clear which projects we are to involve ourselves in, and which are best left alone or delegated.

A truly successful working life is an expansive experience – for ourselves and for everyone we come into contact with. It can be suffocating to be around a boss who insists on being involved in every aspect of everything that is happening. When we are controlling, often we lose perspective. The quality and output of our work suffers, and we start to make poor decisions. We also stifle a whole raft of opportunities for ourselves within and beyond work. We might be an excellent accountant or warehouse manager, but we might also have the potential to shape new policies or to enhance reporting systems at work. But if we don't learn to let go a little, we're never going to find the time to realise these additional opportunities, and will instead become stale and resentful.

To be an effective leader, we need to know when to take charge and when to give others a chance to prove themselves. This doesn't mean we should abdicate our responsibility – there's a big difference between enabling someone to complete a project successfully, and allowing them to sink or swim. Depending on their experience, certain individuals might at first need a high level of supervision. Mistakes will sometimes be made, and progress might initially be slower than if we took the project on ourselves, yet when we can create a supportive environment, new ideas and approaches are able to take shape and over time everyone wins.

How would we describe our leadership style right now? Is it expansive and life-enhancing, or have we become lost in the detail? If our leadership isn't all we might hope for, let us take a moment to imagine what a more expansive style of management might look like, and what it might *feel* like. As we glimpse these possibilities, we can begin to get a sense of how we can make this life-enhancing approach to leadership a reality. Why not write down what more you would like to achieve in your job? What activities and responsibilities can be delegated to make this happen? Which team members are best suited to each of these tasks? How can you introduce them to these duties? What backup will they need? How long will it take them to get up to speed? What resources and support will you need for your initiatives? Where might they come from? What are the desired outcomes of these changes?

When we can plan thoroughly, the way forward will be smoother, and we are likely to achieve our goals.

WE WON'T ALWAYS GET IT RIGHT

Even when we manage well, mistakes will still be made, and so if we want to keep our team strong and motivated, we must ensure they focus on problem-solving and not on cover-ups. There is a huge difference between a culture of accountability and one of blame. In a culture of blame, individuals are often paralysed by anxiety, and so all their energy goes into concealing their errors instead of fixing them. We must never allow our fear of making mistakes to prevent us or our team from forging ahead. Naturally, we need to know how to promote accuracy and the ability to make good decisions. And when something does go wrong it is best always to ensure that we, or someone we nominate, are the *first* person to be told. If we are smart we will create the climate and systems that will help minimise errors and enable our team to deal swiftly and positively with them as they occur. Fewer mistakes will then be made, because those who work with us will be more motivated to get things right and keep up the momentum. When people can openly admit they have missed a beat, they will rarely make the same mistake again.

We too will get things wrong. As a leader, it can be extremely painful to face up to the fact that we have made a bad decision or taken a wrong direction, because what we do affects those around us. Often we're afraid to admit we are wrong, because we fear we will lose staff respect and loyalty, yet when we have made a mistake it is important we acknowledge it – our unwillingness to do so will only alienate our team and discourage them from being honest with us. When we can admit we are wrong, we demonstrate character and courage. Before we speak with the team, it helps to take a couple of minutes to turn our attention within and ask for the right words to heal the situation as quickly and painlessly as possible, because the words we choose will be critical. A brief explanation is all that is needed. When we dare to show that we are human, we create a greater bond with our team and further demonstrate the importance of being up-front.

PUTTING IN TIME WITH THE STAFF

So much of leadership is about communication. Some days we are full of optimism and it is easy to communicate with staff, but when we're tired and stressed it is tempting simply to order staff around without any discussion. Regardless of our commitments, it is vital we are consistent in the way we interact with our staff, and that we give them the respect and consideration we would hope for ourselves. Even a five-minute conversation can make all the difference. We might then discover that a seemingly unworkable suggestion might have merit, or that while we can't provide the resources requested, there are other resources available. The working day won't always unfold as we would like, but the outcome will be more favourable when we behave decently and respectfully towards our staff.

Explaining what we're up to can be time-consuming and exhausting, but not nearly as exhausting as getting staff offside. When we are battling on several fronts, we might be tempted to send out staff memos and emails. Again, the question of how we communicate gets back to respect. The memo or email is an excellent way to reinforce a message by setting out the detail of what has already been discussed, but it can easily signal a lack of respect, and without respect there can be little ongoing loyalty.

Elio worked for a leading advertising agency. He and his workmates were devastated to learn by email that their CEO of several years had been dismissed. 'Everyone was not only angry, we felt betrayed, especially as we couldn't hide behind our emails. We then had to cope with the backlash from our clients and competitors.' When we can put in the extra time and effort with staff, we will reap the benefits.

This does not mean we should indulge high-maintenance staff, who will soak up as much attention as we are able to give them. It is important to be aware of those who demand more time, and to be clear about why this is happening. If we don't, we can end up indulging their behaviour without even realising it. This category of staff needs to be aware that our time is not to be wasted. It is up to us to insist they be succinct. And if they have a tendency to come up with a never-ending string of problems, then it is best to encourage them to think through possible solutions before talking with us. As their behaviour is focused on getting attention, and not on finding solutions, this is often an effective deterrent to time-wasting. When we can take this approach, we help them to be less needy, and then we all have more time for issues that matter.

MAKING TIME FOR OUR WORK

Leaders can spend a great deal of time on decision-making, coaching, resourcing and handling difficult situations, especially when taking on a new team. Still it is vital to set aside time for our own work if we want to be effective. Ultimately, we will be judged on our ability to handle our own workload and to honour our own deadlines, as well as those of our staff. We also need enough space within our jobs to be the inspired professionals we aim to be. When we get lost in the detail, there is little or no time to be innovative – to make new contacts, to refine systems, to discover new resources. And when we become stale, sooner or later this lethargy will creep into our team, until they lack dynamism. Learning to close our office door helps set boundaries. We might also need the occasional day out of the office for planning and for getting out into the field, so that we can maintain our vision of the big picture.

MAKING TOUGH DECISIONS

Even when we have established a good team, we will still have to make some difficult decisions. Whatever our decision, it should be grounded in sound business practices, and charged with goodness and decency. Whenever we are tempted to act only for expediency or to take the easy way out, we can be sure we have lost our way, and that sooner or later our motivations and work practices will become evident to those around us. Daring to take a tough decision requires strength and delicacy. It's easy to be manipulative or to throw our weight around, but to make a firm stand with humanity requires a different approach. Truly courageous decisions honour the needs of *everyone* involved – even if the outcome might not be what some had hoped for. When we are able to take this wider perspective, the final decision cannot help but be more intelligent and fair, because it will take into account the intricacy and complexities of working life.

For too long we have equated brutal decisions in the workplace with being high-powered and on track. We have applauded decisions that have been based purely on the bottom line, giving little or no thought to the impact such decisions have on people's lives, the work culture or the company's reputation. When we operate in this way, we are being short-sighted, not tough. Genuine leadership is about daring to take others with us – not just the strong and the brave, but those who rely on us to help them get past the post. When we're faced with a challenging situation, we need to be clear we are operating from the wisdom of our divine selves, and not from the fears and insecurities of our little selves. Our divine selves will always honour the *greater* needs, pointing us towards the fairest and best solution, while our little selves will do whatever is required to survive. Organisations the world over are peopled by those whose little selves rule the day, and that is why so many workplaces stagger from crisis to crisis.

KEEPING OUR FEET ON THE GROUND

Part of embracing our humanity at work is being prepared to stay grounded no matter how elevated our position. In times past, people rose through the ranks and their success was based on a deep respect for where they had come from. Now we enjoy senior positions early, without any grassroots training. This approach often encourages us to separate ourselves from those more junior, but we all need to remain grounded in the everyday, because we never operate in isolation. When we don't keep in touch with the grassroots we become vulnerable, because we no longer know our constituency. How can we make informed decisions when we have no idea what is really concerning our staff or our clients? When we *do* allow those around us into our lives, they not only share our journey, they help us on our wider quest to become loving and wise.

MAINTAINING OUR HUMANITY

The soul path of a leader is often steeper and more demanding, because there are so many distractions that can take us away from operating from the wisdom of our divine selves. All the great spiritual traditions remind us that it is not the choice of profession that matters, but *how* we work, because our conduct and ethics are all. There is a big difference between being a strong leader and being a leader who behaves inhumanely. Regardless of our status or salary package, we are still subject to the law of cause and effect. Every indecent act we perform now will come back to us in the future. We might be successful, even spectacularly so, but the time will come when we will be called upon to rectify all the pain we have created. When we place figures before people, manufacturing before our environment, success before decency, knowledge before wisdom, we do great harm. Our Light body contracts – we literally block the life-giving energies that surround us, and prevent them from entering our being. Then as our personal energy drops, our joy and hopefulness fade. We become fearful about ourselves and the future, about our ability to deliver or to stay on top. When we're in this frame of mind, it is almost impossible be even-handed. That's when we start to treat people as numbers, when we move others around as if they were little more than chess pieces.

There are no shortcuts to being a successful leader, but there are certain fundamentals we need to maintain to succeed, and humanity is one of these. When we can allow our humanity to shape our working days, there is little room for regret. Let us contemplate our own leadership style. How are we operating right now? Are we motivated by decency, or have we become fearful and unable to treat others as they deserve? If our leadership is not all we would wish, then how else might we lead? What part might our humanity play in this process?

COMPASSIONATE DISPASSION

For too long the workplace has been a battlefield, where even the wins come at a heavy price. There is another way. We are here on earth to discover the awesome power of goodness, and to demonstrate this in our own lives. When we nurture our humanity as a leader, we automatically choose to operate harmlessly. There is nothing weak about being harmless; it takes strength to be loving and wise when those around us are not. When we dare to take this approach, it will serve us well. Still we speak our minds and are discerning, but when we deal with contentious issues harmlessly, we diffuse the emotion around the issue, cutting through all the confusion and negativity and reaching a solution more swiftly. When we operate harmlessly, we also learn to trust the process. Instead of trying to bend others to our will, we aim to reach the best outcome for everyone. When we are able to work with this level of clarity, we create a safe climate around us, making it easier for us to work well with others and to achieve a great deal.

LONELINESS OF LEADERSHIP

While it is important we remain committed to our team, to be an effective leader we need to maintain some distance from those we work with – only then can we create mutual respect and use this wider perspective to govern well. This does not mean we need to be distant with staff, but that we should respect the team's need for time to themselves. Weak managers find it almost impossible to operate in this way – they thrive on creating dependency. Some become so dependent on those they work with, they scarcely allow their staff out of their sight. Not only does this familiarity breed contempt, it narrows the vision, stifles initiative and drives good people away.

How then do we deal with the isolation of leadership? Certainly it can be helpful to mix with other leaders in our organisation – to share ideas and resources and also to enjoy lighter moments. Yet as our colleagues are equally busy, often their ability to share more meaningful relationships is limited. When we can develop a more intimate connection with our inner self through silence and space, we are able to access our inner guidance and wisdom, which will help us understand ourselves and others more fully. The more we are at home with who we are, the more comfortable we will be at work, enabling staff and colleagues to feel more at ease around us. We can then build on this intimacy by spending time with those of like mind, with those with whom we enjoy a deep and spontaneous connection. Friendships with people with mutual interests beyond work can also be deeply fulfilling. The more we pursue our passion for photography or rock-climbing, the more we are able to make new friends who can stretch our attention beyond work. When we can put all these elements together, we can enjoy a rich and rewarding life within and beyond work.

NURTURING OURSELVES

If we wish to be a good leader, we also need to nurture and support ourselves. We have talked already about many possibilities for self-nurture. Morning meditation not only helps us start our day well, it enables us to operate in a state of relaxed awareness. This relaxed awareness enables us to discern what is going on around us from a space of absolute calm. Meditation also helps us to get past the post with relative ease, because it gives us the clarity to see the most direct route forward, no matter how difficult the terrain. The higher energy we attain during meditation will also help attract to us the people and resources needed to maintain this heightened state. Then instead of constantly driving ourselves to exhaustion by forcing issues, we meet the perfect contact before we have even sought them out, or we get additional resources before we have requested them.

It also helps to see ourselves more objectively – to be aware of our actions and motives, and the effect they are having – so that we don't get caught up in self-defeating behaviour. Once we are aware of how we take our frustration out on others – how we sabotage our relationships with staff by our determination to be right, how we fail to listen or take advice – we can modify our behaviour before it ruins our good work. Another helpful practice is to review our day just before we sleep. As we replay the day's events, we can see where we have made progress, where we have wasted our energy, and where we might have given ourselves more credit. When we resist the temptation to beat ourselves up, and can observe our day objectively, our nightly review will help us see how we might work in a more focused and insightful way, and how we can attain our many goals with more ease and enjoyment.

LETTING GO OF THE NEED TO BE APPRECIATED

One of the most challenging aspects of leadership is realising that regardless of how hard or effectively we work, we won't always gain the appreciation we had hoped for from our team. These situations often coincide with times when we're feeling drained. When we meet opposition in our team, it is important we take a raincheck to ensure we're on track. If we have lost our way, then we need to regroup and reconsider how best we might progress. If we are on track, then we need to keep moving regardless.

On taking over a new buying team in a leading department store, Kris managed to save a couple of jobs. It had been a long battle, but it was worth it. She assumed her new team would be positive and cooperative, but had instead to deal with some of the worst behaviour she had encountered. 'It was a real blow,' she confessed, 'yet as I took a closer look at their aggressive behaviour, I realised everyone had been through so many changes in management that they felt angry and out of control. I couldn't tell them their jobs had been on the line and that they'd got a good deal. The next few months were tough. Somehow I managed to find the strength to treat them decently, even though they were being openly destructive. I had to discipline a number of individuals, yet I was determined to remain positive and to respect where everyone was coming from.

'The first few months were hard. There were no instant solutions, but I did learn the importance of being clear about where we were heading and how to get there, then taking one step at a time to achieve this.' Kris came to realise that one of the ultimate tests of leadership is the ability to continue to be decent, authentic and courageous, even when tested to the limit. She was right to promote positive, life-enhancing attitudes, because when we become tired and discouraged we interrupt the flow of energy through our system. Kris's approach paid off. 'Within a few months my team couldn't have been more supportive. The quality of their work was excellent, as was their motivation, and they'd regained their self-confidence. I benefited from their support as well. The whole process made me stronger and a whole lot wiser.'

ALL GOOD THINGS COME TO AN END

As a leader, there is nothing more gratifying than helping those who work with us to extend themselves, yet when we work closely with our team, we can assume they owe us in some way. Then when these individuals choose to move on, we often feel angry or distressed, forgetting that everyone's life is their own. We do not know the soul path of another, and if we don't get a grip on our negative feelings, we will destroy what was an excellent relationship. There may be issues to face when staff leave; if so, we need to know what they are. We may then discover that our management style or decisions have been problematic, or that our expectations have been unrealistic. Whatever the issue, if a staff member has the courage to be honest with us, then we need to value this honesty and take a good look at how we are operating. This valuable feedback might then prevent other people in the team from leaving.

When a staff member resigns, the spotlight will be on us, and so even if their leaving is difficult or potentially destructive, still we need to be even-handed. If we handle this challenge wisely, then everyone benefits.

Rubi took on the difficult brief of bringing two separate teams together after two government departments amalgamated. After a year, everyone was motivated, their work was excellent, productivity was up and their future seemed secure. Another year passed and the department continued to exceed expectations. Then people started to resign. Rubi was devastated. She had worked so hard to make her department's culture a vibrant one, she felt personally responsible for the resignations. But when Rubi took a step back, she realised that her staff were leaving to take up more senior positions and that it was a great credit to her input and expertise. 'While I was sad to see those who worked with me move on, I began to realise how much each person had brought to my working life. That way there were only positive feelings between us. I also discovered that when I enabled one wonderful person to leave without feeling guilty, someone equally special was waiting to take their place.'

When good people leave we have the satisfaction of seeing the values we have fostered carried into other organisations, enabling others to enjoy a more soulful way of working. Sometimes it might be the wider climate at work that has motivated a staff member to leave. Again, we need to be sensitive to this.

Daryl had also worked hard to build up a good team, then just when he was feeling he could relax, his staff started to leave. 'Initially I panicked and gave those who resigned a hard time. But when I started to look around, I began to realise what was going on. We'd had a change of CEO and that altered the whole culture. I then realised that by expecting my staff to stay, I was asking them to stay in an environment that wasn't that good for them.'

Every situation we face as a leader has the capacity to reveal a great deal. When a staff member resigns, our ability to take the wider view can help us see the strengths and flaws in our leadership and in our work culture, enabling us to finetune how we might work. We can regard a resignation as betrayal or as a window opening onto a whole new set of opportunities. What we expect is generally what we get – the choice is ours.

OUR LEADERSHIP CAN MAKE A DIFFERENCE

If we are going to be a leader that matters, then we need to connect genuinely and profoundly with the people we work with. When we can nurture strong bonds with our team, we are far more able to weather the storms that we will inevitably face. Good leaders empower those they work with. Still their goals might be exacting, but not only will they acknowledge this, they will honour the effort needed to achieve these goals, and will assist their staff to get past the post. When we create a culture of nurture and trust, we encourage everyone to play a meaningful part in our organisation and to reach their full potential. The more we can honour those we work with, the more they will be motivated to go the extra mile, to come up with new and effective ways to work, and to be excellent ambassadors, regardless of their status. Successful organisations are those that know who they are and where they are going, and enjoy the process of getting there. When we can help bring this kind of culture about, we will create an organisation that naturally attracts customers and that has the imagination and capacity to move forward more easily within this ever-changing world.

⊷

A prayer for inspired leadership

'O Great Spirit, there is much I want to achieve as a leader, but often I get distracted and disappointed by what is going on around me. Help me always to take a wider view – to work with excellence, intelligence and foresight for the highest good. Give me the courage to hold onto the vision, so that all I undertake at work will not be in vain.'

retrenching others

Experience is not what happens to a man;
it is what a man does with what happens to him.
ALDOUS HUXLEY, TEXTS AND PRETEXTS

PEOPLE VERSUS MONEY

One of the most challenging aspects of contemporary working life is the constant loss of jobs. While most of us agree that individuals are more important than money, these are not the values we tend to espouse at work. As the demands of the balance sheet have become paramount, downsizing has become a fact of life. People continue to lose jobs and there seems no end in sight to this trend. Many of us have worked in companies where staff cuts have become the standard solution to making the figures look good, and we have also seen the long-term fallout of this approach. There are times when job loss is the only way forward, but often companies lack the moral rigour or imagination to ensure this step is absolutely necessary. Far too many decisions to retrench are based on fear and on an inability to take a wider view. When we spend our working lives protecting our own interests – or trying to keeping our superiors happy – we are hardly likely to enjoy a more creative, life-affirming way of working. No matter how much we attempt to sanitise our actions, we cannot escape the fact that retrenchment is inhumane – that it not only damages individuals, but also destroys so much of what is good within organisations.

WHAT WILL IT TAKE FOR US TO COOPERATE?

Increasingly, the ability to get rid of staff is a measure of how effective we are as leaders. The more prevalent this viewpoint, the less we ask ourselves what kinds of people would promote such views. Career advancement is one thing, but devastating the lives of others to prove we have got what it takes is something else. What, apart from solving bottom-line issues, are we doing when considering retrenchment? What impact will this course of action have on those whose jobs are on the line and on those who remain? And in agreeing to a round of retrenchments, are we supporting the abuse of remaining staff by expecting them to do more work than is reasonable? These questions might cause some discomfort, but they need to be considered.

Those who currently pull the strings within many organisations are arch-manipulators. Motivated largely by self-interest and self-aggrandisement they gather around them those who will cooperate. They are careful always to get others to do their unpleasant work, and so adept are they at getting what they want, they will use whatever it takes to get us to cooperate. It is important that we are aware of our susceptibility to these kinds of pressures, because we can become so clouded by our own ambitions or by the opinions of others, that we lose sight of what is right. Then we get drawn into all kinds of questionable behaviour.

Recently Adrian was shocked to discover a fellow advertising executive had taken delivery of a top-of-the-range company car the same day he retrenched his most senior staff member to cut costs. Not all deals are so blatant, but frequently the result is the same – someone prospers at the expense of others. There are many ways in which we can end up selling our souls at work, and our willingness to get rid of others can be one of them.

We won't always save the jobs we are fighting for, but it is important to be meticulous about our motivation and behaviour when the question of retrenchment is before us. Our response to such requests is also dependent on a clear understanding of the options available to us.

Dez explains, 'In my early days as a manager I was as influenced by edicts from above to retrench as the next person, because I'd no idea how I could fight these decisions. I protested, but that was all I felt I could do, and so jobs were lost. Once I realised there were other ways to proceed, I was then able to take a different tack. There were a number of times after this I was asked to get rid of staff, but I was able to save those jobs by finding workable solutions to the problem. I also made sure I demonstrated the ongoing worth of the people whose jobs I'd saved.'

When we are faced with the decision to retrench, we need to understand what is being asked of us and have the strength and imagination to consider the alternatives.

NEW WAYS FORWARD

True courage lies in doing what is for the highest good of our staff and our organisation. When we can make decisions that are intelligent and courageous, everyone benefits. These are the foundations upon which we build a far more meaningful and successful work culture. To dare to suggest another way out of our company's bottom-line problems, and to have the courage to take responsibility for the decision to save jobs, is where true strength lies. Not only are these approaches courageous, they are far-sighted, because they honour the need for stability and continuity. They also demonstrate a willingness to work hard to obtain the desired result. We might still have significant hurdles to overcome to satisfy the organisation's bottom-line issues, but when we can move forward with wisdom and higher intent, we can achieve the extraordinary.

FACING THE FALLOUT

Part of our difficulty in dealing effectively with the sugges-tion of retrenchment lies in our focus. So preoccupied have we become with material goals and resources, we have lost sight of the importance of our *human* resource, and of how devastated our department or organisation is when we shed staff. Not only do these kinds of decisions destroy the lives and families of those whose jobs have gone, they can be equally detrimental to remain-ing staff and customers. Every time someone is retrenched, the workplace changes. Not only does productivity fall, so too does personal motivation. At the same time, whatever loyalty and respect staff held for the organisation and its leaders is eroded, as they worry that they might be next. Frequently there is also a keen sense of guilt felt by the staff who remain.

So out of touch are many managers, that they fail to notice the change in attitudes taking place after a round of retrenchments. Rarely do they see that beneath the veneer of politeness, staff are appalled by the inhumanity of their leader's actions. Such managers also fail to realise that much of the goodwill and pride in achievements has been swept away, and that now their staff are giving only what is required of them. When managers do discern a change in attitude, they tend to regard such responses as subversive, and react accordingly. The more we abandon our humanity, the more we fail to recognise it in others. When we then fail to see that our staff are responding in this way because they have been wounded, instead of assisting them to progress beyond this wounding, we perpetuate the pain by punishing them.

SEEING CLEARLY

In recent years we have not only formalised inhumane behaviour, we have made it acceptable, and so increasingly companies are not even providing counselling or other support services for those asked to leave. To be sorrowful or disappointed by the loss of workmates is regarded as weakness, and so not only do we submerge our humanity, we attempt to stifle it in others. The tragedy of this approach is that it is our humanity that enables us to be great. It gives us the courage and the vision to look beyond ourselves, to help make the world a better place. When organisations focus on material goals at the expense of their ethics and humanity, theirs becomes a life-denying culture. When recalling to me their experience of retrenchment, people spoke repeatedly of the desperate ways individuals were often dealt with.

This was certainly the case for Kerryn, who worked in local government. 'It was hard having to watch people who had worked hard and been loyal being kicked out,' she confessed. 'One day they were at work, and the next they'd disappeared. Some were close to retirement, others were parents with families and mortgages. Their only crime was to be on the wrong side of the head count. It was so degrading.' Often the fallout from these kinds of decisions becomes the catalyst for the best people to move on. Their move then stimulates those of like mind to consider leaving, and a year or two down the track many of our most valuable staff have taken their knowledge and skills elsewhere. The loss of this level of expertise and commitment can take years to recoup, placing even more strain on those who remain.

INTENT IS ALL

There are times when, having exhausted all possibilities, we have no option but to retrench. How we proceed then is critical. Whatever intent we apply to our actions will become the energy embedded within the workplace culture as the company attempts to move forward. If we are operating from fear, then that will be our overriding experience within the company. This self-defeating energy will continue to permeate our actions and thinking, causing our future endeavours to be imbued with fear and fraught with further difficulties. The philosopher George Santayana warned that those who fail to learn the lessons of history are destined to repeat them. The slash and burn approach to our bottom-line issues is the same one we have taken to so many of the problems facing humankind over the centuries, but it has never created lasting success. Surely there is a message for us here.

If we believe in the dignity of life, then whenever the question of retrenchment arises, we are challenged to summon the courage and imagination to see how else we might come up with the resources needed to satisfy the demands of the bottom line. As we allow our inner wisdom to come to the fore, lateral solutions will often become apparent.

This was Larissa's experience when asked to get rid of one of her key performers because he had become too expensive. 'I didn't want Simon to leave, because he was my most experienced member of staff – his output was high and his work was excellent. He was also a great mentor for junior members of staff. The most infuriating aspect of this directive was that it came from someone in head office who didn't even know Simon, or the fact that he was already doing two jobs.' Even though Larissa knew the decision was wrong, she also knew that the odds were stacked against her.

'Part of me felt I was crazy to even try to save Simon's job,' she confessed, 'but I just knew I had to fight for him. When I spoke with my boss, I emphasised Simon's talents and made it very clear that losing him was a last resort. While my boss wasn't delighted with the news, he didn't dismiss my take on the situation either. We agreed to meet the following day. That night I went home and prayed we might find the best solution possible. When I got in the next day my boss asked if Simon would be willing to take a small cut in his package. When I put this to Simon he agreed, in exchange for other concessions. The situation ended up working well for everyone. Simon gained continuity of employment and we benefited from his ongoing experience and loyalty.'

MIRACLES CAN HAPPEN
When faced with these kinds of dilemmas it is essential we give ourselves the space to access our inner wisdom, so we can find a solution that will work for *everyone*. Each and every one of us has the capacity to find the best solution; it is only our anxieties and preconceptions that prevent us from accessing it. We still need to be across the issues, but when we can be less anxious and controlling, it's a whole lot easier to arrive at the best solution. By setting our intent then letting go, we help to take the pain and confusion out of the situation, so we can draw the requisite details and resources to us. The more relaxed and clear we are about the solution we want, the less fearful will be those we are dealing with. As their fear subsides, they will become more willing to be part of the solution. When we dare

to tackle such situations differently, often we are amazed at what can happen.

One friend who worked for an oil company learned that he was going to have to cut his team by one. Gerry knew which team member would have to go. 'It was still against everything I stood for,' he confessed. 'I felt desperate, and so I meditated on this whole issue. Days passed and nothing happened. Then we had staff appraisals, and the staff member who was the likely target for redundancy admitted it was time to move on. His response was totally unprompted. I can't tell you the relief I felt at not having to get rid of someone who'd worked hard for the company for a number of years.'

Margot found herself in a similar situation when working in retail. She too was asked to retrench a member of staff. 'My heart was so heavy I felt like it would burst,' she admitted. 'I prayed for Abigail, because I respected her and would never knowingly do anything to harm her. Before I had the chance to speak to her, she told me she was pregnant and, as she and her husband wanted to enjoy her pregnancy, she was resigning.'

When we have the courage to *want* to do what is right, then we help activate a divine energy that sets in place the best outcome for all concerned. Although we might not consciously be aware of these principles, we might already be working with them by following our instincts to do what we feel is right.

This was Damien's experience when fighting to save one of his team from retrenchment. 'There was nothing wrong with Bill's work or his presentation,' he recalls. 'His clients loved him and he got the results – that was enough for me. I fought for his job, and while I had a lot of resistance, I won in the end. I never regretted my decision.' However when Damien resigned a couple of years later, he was concerned that Bill's job was likely to go. To his surprise, Bill marched into his office the same day. 'I'm going too,' he declared. 'I've finally got enough money for a house out of town and I have a job to go to as well.' Damien couldn't believe what he was hearing. 'I was so relieved I'd had the guts to do the right thing by Bill,' he confessed. 'It was weird that my timing worked for him as well.'

ASKING OTHERS TO DO MORE

When a retrenchment is under way, it is easy to forget how tough this situation can be on those who remain.

Rob, who worked for a leading packager, spoke about the almost impossible workload he faced after yet another round of retrenchments. 'It wasn't just the amount of work they wanted out of us, it was the constant damage-control we had to face with customers and competitors. We were expected to be loyal and hardworking and to act as if nothing had happened, yet we were also under constant pressure to produce more. We felt like we were being stretched to the limit, with little or no appreciation of what we were going through. It was an absolute nightmare.'

Before we ask those who remain to work harder, we need to examine our motivations. Is our willingness to put more pressure on others a desire to go with the status quo – to win at all costs? Or are we prepared to say no if the situation has the potential to be abusive? If times are genuinely tough and we do need everyone to put in more effort, are we prepared to work with our staff to assist them through this difficult time? Again, our responsibility is not just to manage the situation, but to do what is decent by rolling up our sleeves and giving those around us a hand.

BREAKING THE NEWS

Even when we fail to save jobs, it is vital we hold onto the belief that out of all this pain good will prevail, then work to bring this about. It is equally important to take full responsibility for what is happening. If we are party to the retrenchment, then we must be honest. As we get ready to talk to those about to lose their jobs, we can prepare the venue concerned by filling it with Light and asking that everyone involved be surrounded by healing Light. We can also ask that the appropriate words and actions be made apparent to us. This preparation can be very healing when our motives are pure. Directly before the meeting, it is important to take a moment to centre ourselves by breathing deeply and then asking that we be surrounded and suffused with the Light of goodness and decency. Again, our aim is to reach a situation that is for the highest good of everyone concerned. We might even like to say a short prayer.

❦

'O Great Spirit, help me to say and do what is best, so that the outcome will be for the greatest good. Out of sorrow may there be joy, out of fear may there be renewed hopefulness, and out of despair may a new and wonderful vision for the future emerge.'

❦

Once the meeting gets under way, it is essential to allow our inner wisdom to guide us. We cannot anticipate how others will respond, because everyone has different ways of dealing with pain. Sometimes there will be an immediate emotional outburst, sometimes it will occur later, sometimes not at all. It is vital we remain harmless and respectful, no matter how volatile the situation gets. This means allowing the retrenched person to articulate their anger, fear and despair. We also need to maintain our sacred space during such encounters. If we don't, the shock around the situation can cause us to be drawn into the extreme emotions of those around us, allowing the impossibly fine threads of our Light body to be ripped and torn, and making it much harder for us to maintain our equilibrium, let alone find the best way forward. When the meeting is over, we can further assist those asked to leave, by asking that the healing Light remain with them, protecting and guiding them at this difficult time. Where we go to from here is of equal importance. Marching people out of the office at the end of the day is an extremely destructive approach, unless there are genuine concerns about security, and cannot fail to bring out further negative behaviours and responses.

At the end of such days, it is a good idea to go for a walk. Once we're home, it also helps to fill our homes consciously with Light by meditating and lighting candles, and by playing uplifting music. Bathing is helpful around times of extreme stress; as we bathe, we should visualise any residual negative energies being washed away. While we might be tempted to turn to alcohol, it is not a good time to drink, because it will only magnify our emotions and dull our responses. The path of spirit is always about clarity. In such times we need to see the way forward clearly and release ourselves from unhelpful thoughts and feelings. Before we sleep, it helps to contemplate the day, asking that what has taken place be transformed with healing Light, and that all concerned be released to their highest good.

HELPING THOSE LEAVING TO MOVE ON

The process of leaving is often easiest when people are allowed to continue to work for a while, because it gives staff a chance for closure and enables the person concerned to make the transition more easily. If our culture is one of fear, this might be difficult to pull off. We might still be able to achieve this if we are prepared to take personal responsibility for the person who is leaving while they remain with the organisation. Naturally, if the person would prefer to leave immediately or within a few days, we should try to accommodate this. All these ways forward are about upholding a person's dignity with our trust. As organisations are living entities, they too create their own karma. The way we dispose of staff impacts on the remaining staff and the work culture, and on the opportunities or challenges we as an individual and as an organisation will draw to us in the future. When we choose the path of respect and goodness, these positive outcomes will return to us.

GENERATING THE ASSISTANCE NEEDED

Those leaving have the right to respect and genuine support, and so rather than isolating them, we would do well to encourage our team to assist them. This then helps our team to cope positively with the changes, and might mean anything from organising informal social activities to helping those leaving to pack, or to prepare their résumé and portfolio. The offer of professional counselling or assistance with career options is also important. We can also help by ensuring that those leaving are given the chance to finish their projects and undertake a formal handover. When people lose jobs they care about, they are often as distressed about the possibility of their work and customers being neglected as they are about themselves. When we involve them in this process, they can gain positive closure.

We can also assist remaining staff to move beyond their fears and sense of loss by ensuring that those leaving get a genuine and heartfelt send-off, and that their final day unfolds in a supportive atmosphere. One company I worked with would give the departing person a scrapbook filled with handwritten comments and illustrated with photos and graphics out of magazines or from greeting cards. These kinds of gestures bring human warmth to an otherwise desperate situation. It is also a courteous and loving touch to nominate someone to accompany the person who is leaving back to their home. These gestures honour the person concerned and send them off on the next chapter of their life with more positive memories and goodwill. When we make such gestures, we bless our collective futures, enabling everyone to feel more satisfied. We also help get the process of healing under way.

SUPPORTING THOSE WHO HAVE LOST THEIR JOBS

Retrenchment creates a form of bereavement that often touches a large number of people, because at the stroke of a pen it changes the chemistry of our workplace forever. Those who remain often feel a mixture of anger and despair, and in a genuine attempt not to make things worse for those leaving, they avoid them altogether. This then leaves the person who has been retrenched feeling even more isolated and ashamed, because they interpret this silence as disdain or disinterest.

We don't have to be counsellors to assist those leaving; we simply have to allow our compassion and inner wisdom to come to the fore. When we do so, it will become clear how we might help. If we are concerned the person might not want to see us at present, then we can drop them a note to thank them for all they have done, sending them our best wishes. If we do meet we can offer them genuine love and backup. While those who have lost their jobs unexpectedly will often want to cover old ground, we assist them to move forward when we are able to acknowledge their pain, then mirror back to them their many wonderful talents and achievements and recall wonderful times we have shared. This helps them to reconnect with their inner Light and to regain their personal vision.

In such tender situations it is critical we observe right speech. Before we meet with the person who has lost their job, it helps to ask that we be given the words and gestures that will be most healing. It pays also to give some thought as to the location of the meeting – an uplifting location such as a park is often best, because then we are able to share the healing power of nature as we spend time together. Often we may have information about our organisation, or certain individuals within that organisation, that might inflame the issue. There is little to be gained by mentioning such things. It is far better to assist the person concerned by thinking, speaking and acting in a way that warms and nurtures their spirit. When we can create this kind of space for those needing our support, we illuminate their lives, literally and figuratively.

We need also to remember that healing is an intangible process. Even when we might feel like we aren't making an impact, our goodness *will* touch them physically, mentally or spiritually. When we can marry this goodness with the practical assistance of sharing a meal, or sending heart-warming notes, or helping them with their résumé, we become a conduit for the Light in their lives, allowing life-enhancing principles to penetrate even the darkest situations. To continue to hold a good space for others when the atmosphere is thick with fear can be demanding. When we have the wisdom to realise that out of the most desperate situation great good can come, we can maintain our commitment to supporting the human spirit with relative ease. This is the space that His Holiness the Dalai Lama has been holding for years. Not only was he exiled from his country, but his people have been displaced, tortured and even murdered. Yet still he continues to inspire people the world over with his unwavering goodness and profound insights. He holds this space not just for Tibetans or for Buddhists, but for everyone, including the Chinese, because as desperate as life can be, no-one is beyond the healing powers of the Light.

EVALUATING THE REASONS FOR RETRENCHMENT

When the retrenchment is behind us, it is important to take time to reflect on what in the midst of all the pain and confusion we have learned, so that we can we be clear about what went wrong. When senior managers fail to manage well, or accept jobs for which they lack experience, or operate in a cavalier or ill-informed way, profits fall, jobs go and others suffer. If we have helped create this situation, we need to face up to the pain we have caused and take a good look at how we have been operating, to ensure we never create this kind of fallout again. If we work around people who are prone to hubris or bad decision-making, then we need to be more vigilant about allowing unfortunate decisions to be made. While we can't run other departments, often there are opportunities for us to give advice or voice our concerns before the situation becomes critical.

MAINTAINING OUR WORK ETHIC

In the midst of all this drama we still have to get on with our work. It is critical we continue to work honourably, regardless of the climate. We might also have to deal with a variety of responses, not only from those who are leaving and from staff members, but from our CEO or board members. In these situations, our ability to hold everything together is critical if we are to bring the situation to a positive conclusion. When we can work to enhance the human spirit as well as the bottom line, we begin to realise how liberating it is to leave our fear behind and to work more completely. The solutions are always there for those who dare to look for them.

⸻

A prayer to assist us when facing retrenchment

'O Great Spirit, I'm feeling desperate right now, because I have been asked to retrench some of my staff and I can't see my way forward. I would never knowingly harm another. Help me to find the creativity, courage and clarity to reach a solution that will be the best for everyone involved, so that out of this dark situation great good might come.'

disciplinary actions and dismissal

Exactly at the instant when hope ceases to be reasonable
it begins to be useful.
G.K. CHESTERTON, *HERETICS*

TO DISMISS OR NOT TO DISMISS

As managers, sooner or later we are likely to face the unhappy
task of having to let someone go, because of their behaviour or
standards at work. This is not an easy situation to be in, yet still
we must take great care never to let go of someone without due
cause. We need also to be meticulous about our motivations,
because while legislation makes it harder for people to be dismissed unfairly, individuals can still be let go for reasons that are
slender at best. If we feel the point has come where we do need
to dismiss a person, or if we are asked to remove someone, we
must examine *our* thoughts and feelings thoroughly to ensure our
decision is based on pure and reasonable motives. These steps
are necessary, because we are dealing with the life of another
human being and have to take full material and spiritual responsibility for our actions.

TAKING A MORE COMPASSIONATE VIEW

Having to deal with anyone whose performance or behaviour is questionable can be stretching, particularly as so many of us are emotionally exhausted at work. Yet regardless of how much trouble or how many mistakes the person has made, they still deserve our full consideration. It is only when we have the wisdom to sit and consider the circumstance before us that we will be able to decide whether there might be ways other than dismissal to deal with this issue. This means summoning the imagination to move beyond our own opinions and emotions, so that we can understand what is really going on. When we take the time to be more thorough, we are better able to gauge the person's *potential*, as well as their current challenges. Then and only then do we have any real idea of whether dismissal is appropriate. When we go through this exercise, we may discover that this person shouldn't be fired so much as assigned different tasks, or be working in another part of our organisation. If there is an opportunity to bring this about, why would we not help make it happen?

SEEING THE SITUATION AS IT REALLY IS

When we are stressed and exhausted, or under pressure from above to get rid of someone, often dismissal can seem the only way out. But even in situations that are clearly contentious, we are often not aware of the full story.

This was Jordan's experience when working in the head office of a major hotel refurbishment company. One of his team, who was located in another branch, was attracting increasing criticism. 'Brad was a bit of a loner, but he was also good at what he did,' Jordan recalled. 'There was a growing feeling he should be asked to leave, because he'd become uncooperative. The weird thing was that I always found Brad passionate about his work and willing to go the extra mile. As I delved deeper into Brad's work relationships, I discovered that whenever there'd been a problem, everyone would talk *about* him, but they'd never voice their concerns *to* him, and so Brad had become increasingly isolated. No-one had noticed his workload was becoming unbearable, and when he tried to protest no-one listened, so the only way he could vent his frustration was by being difficult.

'As Brad explained his situation to me, I thought I understood what was going on,' Jordan confessed. 'Then he dropped the bombshell. Brad was a Vietnam vet, and although he'd been working in the same branch for years, he'd never felt he could mention this to anyone. The pain this isolation caused him was obvious. There were still disciplinary issues I had to deal with, but our conversation proved a turning point. The senior managers in Brad's branch were shocked to learn of his background, and were willing to be more inclusive.' Brad kept his job and enjoyed a far better relationship with those in his branch. A couple of years later he died of cancer, and everyone supported him during his illness.

How often do we assume we understand far more about a person or situation at work than we actually do? It would have been tragic had Jordan simply accepted the prevailing view about Brad and sacked him – tragic not only from a work perspective, but also from a human one – but that's what we so often do. If we are facing a similar dilemma at work right now, are we sure we are across the *whole* issue, or is it possible there is some vital part of the scenario we have missed? How can we ensure we have the full picture?

ENSURING THERE ARE SUFFICIENT RESOURCES

Sometimes people are made to leave because they were never given the support or structures to do their jobs well. While micro-management isn't helpful, increasingly staff lack the management and on-the-job training to do their jobs well, because their managers are so busy, and because organisations are unwilling to invest in proper staff training. Then when things go wrong, people end up getting dismissed through no fault of their own. When we take time to examine the pattern of dismissals within organisations, we will often see the same managers resorting to dismissal as the *first* course of action rather than the last, because it takes time and effort to turn people around. Rarely are these individuals good people managers, let alone good managers. How can they be when they have so little regard for their staff? Even more rarely do their superiors discuss their shortcomings with them, because they are also busy, and so the cycle of pain continues.

The relationship between a manager and their staff is crucial. Our attitude and work habits will have a *huge* impact on those we work with.

Some time ago, Bridie joined a property management company and was soon regarded as one of their most valuable members of staff. Then when the company was bought out, Bridie got a new boss. In a matter of months, Bridie went from being a highly effective, motivated member of the team to someone who had little or no confidence, because her new boss gave her little time and even less guidance, but was quick to apportion blame. Fortunately Bridie realised what was happening, resigned, and was soon working for another property management company. It was remarkable how quickly she reverted to being a happy, motivated individual. While this story ended well for Bridie, one cannot help but wonder if her former manager is continuing to devastate the lives of those unlucky enough to work with him.

Sadly, this problem is not isolated to a few managers – there are whole organisations around that not only disempower good staff, they make them virtually unemployable. In considering our own way forward, let us examine our management skills. Are we there for our staff, directing and encouraging them, or are we contributing to their downfall by our ineptitude or lack of interest? If we do need to lift our game and be there for our staff, how can we do this quickly and effectively before we destroy all the good that has been achieved?

BEING CLEAR ABOUT OUR STYLE OF MANAGEMENT

Regardless of how capable or experienced our staff are, they still need to know clearly what is required of them, especially as the contemporary workplace continues to change around them. We in turn need to know if what we are asking of them is achievable. We also need to ensure that our staff have the resources and ongoing attention to continue to work effectively and enjoy what they do. There will be times when we can't be available for staff, but in these instances we can delegate to someone within the team who can be relied upon to make the right call. When we give our staff good support, we will know whether a person is genuinely unable to do their job or whether they are hampered by a lack of resources or direction.

It is vital we continue to monitor the resources our staff have to work with, to ensure our team can work well. If more resources are needed, then the onus is on us to find them. This might mean reconfiguring our budget, or lobbying for additional resources. Sometimes managers are reluctant to canvass the need for additional resources, as this isn't always the most popular topic of conversation with those more senior. Certainly we won't get anywhere if those we work with know we are a pushover, but if we are respected and have a reputation for asking only for what is sensible, then we probably have a fighting chance of getting what we need. If resources are genuinely scarce within our organisation, then we might have to revisit our expectations of what each individual can realistically produce, or we might find that by taking a closer look at their job, we can assist them in streamlining their work.

THE GIFT OF LEADERSHIP

While the pressures continue to mount for us as managers, it helps to remind ourselves that we chose this path – not just for our career prospects, but for our soul growth. In giving our staff the support they need, we stretch our capacity for wisdom and compassion. When we can remain supportive and approachable, and are aware of the day-to-day performance of our staff, it is far easier for us to steer them in the right direction. We can also help avoid painful situations by remaining aware of the tasks our staff struggle with and those they are good at. It is much easier to accommodate staff when things are going well, but when we are stretched we are tempted to become more autocratic. Yet whenever we are controlling, we are fearful, and then we create an intimidating climate in which it is hard for staff to work well. When we can remain open-minded and respectful, even on the days we would rather not, we give others a chance by giving them proper guidance. When we can push aside our frustration for those we work with, remarkable things can happen – the person we feel desperate about might, with firm management, turn out to be a star performer.

APPLYING LOVE TO THE PROBLEM

As we wrestle with how best to handle someone who is problematic, it helps to remember that frequently those who are difficult lack confidence, and when they find themselves in an unsupportive work environment their behaviour and perform-ance can deteriorate. When they are given the chance to work with encouragement and clear direction, they are more likely to produce good work. Love is not something we talk about much at work, which is a pity, because love is the antidote to fear and is also a great healer. The path of the spirit is one of love, and is equally applicable to work as to the rest of our lives. We should understand love to mean to a profound regard for each human being. When we can respect others deeply, we begin to see them more completely and recognise their redeeming qualities, even though they might at first glance appear to have none. This depth of regard for others enables us to see extraordinary possibilities in the most difficult situations, inspiring us to deal intelligently and humanely with everyone. This approach demands the high-est standards of us, because it requires us to maintain our respect for others, regardless of the way they are behaving.

One of the most fruitful ways we can express our regard for others at work is by creating a genuinely nurturing space for *all* who work with us, and by being firm and focused, supportive and fair. Still there will be times when disciplinary action or dismissal is called for, but when we are able to maintain our regard for others, we will never deal with anyone carelessly or harmfully. When in spite of ambitions, politics and conflicting emotions, we can see beyond where a person is at to their wider potential and assist them to reach it, we turn disappointment and low self-esteem into confidence and success. As we begin to activate new possibilities in those we work with, together we begin to create a vibrant, life-affirming culture, which not only achieves its material goals, but also honours and nurtures the human spirit.

DEALING WITH REQUESTS FOR DISMISSAL

Even when we are under pressure from superiors to let staff go, we still need all the clarity we can muster to ensure that fearful or mischievous intentions are not in motion. Frequently, such directives are generated by anger, fear or plain dislike.

Adele was working for a large textile corporation when her CEO asked to see her. 'I was told that I had to get rid of a staff member because he'd worn a casual jacket to a high-profile function,' explained Adele. 'I was also told my future prospects with the company would be judged on how I conducted this dismissal.' Understandably, Adele was as much shocked by the reason for the request, as the request itself. 'It was fortunate I was just back from holiday and was relaxed enough to see how ridiculous this was. I was happy to have a serious talk to Stephen about his dress, but I wasn't prepared to sack him. My boss was less than impressed, but as it turned out Stephen kept his job and I was fine. Interestingly, the guest of honour at the function concerned was so impressed by Stephen, he sent him a hamper, so he hadn't been fazed by the jacket!' Adele subsequently learned that her CEO had a reputation for taking a dislike to people, then getting others to move them on. It is easy to be intimidated by dictates from above, but while we might worry about jeopardising our position, we also need to consider the fallout when we fail to do what is right. Daring to live authentically means having the courage to step outside our own comfort zone and say and do what we know to be right. When we compromise ourselves by operating inauthentically, yet another part of our intricate being shuts down, and our capacity to enjoy our work and to draw positive experiences to us is greatly impaired.

NOW IS THE MOMENT

By the time we face the question of dismissal, an individual's actions or behaviour are often already out of control. Not only do we need to get the situation back on track, we need to be clear about how it got to this stage in the first place. Is this individual aware that their actions or behaviour have been unacceptable for some time, or have they been allowed to go their own way? Again, with the increased pressure on managers, we often don't spend sufficient time managing and counselling our staff. Whatever the problems with a person's performance or attitude, they must be canvassed at the time of the incident. If we fail to do this, we can hardly be surprised if the situation deteriorates. We don't help anyone by hoping that unsatisfactory work or behaviour will go away, or by dealing with the difficulty weeks down the track. Again, before any meeting with the person in question, it helps not only to have the salient information to hand, but to take the time to prepare ourselves and the meeting place energetically. As we talk, we must be straightforward, making sure that we confine our remarks to the current situation. Dredging up past misdemeanours is unhelpful and likely to cause resentment. While it is important to communicate clearly, we must also give the person the right of reply.

It helps to begin these kinds of discussions by outlining whatever contributions the person has made to date. When we can do this authentically, we help affirm their sense of self. Then, having laid this positive foundation, we can move on to the areas where there are problems, and assist the person to see how they are jeopardising their achievements by their behaviour or work. Respect is central to the way we handle this meeting. Whatever the topics covered, it is important for the person to know that certain matters need to be addressed, but we in no way seek to harm them.

PROVIDING ONGOING SUPPORT

Once our session is over it is up to us to ensure that the individual concerned is clear about the problems to be addressed and about the way forward. The best thing we can do at the end of the meeting is leave them with a sense of the possibilities ahead, rather than with a whole catalogue of criticisms or with a feeling that they have been set up to fail. Then having given them direction, it is vital we continue to work closely with them to ensure they stay on track. We do this by scheduling regular meetings and by being as accessible as possible – or by nominating someone to help mentor and supervise them if we are not available. When we can hold up a mirror to someone and give them a sense of their potential, this, combined with our support, will do much to nurture their spirit and to help spur them on.

DEALING WISELY WITH DISMISSALS

If, having followed these steps, there is little or insufficient improvement, we may have to proceed with dismissal. Taking the next step, while difficult, is very different from forcing someone to leave without having given them a chance. The steps needed to conduct the dismissal decently are the same as those outlined in the previous chapter on retrenchment. Our attitude throughout this process is crucial. If we can maintain good intent, we ease the departure, not only for the individual who is to leave, but for those who remain. When we can continue to demonstrate our ongoing respect and goodwill towards the person leaving, in spite of the circumstances, we help empower them for their journey ahead.

NO SITUATION IS TOO DIRE

If the dismissal is for a breach of trust or for some other kind of dishonesty, then we have little choice than to dismiss the person immediately. These kinds of situation often require that we follow legal advice and that we sever all contact with the person once they have been dismissed. Even in these circumstances we can still allow our humanity to come to the fore by making a clear distinction between the person and their misdemeanour. While we may never know this person's future direction, we can still hold a good space for them or even pray for them. This is not easy when someone has been destructive, but it is the path that honours the potential of the human spirit. Again the purer our motivation, the better the outcome.

FINDING A PATH THROUGH

Why not take some time out to be alone with your thoughts. Then as you consider how best to proceed, allow your breathing to slow. If you are feeling stressed or emotionally exhausted right now, close your eyes for a moment. As you breathe in, feel yourself being filled with life-giving energies. Then as you breathe out, allow any stress to dissolve. When you feel ready, you might like to consider the following questions.

- How did this situation arise?
- What were the specific circumstances – the people and emotions – involved?
- Was there something more you could have done to diffuse this issue?
- Is the situation retrievable?
- If so, what steps do you need to put in place to fix it?
- What will the person concerned need to do to turn themselves around?
- What is a reasonable time frame for this situation to be remedied?
- What provisos do you want to put in place?

- How best might you communicate these to the person concerned?
- How do you plan to handle ongoing counselling and guidance?
- Who else in the team might help support this person to get back on track?
- If the person has to leave, what is the best way forward?
- Do you need to solicit advice from others before you go ahead?
- When will you do this?
- How can you best manage the person who is leaving?
- What actions might you undertake for those who remain?

surviving the
takeover

A man of great character and strength . . .
knows when to go forward, when to retreat,
nothing can harm such a man.
CHONG TSE

FACING THE CHANGES AHEAD

The challenges we face at work take many forms, but there are few that will test us more than going through a takeover. It doesn't matter which side of the fence we are on; once the take-over is in motion, our lives will invariably be altered in some way. Our workmates if not our workplace will change, as will the ways we are used to getting things done, and whether we like it or not, we will be expected to adjust to these changes. Few of us like change, even though it is the nature of life. Yet the more we are able to move with the changes a takeover brings, the less we will feel as if everything is collapsing around us. Many cultures recognise and celebrate the impermanence of life, which enables them to accept change more easily. We live with the illusion that we are always in control and are shocked when this proves not to be the case. Our lives are full of change, but often we don't notice these changes, because they bring us many good things. It's unwelcome change that terrifies us. Yet even unwelcome change can be of benefit. The very fact we are facing a takeover means that on a soul level we have attracted this situation to us to expand our awareness in some way, and when instead of trying to hold back the tide, we can respond positively to what lies ahead, we conserve our energy for the next stage of our journey.

EMBRACING LIFE'S FLOW

Part of the secret of handling a takeover well is learning to go with the flow. This might seem obvious, but frequently we're not as flexible as we could be, because we have become wedded to our work routine. Most of us love the fact we know what we are doing and where we are heading. The difficulty comes when we cling to these things in the expectation they will keep us safe, because during a takeover it is those aspects of our job that are most likely to change or be dismantled. Even though we might fear we are losing control, sometimes there has to be a complete end to what has been before our lives can be enhanced. If we can find the courage to live with this discomfort and see where it leads us, often a whole new level of understanding and fulfilment can be ours. If we continue to cling to what has been, we will cause ourselves and others great pain. As we prepare ourselves for the takeover, it is important to acknowledge any grief or disappointment we may feel at having to leave our familiar world behind. Even if we are optimistic about the future, the chapter that is closing deserves to be honoured. Why not take a moment now to acknowledge any grief or disappointment at the end of this era? Also remember all the wonderful things – the people and the achievements – your job brought to you; there are so many things to be grateful for. Know that this part of your life is closing because there is something better ahead.

MOVING FORWARD WITH CONFIDENCE

When the takeover gets under way, often different people will be running the company. There will be new systems and decisions to accommodate, and not everything will unfold as we might hope. This doesn't mean that all the changes will be detrimental, but that many will be unfamiliar or might at first seem illogical. This is when our fragile egos can jeopardise the possibilities ahead by encouraging us to be uncooperative or destructive. While these changes might at first glance seem unnerving, it helps to remember that we can't see the full picture and that the takeover isn't just about us. It is a journey we have embarked on with a whole range of people, with their different personalities, their fragilities and egos, their skills and shortcomings, and there is much we can learn from this journey.

Often during times of major change we feel threatened. Everyone withdraws, and so we all end up in a holding pattern. However, when we can continue to work well and interact positively with others, we help find new and positive ways forward. By learning to operate beyond the rumours and raging emotions, we can begin to see the challenges and possibilities ahead, to discern what is of value and what is peripheral to our work, then set our direction accordingly. When we work with this level of insight, we are more able to find the courage to be diligent and professional, regardless of whether the sales figures are in the format we are used to or whether we still have the same work area.

STANDING IN OUR OWN SPACE

Once the takeover begins, new factions often emerge because everyone is so scared. Yet if we have a clear sense of who we are and what brings us joy, we don't need to join a faction. Instead, we can focus on finding new ways to work with *everyone* in our new team and treat them with respect. When we make the effort to be consistent and fair, even when others are not, those we work with will have nothing to fear from us. There is no better space to occupy during a takeover, because when we remove fear from the equation, those we work with will begin to take us into their confidence and to solicit our ideas and opinions, enabling us to give our best and to feel our effort is worthwhile. This enables us to enjoy more freedom at work, because we are able to move forward with less baggage. We are then more able to speak up about difficult issues and be taken seriously.

FACING THE CHANGES AHEAD

This approach is not about denying what is happening, but about applying our insight and wisdom to the situation, so we can move forward with strength. The path ahead may have difficult moments, but the very fact we can recognise this helps lessen the impact of such challenges. And as life is ever-changing, we can take comfort from the fact that even the most trying episodes will pass. We are then free to consider how best to proceed. We can rely on our own efforts to see us through, or we can open ourselves up to the wisdom and resources of the universe. Most of us would prefer to see what lies ahead before we commit ourselves, but life is about *conscious* choice. What then are we going to choose? If we join forces with the universe, our difficulties won't disappear, but we will be shown the most direct route forward.

Basically, the takeover is just another backdrop for our soul's growth. How our lives will unfold during the takeover will be different for each of us. Some of us will stay, while others might move on. The more fluid our outlook, the more life is able to direct us and ensure we are in the right place at the right time. Then even when there is a great deal of fear and uncertainty, we won't get caught up in this fear, because we know events are unfolding as they should. We might find it difficult at first to locate this underlying sense of rightness in all that is happening during the takeover, but the more we trust life, the more we are able to move beyond being a victim, and see the good in each moment. This does not mean that everything that happens will be ethical or humane, but that in spite of the dark moments, we will have a sense of who we are and who we might yet be. The perfect affirmation at this time is 'Whatever I need will come to me'. This is a powerful statement because it acknowledges our belief that in spite of the takeover, the universe is a safe and supportive place. Because we ask for *everything* we need to come to us, we open ourselves up to the *whole* spectrum of possibilities inherent in this new situation rather than just some of them.

TAKING THE WIDER VIEW

It is easy to be overwhelmed by the immense detail of a takeover, yet when we can take a more expansive approach, we are more able to deal with all the work that needs to be done. When we believe that *all* we need will come to us, instead of worrying about how everything is going to work out, we can focus on whatever is directly before us and can complete it, then move on to the next task and the next. When we can keep our eye on the ball, when we can be consistent and patient and put one step carefully in front of the next, we are far more likely to reach our desired goal.

There will still be times when we will feel nervous or alone, when we have to walk through the darkness, or when we have to remain patiently where we are. Such times can take us to the limit, but only when we fight the process. When we can be guided by our innate wisdom, we are able to respond intelligently and harmlessly to whatever is before us, surprising ourselves and others with our courage and creativity. The line, 'Thou preparest a table before me in the presence of mine enemies' from Psalm 23 helps remind us that no matter how desperate the moment, life will furnish *all* we need, as long as we are open to this possibility. When we dare to step outside our comfort zone and work towards the best outcome for all, we discover the hero within. Now more than ever we need all the corporate heroes and heroines we can get. We each have the capacity to achieve wonderful outcomes at work – perhaps this takeover is the perfect time for us to awaken these possibilities.

SUSTAINING OURSELVES THROUGH THE INEVITABLE UPS AND DOWNS
Having set our course, how do we then put the right building blocks in place to ensure we can work effectively through the takeover without wearing ourselves out? Simply hoping things will turn out well, or praying that someone will rescue us isn't enough. Life requires that we help create the future we long for. As well as drawing on our job skills, it is essential to meditate and make time each day for a little silence and space. This helps us access the solace and insight we need to observe events as they unfold with more clarity. We should still work hard and plan ahead, but this wider perspective will enable us to draw to us whatever resources we need. When we can work with this level of ease, we are able to locate all that is good and positive in the moment and discard the rest.

CHERISHING THE MOMENT
Even in the middle of a takeover, *this* moment is all we have. When we can learn to cherish this moment, we cannot help but

be good at what we do. When we pay attention to the moment, we are also able to recognise the signposts that are there for us, and thus accomplish our goals more readily. These signposts might come in the form of a slogan on a billboard, an article in a discarded magazine, or a chance remark made by a work-mate. One friend was in a client's office when a motivational book literally fell off the bookshelf and hit her on the head. The book's title was enough to get her moving in the right direction. Another journalist friend changed course after an interview with someone whose take on life touched her profoundly. When we dare to work more insightfully, we create the circumstances we need not only to thrive, but to take us to the next level. We then realise that regardless of what is happening at work, or of what the powers that be have in mind, we will remain at our current workplace until it is time for *us* to move on. When we work with the universe, we are no longer in such a hurry, because we realise the importance of being in the right place at exactly the right time.

Once Roberto's magazine house was taken over, he decided to resign, but the day he went to resign, he discovered his CEO had been called overseas for a few days. Roberto felt angry and frustrated by this, but as it turned out, the intervening week gave him the chance to reassess his decision. During this time, he picked up a card that said, 'I will remain where I am until the good of this experience is revealed to me.' Even though this wasn't what Roberto wanted to hear, the message made him realise that in spite of the way things looked, he was meant to remain where he was. 'Looking back, I guess I panicked because things were so grim,' he confessed. 'I'm just grateful I got the chance to reconsider, because the moment I decided to stay, everything began to improve.' Roberto went on to have several rewarding years with his company that he would otherwise have missed out on.

Even if your work might seem a little grim right now, are there signposts you have been ignoring? Do you have the courage to listen to what they are telling you and to act on their guidance? Or do you prefer to go your own way?

THE POWER OF INTENTION

We each have the capacity to embrace the moment and live and work fully, even when everything around us is in chaos. We achieve this best when we can work with clear intent. As we have already discussed, we establish our intent when we can define the qualities *we* would like in our day and then invite them to be present in our lives. During a takeover, we might like to concentrate on inviting such qualities as peace and respect, safety, joy, new possibilities, harmony and clarity to be present for us at work. Again, as we invite these qualities into our lives, it is important to note the *feel* of each energy, because the more we are able to experience these life-enhancing energies, the more they become part of us.

We can enhance this process by contemplating what a *peaceful* day at work might look and feel like, as we visualise ourselves working in the midst of the takeover without conflict. Then as we visualise ourselves being *respected* at work, we might like to experience how satisfying it would be if we could not only receive acknowledgement, but treat others well in return. Similarly, when we think about *safety*, we might imagine ourselves working productively and expressing our ideas and concerns without any fear of reprisal, which in turn enhances our commitment and enjoyment of work. When we can visualise how each quality might be applied to our working day, we are more able to bring our dreams to fruition.

OVERCOMING OUR SENSE OF HELPLESSNESS
TO WORK WELL WITH *EVERYONE*

Often we assume that our experience of a takeover is bound to be unpleasant, and so we deny ourselves the joy of becoming part of a new community. There will be times when we desperately want things to be different from the way they are – when our working days will seem like a life sentence – yet when we can step outside *our* concerns and think about those around us for a moment, we will gain more perspective and feel better as a result. We might then be inspired to do more for those around us – to pass on an uplifting book or quote, share a pizza, organise tickets to the movies or a night out ten-pin bowling, or bring flowers to work to brighten our shared space. There are literally thousands of ways we can lift the darkness of a difficult moment.

Although Kylie had a relatively junior job in a printing company, when her takeover was under way she felt compelled to do something. 'I wanted to make things better, so I bought doughnuts for everyone and wrote emails to anyone who was having a hard time. I was amazed at how many people appreciated this. A couple even cried, they were so touched.'

These kinds of gestures *matter*, because they warm our lives, transforming our fear and uncertainty into optimism. They also give us a chance to raise our heads for a moment and reflect on all that is positive about where we work.

Susan wanted to create a sense of belonging for her newly blended team, so she acquired a round table for their new work space. 'I had a hunch it might work,' she explained. Over the following months, the table proved invaluable in bringing the team together. 'There have been lots of changes to the space since then, but the table's still there. The team was given the option of more space for themselves or keeping the table; they voted to keep the table, because they love getting together.'

Often it is the *subtleties* that transform the moment. How then might we reach out to those we work with? What tiny gesture can we make that might just help everyone to move beyond the pain and uncertainty?

TAKING STOCK

When the takeover is finally behind us, it is important to take time to contemplate what it has brought to our lives. There will be things we would rather have done differently, but when instead of getting lost in regret we can learn from our mistakes, we can be more effective in the future. There will probably also be the gifts of new friendships and community and of additional experience; as we savour these things, we realise how much richer our understanding of ourselves and our working life now is. If we are fortunate, we will also have discovered new depths to our courage and compassion and will have experienced how they have helped us travel still further in our work. If a takeover lies ahead of us, it is important never to lose sight of our choices and our ability to shape our own future. We can allow ourselves to be damaged or broken by the changes ahead, or we can consciously immerse ourselves in the experience, seeking all that is good there. Then when we emerge, we cannot help but be wiser, stronger, and more able to appreciate the moment and to live and work more productively and meaningfully.

❦

A prayer to illuminate the way ahead
'O Great Spirit, I'm feeling scared because everything that is familiar to me is being dismantled. While I want to step

confidently into the future, part of me wants to cling to what has been. Help me to begin each working day with all the enthusiasm and open-mindedness I had when first I started work. Help me also to see the good in each moment – and in the new people and systems I'm working with – so that I may become stronger and wiser. And in those moments when I feel like I'm sinking, help me to remember I'm not alone. Help me to continue to reach out to others, enabling us to create a better future for us all.'

losing our job

We must be willing to get rid of the life we've planned,
so as to have the life that is waiting for us.
JOSEPH CAMPBELL

FACING THE FACTS

There are many beginnings and endings in life, but few as painful as losing our job. When we lose our job, we don't just lose our position, we lose our income, status and sense of self. And yet, even when devastated by the trauma of the loss of work, most of us would willingly turn back the clock rather than embrace a new opportunity. The painful fact is, however, once we've lost our job there can be no turning back. Often it is the finality of this situation that daunts us most, because our work isn't just our livelihood, it's an important part of our sense of community. Overnight, we lose contact with those whose talents and foibles have made our lives interesting. And while the world continues on around us, we are left with whole days to fill, as we try to deal with our hurt and outrage. Often we want to lash out – to have someone to blame, or we feel such a sense of shame that we seek to punish ourselves.

264

WHY DID THIS HAVE TO HAPPEN TO US?

At the centre of our unhappiness is the question of why *we* had to lose our job. We can spend days, weeks or even months torturing ourselves with the many answers to this question. Perhaps the practical or political explanation of our situation is already apparent to us, but regardless of our personal circumstances, the real reason we are no longer in our former position is that our job no longer serves who we *are*. This might seem an extraordinary statement, but this is the truth of our situation. If we can summon up the courage to explore this more completely, then instead of feeling diminished by recent events, we can instead begin to focus on all that awaits us. This is not so much about putting on a brave face or being optimistic, as it is about moving beyond the stress and grief so we can begin to see ourselves in a new light. We are an extraordinary combination of mind, body and spirit tasting the richness of the human experience. While life might be painful right now, our divine self remains untouched by our current circumstances, because no matter what others have said or done, we are *still* incredible beings. Even in this moment, life hasn't abandoned us or let us down – rather, it is stretching our vision and imagination, so that we can discover who we might yet be.

REGAINING OUR MOMENTUM

While this sounds encouraging, most of us still need to get ourselves together and find another job. To achieve this, we need to summon the courage to leave the past and all we had hoped for behind, so that we can concentrate on this moment and all that it offers. Let us take a moment now to become aware of how we are feeling and note any parts of our bodies that feel tense. As we begin to breathe into these areas, we allow them to relax.

Then as our breathing deepens, we can visualise ourselves lying on beautiful golden sand in the comforting warmth of the sun. The gentle radiance of the sun fills every part of us with its soft golden light. As we lose ourselves in the gentleness of this highly charged energy, we can ask to see our life more completely. Then as we examine the landscape of our life, we begin to realise how much we have given away to our work, depleting ourselves over and over. In this moment of insight, we ask that all we have given to our work may come back to us. We can visualise our life energy in the form of ribbons of Light. Dozens upon dozens of filaments of Light stream back to us, until we are swathed in a massive cocoon of Light. As we explore our new lightness of being, we realise how much better we feel, and are inspired then to give thanks for our life and all it enables us to do. Let us make a pact with ourselves in this golden moment to take better care of our life's energy in future. As we contemplate how we might do this, we feel a sense of excitement at the possibilities ahead.

WAKING UP TO THE MOMENT

When we are seeking to reclaim our energy, focus and zest for living, a good start is to look at our current routine more closely. As we continue to walk the dog, drop the kids at school and get the groceries, we begin to realise that all these seemingly mundane activities are precious beyond belief, because they help us *engage* with life, embrace our humanity, and live more fully in the present moment. These and many other of our little daily tasks are the bedrock of our existence; if we allow them, they will give our days shape and meaning, provide us with moments of contemplation and help us to belong. As we ground ourselves in these everyday moments, we see that here and now we have the opportunity to *recreate* ourselves. In this moment, we have been given the chance to step off the treadmill and redress the imbalance in our lives. We do this by immersing ourselves in the *simplicity* of daily life and allowing it to feed and nurture us.

COMING ALIVE

When nothing seems ordinary any more, we can begin to explore further possibilities that are available to us right now. Let us set aside an hour to go somewhere we haven't been in a long time – to enjoy a cup of coffee or a bowl of soup at the corner café – purely for our *enjoyment*. Why? Because we *deserve* it. It is important to do something *today*, so that we can start to live more *intimately* within our being, so that those parts of us that are broken can begin to heal. By immersing ourselves in those things that delight us, we allow ourselves to come to life again. What would we like to do today to lift our spirit and make our soul sing? Let us write them down – all of them – because each and every possibility is a potential moment of happiness awaiting us. Whatever we choose need only be limited by our *imagination*. The important thing is to dare to do the things we love *willingly* and *unselfconsciously*, so that we can bring to life those parts of us that have been overtaken by hurt or fear.

One of the best ways to get inspired is to take the time to walk each day. When we walk, our sense of isolation dissolves; as we take in the air, the people and the places around us, we begin to re-establish our connectedness with the earth and all living things. For far too long our lives have been little more than a blur, but *now* we are being given the opportunity to discover what lies *beyond* the freneticism. The more we open ourselves up to the world around us, the more we are likely to feel as if we are experiencing our surroundings for the very first time. When we are alive to the moment, each day is not just another day, but a *unique* day in this extraordinary adventure we call life. Some time ago, a friend who was between jobs was on a bus when she caught sight of the sky. 'I know it sounds mad,' she confessed, 'but the sky was so beautiful, it blew my mind. I couldn't take my eyes off it – I guess that's because I hadn't noticed the sky for years.' When we immerse ourselves in the detail of daily life, we discover that every nuance has something for us. It is in such details that the inspiration was found for many great works of art and thought. It is in the gift of such moments that we find the momentum to live more completely.

When we make the space for such experiences, we start to remember all the things that make us laugh and that intrigue us, prompting us to take more interest in the *substance* of our lives. Then as we wake up, we begin to rediscover those we know and love, to appreciate the many aspects that make them special – their idiosyncrasies, fragilities, and talents. As we savour those we love, we are reminded of all they bring to our lives, and we realise that we are already blessed. This is a far better space to occupy when seeking another job than that of a person who is lost and angry.

GETTING THE HELP WE NEED

We might still need help to put the past behind us. No matter how brave or clever we might be, most of us cannot deal with losing our job without assistance, and so a valuable part of our time out of work may be spent in actively healing the past. It is important to deal with the many emotions around our job loss – if we don't, we're likely to sabotage ourselves.

Douglas was CEO of a major building company, which had just emerged from a recession when the board decided they needed someone else at the helm. 'For months I was so angry that they could do this, that I couldn't get what had happened out of my mind – it affected my whole life,' Douglas confessed. 'The interviews I went for were disastrous, and most friends stopped calling. It wasn't until my wife said she couldn't take it any more that I realised I had to get over it. That's when I got help to deal with my anger. I can't describe the relief I felt when I was able to move beyond all the bitterness.'

Seeking assistance might mean talking with friends or professionals, or booking a session with a shiatsu or acupuncture practitioner, to help to get rid of our stress and clear our heads. Kinesiology is also very good, because it surpasses the mental chatter, allowing our bodies to tell us what is most needed to heal ourselves. It has enabled me to make some major breakthroughs at critical points in my own working life. Even when we take advice and comfort from others, we must always be sure that what is suggested feels right for *us*, because our inner wisdom knows best. The following prayer might also be helpful.

⤖⤖

'O Great Spirit, so much of what I have come to rely on has been taken away from me. Help me to see that this too is part of the greater plan for my life, so I can find the courage and strength to move forward without fear.'

⤖⤖

DEALING WITH THE PAIN

It is not only our anger we have to face at such times. Often there can be a lot of grief around the loss of work. One of the difficulties with grief is that it creeps up on us unawares, and just when we thought we were over it, our hurt returns to overwhelm us. We need not be fearful of or frustrated by our grief – it is simply a build-up of energy that needs release. And even when we feel grief-stricken, it helps to know that it is our little self, or ego, that grieves. Our divine self remains untouched by what has happened, because it operates *beyond* the many limitations we place on ourselves. Once we know this, we can recognise that when we're feeling down, we can help assuage our grief by comforting our little self: 'I know you are worried about what is going to happen, little self. You're probably concerned about the way others see you right now. Even though you're hurt, everything is okay, because you're not alone. I will help you through this time, so that you can discover all the wonderful things that await you.' This process is not about denying our hurt, but about making the distinction between the part of us that is grieving and the divine self, which is beyond pain of any kind. When we can shift our focus and identify with our divine self, we can move forward with far greater insight and confidence.

WHAT HAVE WE GAINED?

As we move beyond the pull of our emotions, we can start to look back at our former workplace to see what it can teach us. What would we do differently at work in the future? Would we avoid confrontations? Would we work smarter, not harder? Would we ensure there was more time for friends or for ourselves? Would we speak out for ourselves and others?

For each of us the lessons will be different, but the insights will be valuable nonetheless. No matter how scorching our story, when we are able to gather up all the experience we have gained from our previous workplace, we help propel ourselves into a new space. Then we can discern the many blessings that were there for us, such as the skills we gained and the people who supported us regardless of internal politics or our results, who made us laugh, who gave us their confidences and their friendship. We might like to send them a note, or to thank them in person, knowing that by allowing the good we have gained to flow on, we will open the way for more good to enter our lives.

WHAT TO DO WHEN THE NEXT JOB ISN'T HAPPENING

However much work we do on ourselves, it won't ensure that we'll have a job today or next week, because so much of life is about timing. The job that awaits us might not be available yet – so what can we do? If we need to keep busy, then we might wish to volunteer our services. If we need an income, then we might want to consider a part-time job or some contract work. Not only does this work give us some cash, but our future job might well emerge from it.

When the clothing company Daniel was working for went to the wall, his family was still young. 'There was no chance for me to have time out. I needed another job as soon as possible, so I called up the agency who'd supplied most of our staff. They had a two-month assignment with a company I knew. It wasn't a company I would normally have considered, but the job seemed interesting enough. Once I was there they offered me a full-time position, and because I was enjoying myself I took it, and I'm still there.'

If we are able to take a break, then we can use this time to reassess.

When Katarina lost her marketing job, she went for a number of interviews, but without success, so she took a break. It was only then that she realised she'd had enough of corporate life, and so she decided to open a bookshop. Several years and a number of awards later, Katarina has a thriving bookstore that has made a major contribution to the cultural life of its neighbourhood, and which provides income for over a dozen staff. 'Had I been offered a job immediately I'd still be doing the same kind of work I'd done for years. While I was good at what I did, I was bored, but was too busy to realise it. By being forced to take a break, I was able to see what else was there for me,' she explained.

When we can find the courage to continue to get out of bed in the morning and dare to dream again, then regardless of what has happened we help draw the next chapter of our working life to us.

AMAZING GRACE

As we seek to move forward, we need to be clear about how we are going to handle our situation with former workmates and with family and friends, because at this time our good work can so easily come unstuck. When we talk to those who are sympathetic, it is tempting slip into the role of victim or to retaliate by being poisonous. We can instead choose the healing path of *grace*. Grace is non-combative and teaches us to move beyond wanting to hurt or blame ourselves and others. It helps us deal with our pain with dignity, so that we can begin to leave our trauma behind. It takes great courage to be gracious in a world that often lacks grace. When with the help of grace we can gather up all our pain and disappointment, our suffering will be replaced over time by a profound sense of peace and purpose. Then instead of filling our spare time with gossip and spite, we are inspired to embrace life's painful episodes and to start to move beyond them, becoming wiser and more discerning.

We personify grace when we don't allow ourselves to be poisoned by negativity, and can maintain a light-filled space even when life looks grim. We then draw people and experiences to us that are of the Light. The great spiritual traditions take us further; they teach us to pray for those who have done us wrong, asking that they too may find enlightenment. This is no easy step when we have lost our job, but it is a profound one. The gift of grace ensures that nothing negative that happens to us can remain with us – with practice we are able simply to observe our hurt and disappointment, then move on.

<hr />

A meditation to assist us in moving forward

Find a relaxing space where you can be quiet. Then as you allow your attention to move within, note the steady flow of your breath. As you follow your breath in and out of your body, be aware of any parts of your body that feel tense. Pay particular attention to the muscles around your mouth and shoulders, stomach and lower back. Allow each of these parts of your body to relax. Then as you reach a new level of calm, it is time to step into the future, and see yourself in thirty years' time.

Take a moment to allow the image of your older, wiser self to take shape. Welcome it – embrace it. What do you notice about your older self? What do you look like? What interests you? What have you learned? How do you feel at this stage of life? Feel how much you are loved and respected, how surprised you are at the laughter you share. Absorb everything you are experiencing.

Now it is time to ask your older self to give you advice about your current situation. Listen carefully to what your older self has to say. In this moment, there is a lightness in your being, as you are able to take a much wider view of what is happening. Allow yourself to absorb all the goodness, warmth and love that is here for you. Willingly receive all this positive energy and wrap it around you.

When your older self has finally told you all it can, take your older self into your arms and embrace it, as you thank it for all it has given you. As you then separate, bless your older self and ask that all it has given you may return to it many times over. Then as you watch your older self depart, ask that its wisdom might remain with you. Allow yourself to stay in this sacred space for as long as you wish. Then when you are ready, bring your attention back into your body and open your eyes.

Why not write down all that you have learned from your older self, so that you can use the many insights you have gained to help you through the days and weeks ahead?

going for the new job

If we feel our passion draws us to a specific career,
it's not the career itself we're drawn to,
but an energy we think we'll tap into through that career.
DERRICK BELL, *ETHICAL AMBITION*

GETTING OUR ACT TOGETHER

When we are clear that it's time to move on, there is much we can do to prepare for our new job. Naturally we must have the qualifications and experience. We also need to have done our research, so that we know as much as possible about the position before we go into the interview. There are many ways we can get information on a company – from checking out their website to requesting background material from their public affairs department. As we study the job specifications, it helps to make succinct notes, including questions we might be asked during the interview. Once we have this information down and have absorbed it, it is a good idea to rehearse our responses to the likely questions. When we do so out loud, it helps us gain confidence and express our answers more clearly. If we can rehearse while standing, then even better, because standing helps raise our energy.

The preparation of our résumé is critical, because often

our résumé is the key factor in being selected for an interview. A well-written two- or three-page document summarising our experience and including a note on our aspirations and wider interests is essential. This is not something to be hurried. When we can work on our résumé over a number of days, we have the chance to refine the language it uses and information it imparts. There are professionals who can help with résumés, and there are many good books on the subject. Of equal importance is the covering letter we send off with our résumé. While this should be succinct, it needs to encapsulate our experience and aspirations, and give a sense of who we are and what we can bring to the position. A well-constructed letter can make or break our chances of getting an interview. We need to have thought about our referees, and to have obtained approval to use their names – not only because it is courteous, but also because it prepares them for any approach they might get from potential employers. Depending on our profession, we might also have a portfolio of our work. This is something that often requires a lot of preparation, to ensure that the work presented is current and well displayed. As our portfolio is precious, it is best saved for the interview.

Often employers will go through a recruitment company, or will ask for résumés to be sent in. If we are in a position to ring our potential employer and register our interest, then it is vital we have our thoughts together, because people don't want their time wasted. It is critical to prepare a brief summary of our experience and interest in the job. Often we are nervous; we will sound more confident if we make the phone call while standing up – not only are we then able to breathe more easily, but we can also project ourselves more positively. Talking a *little* louder than normal is preferable to talking quietly and sounding as if we lack confidence and energy.

While we have every right to be excited by the possibilities of a new job, if we are overly anxious about getting it, we can often appear desperate and discourage our potential employer. We are more likely to succeed when we can set our intention about finding the right job, do our homework, then let go, so that we don't sabotage ourselves. The night before our interview is best spent quietly, so we can gather our energies. Then before we go to sleep, it helps to run through our notes slowly and thoroughly one last time. This done, we can then surround ourselves with white Light, and request that we rehearse our interview while we sleep. This might seem like a recipe for sleeplessness, but not if we have learned to let go. Frequently, we do not remain in our bodies while we sleep, so we can use our sleeping time for rehearsals. This does not mean we don't still have to do our homework, but that we get the chance to be even more polished when the interview comes around.

GETTING THERE

When we get to the day of the interview, even though we might be nervous, it is important to prepare ourselves energetically by meditating and by allowing ourselves some silence and space before we go in. It is normal to be nervous, but it is important to remember that we're simply facing a new situation, not a firing squad. Instead of suppressing our fear, it helps to locate the source of the fear in our bodies – then as we travel to the centre of our fear, we can begin to focus on this energy, and consciously redirect it to help us give a good performance. Again, we can visualise this energy as a stream of Light, or as an arrow, preparing the way for us so we can perform well. Then every time we feel nervous, we can simply repeat this visualisation.

If we are unsure of the location of our interview, it helps to

277

have a dry run of the trip there a couple of days before. Either way, it is important to get to the interview in plenty of time. That will give us a chance not only to calm ourselves, but also to absorb the vibes of the place before the interview commences. If there is an opportunity to use the bathroom, we can use the quiet to draw our energy in around us, asking that we be given the appropriate words for the interview, and that whatever happens be for everyone's highest good. Then as we bathe ourselves in Light, we can also ask that those who are interviewing us and the room in which the interview is to take place be bathed in Light, so that the space is filled with the most conducive energies possible.

From the moment we arrive in the building we must not forget that we are on trial – how we deal with everyone we meet will be noted and reported back to our prospective boss. Not infrequently individuals arriving for an interview are offhand, if not rude, to the receptionist or junior members of staff. News of this behaviour gets back. Nerves are no excuse; there will always be stressful moments at work. Equally, while we might be eager to fit in, it is also important not to tie staff up by chatting, or asking them inappropriate questions. When we go for an interview we are a *guest* and should treat our time with the organisation as a guest would.

THE INTERVIEW BEGINS

When we enter the interview room it is important to acknowledge everyone present and, once the interview is under way, to maintain eye contact with everyone. Often we regard interviews as exams, because they test our experience and good sense, yet we will be far more effective when we can treat the interview as if it were a stimulating and focused conversation. This doesn't mean we have to hold the floor, but that we show we are able to deal easily and enjoyably with those around us. A lack of confidence or overconfidence is equally off-putting. We serve ourselves best when we can be our *professional* selves.

We also forget that those interviewing us are often nervous and stressed. While the interview is no place for jokes, it helps when we can display a sense of humour, because it sets everyone at ease. I was very impressed with one candidate who arrived for his interview soaking wet. The weather had changed suddenly and he had been caught in a downpour. He apologised for being so wet, then continued with the interview as if he were perfectly dry, indicating just how impressive and resilient he was.

In an interview situation, there is a lot to take in, so it is important to remain focused. It is easy to pre-empt or misinterpret questions due to nervousness. The more clarity we can bring to the interview, the more we are able to pick up on the *nuances* of what we are being asked, enabling us to give excellent answers rather than standard responses. If we don't understand a question, then it is important to ask for clarification. Sometimes we are asked about areas that lie outside our experience; the smart thing is to answer truthfully about gaps in our experience, and to come up with possible solutions. Most employers would rather have a person who lacks certain elements needed for the job, but who is clearly intelligent, enthusiastic and willing to make up any gaps in their knowledge, than someone who is qualified but lacks vitality. As the best interviews are like good conversations, we need to come up with our own list of questions and comments. It is even better when we can come with good ideas for the job. One of the most impressive applicants I had was a young woman who came to her interview with over a dozen creative ideas about how she would operate. These weren't just a set of hastily scribbled notes – her ideas were innovative and workable.

FIELDING TRICKY QUESTIONS

When asked about why we are planning to leave our current workplace, it is important we do not denigrate those we currently work with. Any employer worth considering wants someone who will be loyal and discreet, not someone who is going to share their employer's failings with the world. Sometimes potential employers will attempt to use interviews to solicit information about competitors. Whether we are asked a deliberately inappropriate question or not, it is not our place to give away state secrets. Often we can get around such questions by saying something like, 'While it's not appropriate for me to indicate sales figures, that is certainly a major product for us.'

Even though we have prepared well for the interview, it is important not to inundate our interviewer with anything and everything we know and have ever done. As we are having an exchange, it's just as important to *listen* to what people are saying as it is to sell ourselves. Even if we are very good at what we do, it is always better to relate our successes with a touch of humility. No-one wants to employ someone who feels they are doing the company a favour by accepting the job. As the interview progresses, the interviewer is going to be as interested in our personality as they are in our experience, because a new staff member can make or break a good team.

DON'T WASTE TIME

When we are in interview mode, we can forget that interviews are often squeezed in around a normal working day and workload. It is frustrating for the prospective employer to discover someone hasn't done their homework, is only vaguely interested in the job, or doesn't listen to the questions. Sometimes, as the interview progresses, we realise we mightn't have answered an earlier question as fully as we could. It is acceptable to backtrack, as long as we ask if we might do so, then keep our comments brief.

At the end of the interview it is a good idea to sum up our reasons for wanting the job and what we feel we can bring to the position. We can also ask when we might hear whether we have been short-listed, or have the job. This is not the time, however, to embarrass our interviewer by trying to ascertain whether we have the job. It is courteous to thank them for their time, and we might want to follow up our interview with a brief email or fax to reiterate our thanks and interest, but only if this seems appropriate. It is important to remain respectful – no-one likes to be stalked, whether by phone, email or voice mail. If we are fortunate enough to be selected for a second interview, then we must not be overconfident or complacent. Often there is more homework to be done before this interview. It doesn't hurt to take time to consider some of the questions we were asked the first time more thoroughly. On a number of occasions, I have changed my mind on second interview, simply because the preferred applicant lacked the same level of enthusiasm or focus.

EACH INTERVIEW HAS SOMETHING TO TEACH US

Not every interview we go for will eventuate in a new job. After an interview, either party can get cold feet; it is always important to be aware of this possibility. There are many reasons why we can fail to get a job – and it might be more to do with internal dynamics than with our experience. If we don't get the job, we may have the opportunity for valuable feedback; if so, we should make the most of this opportunity. If it feels appropriate, we can ask to stay in *occasional* contact with the employer to see if any further positions come up. Should we be given this opportunity, it is important not to abuse this relationship – contact more than once or twice a year is intrusive.

Instead of being bitter about failing to get a job, it is more beneficial to focus our energies on dissecting the interview, so we can ascertain any gaps in our experience or presentation that need our attention. While it is natural to feel disappointed, we also need to respect the right of an employer to choose the person *they* want for the job. This ability to let go will help bring us closer to the job that is for us. Equally, a round of interviews might make it clear that we want to recommit to our current workplace instead. Even when we have been offered a job, it is important to give ourselves some silence and space, so we can see how we are really feeling about work in the light of this and other interviews. We don't want to jump out of the frying pan into the fire. There may be a great deal we can contribute, but unless we're passionate about the new job then we're unlikely to end up where we're meant to be.

MOVING ON

When we resign, it is important to be as courteous towards the organisation we are leaving as we are to the company we are moving to. Unless there are extenuating circumstances we should serve out our full notice and continue to be focused and productive until the day we leave. We should also ensure there is a proper handover. Even if there are things about our old workplace that annoy or distress us, it is important to be harmless and generous in our remarks about our former employer. And when we hand in our letter of resignation, it is generous to thank the organisation for all we have learned, and to wish everyone well in the future. When we can get through these final weeks with grace, we will put in place the right energies for the future.

◦

A *prayer to help you find the job that is right for you*

'O Great Spirit, I really love the sound of this job, yet even though it sounds right for me in every way, help me to do my best, then let go of the outcome, so that I do find the job that is best for me in every way.'

◦

PUTTING YOUR BEST FOOT FORWARD

As you prepare your application, here are a number of points to consider.

- Does your résumé encapsulate all you have done at work?
- Are its wording and presentation accessible and inviting?
- Are there qualities or achievements within or beyond your work that should also be mentioned?
- Does your covering letter include all the essential points?
- Is the style suitable for your prospective employer?
- What is your prospective employer likely to get excited about in your application?
- What concerns might they have?
- Are there any attachments you could include with your résumé and covering letter that might be of interest?

GETTING READY FOR THE INTERVIEW

Your interview is scheduled. Here are some questions to help you decide whether you are ready for the interview.

- Do you know where the interview is?
- How can you ensure you get there fifteen minutes early?
- Are there any inside tips you have access to?
- What do you plan to wear?
- Is this suitable attire for the interview or the company?
- Have you got at least two copies of your résumé to take with you to the interview?
- Is your portfolio smart, up-to-date and accessible?
- Are you prepared to leave your portfolio with the company if requested?
- If so, for how long?

ASSESSING YOUR PERFORMANCE

Now the interview is over, it is a good idea to think about how you went.

- How did you go with the introductions?
- How did you perform during the questions?
- Did you engage everyone during the interview?
- Was there anything you misunderstood or failed to give yourself full credit for?
- Are there additional areas you need to follow up on?
- What points do you want to get across if you get a second interview?
- Are there aspects of your résumé, portfolio or presentation that need finetuning?

If you have food in the refrigerator, clothes on your back,
a roof overhead and a place to sleep, you are richer than
75 per cent of this world.

If you woke up this morning with more health than illness,
you are more blessed than the million
who will not survive this week.

If you have money in the bank, in your wallet,
and spare change in a dish,
you are among the top 8 per cent of the world's wealthy.

If you can attend a church meeting without fear
of harassment, arrest, torture, or death,
you are more blessed than three billion people in the world.

If you have never experienced the danger of battle,
the loneliness of imprisonment, the agony of torture,
or the pangs of starvation,
you are ahead of 500 million people in the world.

EDEN PROJECT, CORNWALL
www.edenproject.com

making a difference

No person was ever honored for what he received.
Honor has been the reward for what he gave.
Calvin Coolidge

HOW CAN WE MAKE AN IMPACT?

We are becoming increasingly aware of the massive social, economic and environmental challenges facing our planet. Many of these challenges are fuelled by our expanding global economy, which in turn is fuelled by our consumerism. Rainforests are being destroyed, waterways polluted, and millions upon millions of people, including children, are working in sweatshops for subsistence wages – just so that we can have more for less. Futurists are already warning that the West is becoming so saturated with products that our markets cannot keep pace with the race for ever-increasing profits. For this reason, attention is now turning to the Third World to find ways to boost their economies, so we can flood their markets with our goods. Thus the demands on our tiny planet continue to grow.

While most of us want to leave life better than we found it, often these problems loom so large, and our personal resources seem so slender, that we are left wondering how we can make a genuine difference at work. The good news is that many positive steps are already being taken by individuals and organisations around the world to give back – to be more socially responsible, to balance profitability with charitable support, to be more ecologically sound. And while we might not all be able to save a rainforest single-handedly, we too can make an impact. The hardest decision for most of us is not whether we should do something positive, but where to begin, as we are so busy most of the time. It can be hard enough getting through our work, let alone taking on additional activities, yet wherever we place our intent, the energy and imagination and resources will follow. When we are able to hold onto the dream that we can touch the lives of others in some meaningful way, we invite the universe to work with us to expand the possibilities we can bring to our work, and remarkable things can be achieved.

Before many of us can make positive strides at work, we often need to redress the attitudes that hold us back. So obsessed have many of our organisations become by the bottom line, now we have come to believe that we have to struggle hard to meet our material goals at work, that we don't have the resources to do anything more than this. When we think this way, our whole outlook becomes paralysed by fear. We become afraid that by giving to others there mightn't be enough resources in the future – or that we might be taken advantage of. When we find ourselves unable to give, we are basically operating from a space of *profound* lack. As our fear grows, we hold what we have more tightly – cutting corners and shaving costs – forcing fewer staff to work harder with fewer resources, creating cultures that benefit few and disadvantage many. When we work in this way, we starve the individual and collective spirit. We see the consequences of this in the increase in sickness and staff turnover. Then as every aspect of work becomes more difficult, the joy fades and motivation suffers.

We all realise that there are many goals, financial and otherwise, that need to be met at work. Beyond these concerns is the much neglected question of how *best* we can work. We can remain fearful and self-absorbed, or we can start to achieve far more than we had dreamt of by *expanding* the possibilities for our work. When we can genuinely give to others, we honour the universal flow of energy that demands we give as well as receive. When we allow energy to flow freely, abundance will follow. No-one asks that we squander our resources, simply that we use them to enhance our life experience and the experience of those around us. At the heart of genuine abundance is the ability to live beyond fear – to love ourselves and others, to believe the universe is a supportive place, and to encourage an expansive attitude of mind that inspires us to work for the highest good of *all*.

WE DON'T HAVE TO BE A MULTINATIONAL TO MAKE A DIFFERENCE

Even though we might not be aware of it right now, our capacity to benefit others is immense, and as we start to think about how we might make a difference at work, we are reminded that it's not the size of the gesture that matters so much as the willing-ness to reach out beyond our own concerns. Then as we look at our workplace with fresh eyes, we begin to see the opportunities that are there for us.

John is a local bookseller with modest resources. When he opened his store he was determined to give something back to his local community. Each month he donates books to a local refuge for young women recovering from drug addiction. Not only has this small gesture encouraged these young women to read, they have now elected to have a TV-free night once a week, so they can devote this time to reading. Who is to say what impact a handful of books each month will have on these young women? John and his team might never know. The important thing is that they are reaching out to those who rely on their compassion.

The more we are able to share what benefits life brings through work, the more meaningful our lives become.

Caitlin had been working in toiletries for some time when she discovered that many teenagers in care didn't get a Christmas present. She and her workmates were constantly inundated with samples and leftover stock, so Caitlin rallied her colleagues. They undertook to collect all the samples and stock they didn't need and couldn't sell. As Christmas approached, the toiletries were gift-wrapped and sent to a major institution supporting teenagers in care. By the time Christmas came around they had literally hundreds of toiletries for the teenagers, who would otherwise have had nothing.

These gestures are about honouring the resources we have, about feeling blessed by what we have. One of the best ways to feel better about ourselves is to take a look around. We will then see that even if we are on a modest salary we are way ahead of most in the world, who still struggle to have enough food to eat, to have access to clean water and medical assistance, to be educated.

SHARING OUR EXPERTISE

The resources available to us through work are many, and include our *human* resources. One of Australia's largest law firms, Freehills (www.freehills.com), maintains a strong culture of supporting the community by providing specialist resources that might not otherwise be available to disadvantaged groups and individuals. In the early 1990s, a formal program was established to dispense free legal advice to appropriate organisations and individuals. In Sydney alone, the company supports two community legal centres and provides legal advice to a number of community organisations. The Shopfront Youth Legal Centre in the inner city, which is run by the Salvation Army and the Sydney City Mission, enjoys the services a full-time Freehills solicitor, who gives legal assistance to homeless and disadvantaged youths, and a secretary to coordinate the centre's activities.

In London, the Media Trust (www.mediatrust.co.uk) was established a decade ago to match media professionals willing to donate their skills and time with charities needing their expertise. The Trust now has a register of 1500 professionals, many of whom assist several voluntary organisations over the course of the year. Some advice might only last half an hour, while other groups might need the services of a professional for several hours a month over a number of months. A public relations consultant might work with a non-profit organisation to help them put together a media campaign, or someone experienced in film might help produce a promotional video. The Trust also has an extensive educational program at affordable prices on everything from the design of promotional literature to media training and how best to get coverage in national newspapers.

Most of us do want to work for organisations we can be proud of and that we feel are worthwhile. When we set these kinds of positive gestures in place, everyone benefits. There are many ways we can be an influence for the greater good. As we look around our workplace, we might discover ways to encourage our organisation to recycle more paper, to save water or electricity. Perhaps we can take a new look at key retail periods and institute a giving tree for those in need at Christmas, or set up an opportunity for gift-giving to disadvantaged mothers at Mother's Day.

When Max looked at the resources he had access to in his publishing house, he became aware of how many damaged books were destroyed each month. While most of these books had only minor flaws, they had no commercial value. Rather than see these books pulped, he organised regular shipments of them to state prisons.

With very little additional effort, we might be able to use our distribution system to disseminate much-needed health or educational literature, or we might make an experienced member of our finance team available to help a non-profit organisation establish or streamline their financial systems. One leading Australian bank grants its volunteer firefighting staff twenty paid days a year to fight major fires over the summer months. Alternatively, we might be able to use *our* professional experience to benefit others.

Natasha works in outdoor advertising, selling large-format billboards nationwide and organising her clients' campaigns. She has a large and varied client base and loves her job, although the pace can be frantic. Bali has become a favourite holiday destination, yet every time Natasha travelled there she was saddened by the terrible plight of the street dogs. Then when she was in Bali in 1999, while getting help for a dog with a broken paw, she discovered that a local vet, who had been providing some volunteer care to dogs, was in need of medicines. 'Although I feared I might be biting off more than I could chew, I was convinced people would help if I could get the ball rolling. I asked my friend Paula to help me start a charity for these dogs. She agreed.' To set up a charity, strict guidelines must be adhered to; it took Natasha four months to get a licence to fundraise. The charity would be 100 per cent non-profit, with all donations to be spent on medical supplies for the street dogs. In February 2000, the Bali Street Dog Fund (www.balistreetdogs.org.au) was born.

Natasha has continued to work full-time in advertising, and on weeknights and weekends, she and Paula are on the phone and home computers contacting pharmaceutical companies, asking for donations and printing up newsletters. 'After work and during my lunch hours, I would pick up medical supplies, meet new supporters and volunteer vets, and organise deliveries to Bali.' Some might imagine Natasha's work would have suffered, but in her first year of setting up the Bali Street Dog Fund, she won four awards for top sales executive in her company. 'Setting up the charity has provided me with more satisfaction than any other monetary achievement. It has shown me what we are capable of if our belief is strong enough.' The Bali Street Dog Fund has now enjoyed the services of more than thirty Western volunteer vets. The team works the streets six days a week, and just over 8000 street dogs have now been desexed and treated. Natasha used her considerable organisational and marketing skills and her ability to network to make a difference. 'Don't talk about it – do it. If your belief is strong enough, you can make it happen,' she advises.

RE-EXAMINING OUR WORK PRACTICES

If we are in a position to influence decisions within our company, then we can help by looking more closely at *how* we work. While we might feel heroic about having sourced cheaper products overseas, we rarely give any thought as to why this might be. As we increasingly enter into trade relationships with Third World countries, we cannot allow the competitive pricing of manufactured goods at a suitable quality to be the sole criterion for striking up a commercial partnership. Whole areas of the Third

World, and China in particular, are now huge social and environmental disasters from these kinds of partnerships. Already there are cities blanketed by pollution, poisoned waterways, and millions of people working inhuman hours for subsistence wages. If we enter into these agreements without paying attention to the wider issues, then we too are party to these abuses as surely as if we were perpetrating them. Increasingly, consumers and investors are becoming aware of human rights abuses, and have already actively boycotted big-name brands that fail to respect the right of each human to be treated with dignity. By working decently with potential suppliers, we have the opportunity to influence work practices for good.

The Baltimore-based Global Alliance for Workers and Communities (www.theglobalalliance.org) now devotes its efforts to helping improve the lives, workplaces and communities of young adult workers involved in global manufacturing, particularly young women in China, Vietnam, Thailand and Indonesia. In Britain, retailers such as Monsoon and Marks & Spencer have joined the Ethical Trading Initiative (www.eti.org.uk), which has a code of practice that lays down conditions for those employed in factories in Third World countries and in Britain. This code of conduct includes the right to freedom of employment, safe and hygienic working conditions, living wages, reasonable working hours, and regular employment. Child labour is banned. Labour Behind the Label (www.labourbehindthelabel.org) is another British initiative set up to ensure workers are not exploited during the manufacturing process. These kinds of consciousness-raising initiatives within the workplace might not necessarily bring overnight results, but as we become more aware of the possibilities, we too can be part of the process for change.

The Danish company Novo (www.novo.dk) is a world leader

in diabetes care. Novo employs more than 18 000 people in sixty-eight countries and markets its products in 179 countries. It takes its global social responsibility seriously; the company is engaged in a number of activities designed to help bring proper diabetes care to more people, including the World Diabetes Foundation, and will donate more than €65 million over the next ten years to improve diabetes care in developing countries. Novo has also set up an evaluation system for all of its 7000 suppliers that gives equal consideration to their social and environmental performance, and to their pricing and the quality of their goods. This initiative was taken because the company firmly believes there is a direct correlation between financial results and social and environmental performance.

The Vancouver City Savings Credit Union (www.vancity.com), which places around US$69 million of business with 1500 suppliers, has also made the decision to ensure that they all conform to its ethical policy. Through this policy, the credit union actively seeks suppliers that 'practice progressive employee relations, contribute to the wellbeing of their communities, and respect the environment'. The credit union is also the first financial institution in Canada to introduce a low-interest Clean Air Car Loan to help find solutions to climate change. Loans are being offered for the financing of gas–electric hybrid vehicles up to a maximum of CAN$35 000.

Two excellent resources for environmentally and socially responsible business practices are Business for Social Responsibility (www.bsr.org) based in San Francisco, a global organisation devoted to achieving success by respecting ethical values, people, communities and the environment; and the World Business Council for Sustainable Development (www.wbcsd.ch) in Geneva. The latter organisation has developed a Virtual University for

Sustainability to help prepare managers and decision-makers for the challenges ahead.

ENVIRONMENTAL CONCERNS

In our day-to-day activities, how each of us works also impacts on the environment. Often it is only when we take a step back that we realise just how meaningful our choices can be. Certainly this was the case for Interface Inc. (www.interfaceinc.com), the world's largest manufacturer of commercial floor coverings. Interface Inc. is a world leader in the commercial interiors marketplace and a recognised leader in the sustainability movement. The company began its journey to sustainability in 1996 and has since committed itself to 'achieving sustainability in all of its dimensions, and to become restorative through the power of influence'. When founder and chairman Ray Anderson began his journey, he had no idea that his company would achieve such a national presence, let alone a global one.

In 1994, in spite of his company's immense success, Ray began to realise the impact his then US$500-million-a-year carpet company was having on the ecosphere, so he commissioned a report (www.interfacesustainability.com) to get a clearer sense of the full impact of the Interface product – from the resources needed to make it, to what happened to it at the end of its useful life. Ray discovered that to produce US$802 million worth of carpet tiles, Interface had to extract one billion pounds (450 million kilograms) of natural resources, including nearly 900 million pounds (400 million kilograms) of non-renewable petro-based fossil fuels such as oil, coal and natural gas, which, when burned, discharged emissions into the atmosphere.

Alarmed by what he had discovered, Ray committed his company to a 'mid-course correction'. The Interface Model for Sustainable

Development emerged, and Ray charged his employees to 'convert Interface into a restorative enterprise, first to reach sustainability, then to become restorative – putting back more than we ourselves take and doing good to Earth, not just no harm – by helping or influencing others to reach toward sustainability'.

Interface began its journey by focusing on waste elimination, defining waste as anything that does not provide value to the customer. Cumulative savings from 1995 to 2003 totalled over US$221 million. Improved energy efficiency and conservation efforts have reduced the total energy required to manufacture a square yard of carpet by 30 per cent since 1996, and the total energy consumption per linear yard of fabric is down 18 per cent since 1996. Today, more than 8 per cent of Interface's energy is derived from renewable resources, and more than 20 per cent of Interface's products are manufactured from non-petro-based materials. As of 2002, Interface had reduced its total carbon dioxide emissions by 29 per cent, and its waste to landfills by 66 per cent since 1996. Interface has diverted more than three million square yards (2.5 million square metres) of carpet from landfills since 1994.

In 2003, Interface Flooring Systems was the first flooring company to receive third-party certification for an Environmentally Preferable Product (EPP) from Scientific Certification Systems for its carpet. In that same year, Interface introduced its climate-neutral Cool Carpet™ product. By investing in projects that offset the greenhouse gas emissions associated with the entire life cycle of their Cool Carpet products – from raw material acquisition, through manufacturing, transport and end of life – Interface customers can make climate-neutral carpet purchases. The Cool Carpet products are certified as 'Climate Cool' by the Climate Neutral™ Network (www.climateneutral.com).

CHARITY BEGINS AT HOME

Our ability to get things right begins with our *own* workplace. If we are looking for ways to improve working conditions within our organisation, or at least to have benchmarks against which to track our progress, we can log on to the Gradient Index (www.gradient-index.net) developed by the Institute of Social and Ethical Accountability in Britain. Once into the system, we can input our company's data and see how our organisation fares in terms of social and ethical accountability relative to those who have already contributed their data. This initiative has been put together with the assistance of a number of companies, including FTSE and KPMG.

Another way to make a difference is to find ways to reach out to the underprivileged and handicapped by enabling them access to the dignity of work from home. A recent study conducted by Sustainable Teleworking (SusTel) showed that the creation of more flexible working opportunities at the United Kingdom's leading telecommunications company, BT (www.btplc.com/betterworld), benefited both the staff and the company. The researchers surveyed 1874 (of a total of over 7000) BT staff members, who work from home as flexiworkers on its Workabout scheme. Of these, the overwhelming majority were not only less stressed than when they worked in an office, they were also more productive. A small minority of disadvantaged or disabled employees on the scheme would not have been able to work at all had they not been given the freedom to work from home. Apart from greater productivity, BT now enjoys better employee morale and lower absenteeism. Around 14 per cent of the employees on the scheme said that the workplace flexibility also enabled them to take part in organised community activities.

There are no limits to the ways our organisations can give

297

back. SPC (since merged with Ardmona to form SPC Ardmona, www.spcardmona.com.au), Australia's largest manufacturer and marketer of fruit and vegetables, had major business hurdles in the early 1990s. By the end of the decade not only was the business strong, but the company had established a Community Care Program dedicated to providing 'food aid to the hungry, financial aid to the distressed and assistance to other non-profit organisations operating in the community'. One of their most impressive campaigns is their Operation Share-A-Can project, which feeds the hungry and the homeless. Around 700 employees each year volunteer their time to produce more than 400 000 cans of produce valued at $1 million. The ingredients and services are donated by suppliers, as are the packaging and the twenty-five semi-trailers needed to transport the goods. These are then distributed to the Victorian Relief Committee and Foodbank Victoria, which in turn distribute the food to over 300 Victorian welfare agencies. Unlike some similar schemes, the food used for this huge effort is of the highest quality. While SPC Ardmona initiated this scheme, it is quick to acknowledge that it is only through the support of its many partners that it can undertake this major food relief operation. It is interesting that SPC and Ardmona both began life as growers' cooperatives, and that even after their own business hurdles, together their commitment to the community remains strong.

As we start to think about the possibilities available to us, we may well be inspired to work in different ways. Certainly this was the reasoning behind ACCÍON International (www.accion.org). While most banks around the world seek clients with substantial assets, ACCÍON gives people in the United States, Latin America, the Caribbean and Africa the opportunity to move beyond poverty by providing them with micro-loans and business training. Founded almost forty years ago, ACCÍON frequently lends individuals as little as $100. This is often enough to enable borrowers to break the cycle of poverty. Interest is charged purely to cover the expense of the loan. Most borrowers outside the United States have no collateral – they may even be illiterate – yet with small injections of cash they can begin to earn enough to live on, through farming or other enterprises. This often enables individuals to afford running water, better food and schooling for their children. These gestures are significant in a world where 3 billion people live on less than US$2 a day.

Often women lack collateral and are unable to get further education or get a home business off the ground. In 1992 The Women's Loan Fund, Wahine Putea, was founded in New Zealand to make interest-free loans available to women for study or to establish a tiny business, or to help them towards financial independence. It was inspired by the concept of micro-credit, more common in less developed countries. In the Wellington fund, loans range from NZ$1000 for a personal loan to NZ$1500 for a business loan. The money comes from investors who place lump sums in an interest-free fund. This fund is run by women, who also provide business advice and coaching, and networking and promotion through their newsletter to their clients. Fifteen additional funds in New Zealand have adopted the Wellington model and are now operating independently.

INSTITUTIONALISED GIVING THROUGH WORK

There are many forms of giving back. We can decide as an organisation which charities we would like to support, then institute a direct debit from the gross salary of each staff member wanting to participate. Many companies already have this procedure in place. It is an excellent way to support a charity – and not only are the donations tax deductible, but the charities concerned also have a regular income stream. This method of donation cuts down on their administrative costs, because they receive one combined staff payment from the company each month, rather than donations from a whole range of individuals. For those with even modest amounts to donate, the contributions are worthwhile. In Britain £72 million was generated through payroll giving in the 2001–02 financial year.

Some companies match whatever contributions staff make. The Royal Bank of Scotland raised £4.5 million in 2002 by contributing *double* what its employees donated through the Give As You Earn Scheme. There are many ways companies can fundraise; the UK-based Giving Campaign (www.giving campaign.org.uk) is an excellent resource. Not only do staff feel good about fundraising, their world-view is expanded as they become more aware of those less fortunate. Regular bulletins on the progress of the charities supported can be emailed to staff, or representatives of the charities might even address staff occasionally, allowing an even greater sense of partnership to develop. These gestures need not be time-consuming, but their effects on morale are obvious.

BEING MORE CREATIVE WITH OUR OWN RESOURCES
One of the many questions we also need to ask ourselves is, what do we do with the money we earn at work? Do we make an effort to buy products that are ethically and environmentally sound? Do we further observe the flow of energy in our lives by giving away computers, furniture and other items when we purchase replacements? Local communities are often starved of basic resources. We forget how much they might benefit from having another computer or printer, or some leftover carpet.

When next we get paid, perhaps we can pause for a moment and, instead of spending our money on yet another suit or pair of shoes, we might be a little more generous towards those who don't even have clothes or shoes. Or perhaps we might think more closely about our community – about a neighbour who might need help with their garden or shopping or trips to the doctor, or a community group in need of volunteers. There is no way we can tackle all these possibilities, but each of us can find ways to work towards making our workplace more human, more passionate, more cohesive, with work practices that enhance the human spirit and also benefit the planet. Every step we take has an impact.

A contemplation on work

Just for today I will think less about myself and more about others.

Just for today I will relax a little and remember how blessed I already am.

Just for today I will be less impatient and more hopeful.

Just for today I will allow my imagination to move beyond all I have to do.

Just for today I will take greater care of the resources I have.

Just for today I will do something for someone else.

Because I know that when I take good care of today, tomorrow will take care of itself.

living the dream

Go with the flow, be out of control and the dream will reveal itself to you. Chances are it will probably be nothing like you first envisaged – instead, it'll be ten times better.
Jesse Martin, *Dream On*

HONOURING OUR DREAMS

We live in remarkable times. Unlike our forebears we have the opportunity to enjoy several or more chapters within one lifetime. Often we limit these possibilities by putting our most cherished dreams on hold for our work – as Ralph Waldo Emerson observed in his *Journals*, 'We are always getting ready to live, but never living.' We spend our days waiting for something to happen that will catapult us to where we long to be; we become lost in unrealised dreams. Our lives then narrow, as do our options, as we convince ourselves that because we're a lawyer, a bank clerk or an optometrist, we can't learn to weave or play the saxophone, travel to Tibet or the Yucatán, or enrol in a class in philosophy or psychology. We don't see that as a receptionist we might also become a skilled calligrapher or make handcrafted paper, or that as a sales executive we can also learn to make jewellery or to work with wood or glass.

Our creativity is the voice of our soul – it feeds and uplifts us. When we suppress our creative impulses, our lives feel constricted and lacking fulfilment. Over the years, many people have told me they are desperate to write, but that they can't write while they are still working. They cling to this belief, even though they have been told that most writers have full- or part-time jobs and lead busy lives. New books are born because writers *make* time for their passion – they write on buses and trains, at the kitchen table and in airports. One well-known writer who was the editor of a leading magazine and a mother of four young children would begin writing at 10 p.m. Another writer lives on one of the most remote pastoral properties in the world and gets up at 4 a.m. to put pen to paper before her working day begins. Like so many writers, neither of these women regard their writing as a burden; it feeds the other parts of their lives, enriching the moment and allowing them valuable time to themselves.

DARING TO MAKE OUR DREAMS A REALITY
We often allow work to become our excuse for not pursuing our most cherished dreams. We convince ourselves that it is more appropriate for our lives to be swallowed up by endless meetings and reports and by the next project and the next. But work is no excuse for neglecting our dreams. We can spend our lives talking about having a creative life, or we can start to pursue the things that interest us and allow them to take us to places we haven't dreamt of. Often we fear the new, and yet isn't this what most of us need in our lives right now? Isn't it time we stopped living by rote? If we indulge our fear, it will keep us stuck. As Julia Cameron observes in *The Artist's Way*, answered prayers are scary – scary because we no longer have an excuse for not making our dreams a reality, scary because we might fail, and scary

because we might succeed. We don't have to resign from work to do the things we love, yet often that is how we react when faced with creative possibilities. Often we're also afraid that life will punish us if we dare to do what we love most.

When we take a look at the genuinely successful people at work, they are committed to work and to their lives *beyond* work. They play an instrument or sing in a band, work with fabrics or with metal, or are wonderful cooks or gardeners. They give themselves to a whole manner of pursuits for the sheer *love* of it. Theirs is an expansive way of living, because all they put out comes back to them many times over. Even though they might have families, a busy job, or slender resources, still they continue to screen print, to sing opera or to grow herbs. They pursue their passions beyond work, because they *know* how much these activities benefit their lives. By listening to the promptings of their souls, they enjoy a far greater *intimacy* with themselves and others. And because they are not prepared to sacrifice their wider passions, their working lives are often more focused and less problematic. They still work at the merchant bank, the local kindergarten, the insurance company or the hardware shop, but as they work, their jobs are enriched by their burgeoning life beyond work. The beauty of cultivating a significant other life is that it enables us to balance our time at work and with those we love, with time for *ourselves* and *our* passions.

BECOMING AWARE OF THE OBSTACLES WE CREATE

To neglect to do what we love can prove fatal. Derrick Bell describes the sacrifice of passion as a kind of psychic suicide. Our creative impulses can at first overwhelm us, because they demand that our lives be more fluid, yet when we can step through our fears, we enter a whole new relationship with ourselves and the world. Our dreams help reawaken our capacity for living, our ability to be more spontaneous and our trust in *our* selves. Jesse Martin, the youngest round-the-world solo yachtsman, hints at the way forward when he talks of his own achievements: 'The most satisfying part of the adventure was not the beginning, the end or the physical aspect of sailing. It was in letting go – when all the things you have worried about, feared and dreaded disappear, leaving you alive, happy and living your dream.'

NURTURING THE PROCESS

At some level, we all yearn to realise our dreams, only to end up killing these possibilities through our impatience. We expect to be skilled at whatever we undertake before we have even begun to hone our new skill. Every dream needs patience, courage and a sense of humour. Every time we pursue a new dream, we are embarking on a journey of spirit that will deepen our understanding of life. Our ability to hold this vision will be tested, and people and situations may discourage us, yet once we start to make progress, we will begin to appreciate how much more satisfying our world has become. The more we relax into our dreams, the more we are able to live as we did when we were children – happily embracing each moment, enjoying the journey as well as the destination.

BEING CLEAR ABOUT WHAT WE WANT

To follow any creative dream takes courage, but if we are prepared to put the time in, life will help us find the resources we need to make our dream a reality. We still have to be clear about whether we *do* want to learn to sculpt or to weave, or whether this is just something we like to talk about. When a young aspirant went to see a great spiritual teacher in the hope of finding the meaning of life, the teacher asked him how much he really wanted to learn these things. 'More than anything in the world,' the young man assured him. In that instant the teacher grabbed the young man, dragged him to a nearby river, and pushed the young man's head under the water. Terrified, the young man fought back, until the teacher finally relented. 'I have no doubt you are interested in the meaning of life, but you do not want it enough,' declared the teacher, and sent him on his way. If we're not careful, our wider aspirations can end up being little more than indulgences in which our ego takes refuge when it feels like a boost. We may well talk about helping the homeless, or becoming a vegetarian cook or a quilter, but do we have sufficient passion to get there? Now is the perfect time to take stock, to look at the long list of things we have promised ourselves, and to start to make plans. If our passions have changed, then it's time to put old dreams aside and discover new ones.

TAKING THE CREATIVE LEAP

The universe rewards those who follow the promptings of their souls. To help us get moving, we need to establish some physical and mental space, so we can give birth to our dreams. Often we don't want to set aside the space for our creative endeavours, because it will interfere with our lives or our decor. If this is the case, then we need to decide what's more important – living with more passion, or worrying about how our home looks.

For years, Sophie kept the spare room in her apartment for guests. Even though she had done several courses in weaving, that was as far as she had got, because she had no room at home for a loom. She kept wishing she could afford a bigger apartment, then one day she realised she could use her spare room for her loom. As friends only visited three or four times a year, the rest of the time the spare room sat vacant. Sophie rearranged the furniture, bought a sofa bed and purchased a small loom. After this, she couldn't wait to get home from work to weave – and her friends and visitors were delighted by her weaving.

We mightn't have much space at home, but we can still find ways to make our creative tools readily accessible – if we don't, we're likely to give up. Frequently, all we need is a drawer or a box, or a small area devoted to our raw materials. Or perhaps we need to see our limited space in a new light.

Scott had wanted to garden for years. 'It just didn't occur to me I could still garden, even though I live an apartment,' he explained. When he was finally inspired to create a miniature garden on his balcony, Scott planted herbs, tomatoes and some ornamental bushes. 'Now the garden's established, I couldn't imagine life without it. I now realise why Dad used to spend hours in the backyard fixing up old cars when he got home from work – it clears your mind and gets rid of the stress.' Having time to garden has improved Scott's relationships at home and at work: 'I'm a much better person to be around these days,' he admits.

Meredith has a busy job in sales with a lot of travel; often when she gets home she doesn't have the energy to set up for her stained glass work, so she attaches herself to a local class, where she can have access to a welder. The whole process of working with her hands and absorbing herself in her latest project gives her an immense amount of satisfaction. 'It doesn't matter what you produce – the important thing is that it's come from you,' she reflects.

REALISING OUR POTENTIAL

Whether we're a banker or a social worker, a linesman or a computer analyst, each of us is born with *massive* creative potential, but rarely do we sustain this creativity into adulthood – we become disheartened and distracted along the way. We all have the impulse to strive for *more* – not just for more money or another promotion, but for expressions of who we uniquely are. When we dare to pay attention to this yearning, whole aspects of ourselves that have lain dormant are at last able to emerge. Often when we start out on a creative endeavour, we are terrified that we might not be any good or, worse still, that we might be good. Will this sudden burst of potential perhaps turn our lives upside-down? Will we have to leave our marriage, our kids, our job? When we allow ourselves to be overtaken by these kinds of fantasies, we end up defeated before we've even picked up a paintbrush or tried our hand at a musical instrument. Instead of wasting our energies on such imaginings, we're far better off simply taking the plunge.

A great way to get the creative juices flowing is to develop a ritual that will help us get in the mood. Each writer has their own way of getting their words down; one person might write with a blue pen, another might use lined paper. Some work best writing longhand, while others prefer to key their work straight into a computer. Some love the buzz of writing in cafés, while others need complete silence. Often the first step is hardest. Sir Winston Churchill would always splash paint across the blank canvas to get started. Some people are inspired by certain kinds of music, while others prefer to be alone with their thoughts. Each of us is unique, and so it's important to follow *our* instincts. What might your ritual consist of? What qualities in daily life uplift and inspire you? What gets your creative juices flowing? Once we start to establish our own ritual, it becomes a signal to our subconscious that it's time to get going.

WORKING TOWARDS THE LIFE YOU WANT

When we allow our creative life to come to the fore, we help redress the imbalance often created by work – we can't paint ceramics or work in mosaic if we allow our work to take up all our time. We are then motivated to finetune our systems, to prioritise and to plan ahead, because unless we're organised and getting results, there's no time for our wider passions. Once we do start to support our creativity, we bring all kinds of new possibilities to life that will enrich our work.

Kirky works full-time in the building industry liaising with architects and designers to provide materials for shopping centres and hotels. He fell into art at school, loving the freedom of expression it brought. Kirky went on to art school, but like so many artists wasn't able to paint full-time, so he pursued mainstream work, which he enjoys because it prevents him from becoming isolated. Even though he lives in the city, Kirky was lucky enough to find a home with a shed, which had once been a small millinery factory and is now his studio. He loves creating something as tangible as paint on canvas. He has now held several exhibitions, and has been gratified by the response he has enjoyed from the general public and from clients and workmates. 'It's great to see people buy my paintings, to know they'll end up in other people's homes and add something to their lives.' Kirky describes painting as a meditative experience that enables him to get rid of the stress and angst of work. His passion for painting supports the rest of his life, benefiting him in unexpected ways. When his mother-in-law died a few years back, his painting helped him deal with his grief. 'Get organised, and just do it,' Kirky advises. 'If you don't, you'll always wonder whether you could have done it.'

Di has been a nurse for over thirty years, the past twelve of which she has been a community health nurse, covering an area of around 38 500 square kilometres. Her job is demanding and requires a lot of driving, but Di enjoys what she does. Di also loves colour, pattern and texture, and patchwork and quilting satisfy her need for these things. 'Quilting has enriched my life – I would still rather be sewing pieces of patchwork together than doing anything else. The excitement of putting pieces up on my design wall, or sewing that first block, or seeing all those little pieces joined into a whole new fabric has never faded. I have learned so much about fabrics and threads, design and colour, fabric dyeing, machine quilting and embroidery. Wanting to share my love of patchwork has given me the confidence to teach, which stimulates me creatively. I have no great affection for the finished object; it is the making of it that matters most. I give lots of my stuff away.'

Di has won numerous awards, and one of her pieces was considered for an exhibition at Sydney's Museum of Contemporary Art. Patchwork and quilting have enhanced Di's days, giving her a life apart from work. Her best time for quilting is in the early morning, after taking the dog for a walk. 'I can usually count on an uninterrupted thirty to sixty minutes before my family is up. Some days I might only get a few minutes or none at all. The trick is to try to do a little bit every day. Another trick is to leave your needle in the work ready to start the next day.' Di encourages us to commit to whatever inspires us: 'Practise, practise, practise whatever skills you need for your particular craft. No-one ever got good at anything by doing it once or twice.' The secret of her success clearly lies in her love of what she does: 'Play a lot. Get over the feeling that you must have something to show for your time. You are learning while you are playing. Take a class, read a lot, or surf the net. If you wait till you have a large block of free time, you'll be waiting forever.'

Mark has a high-powered position in finance, dealing with the money market and a whole range of clients. After a number of years devoted to the many demands of his job, he decided to take piano lessons and explore children's writing out of hours. 'Going for what you love is not something that comes easily to most people, especially in today's paced world, where things are only measured in dollars,' Mark admits. 'In making a conscious decision to go for what I love in my own life, I feel I can be a better example for my children – to give them the courage to do the same.' Mark has no doubts about the benefits of his creative pursuits: 'They have enhanced my ability at work. I feel more balanced and rounded. I also feel my energy is much more in the now.' This centredness has proved invaluable to Mark, who spends his days analysing past trends and making projections on where the markets are heading. He also feels this time out has balanced the masculine, results-oriented part of his nature with his more nurturing feminine side: 'Striving to know the whole you is not a luxury but a necessity – the alternative is a shallow existence.'

Elisabeth's private passions are the perfect foil for her work – she runs the Stop Laughing, This Is Serious Gallery, which specialises in cartooning and illustration. She also does a small amount of illustration work and her own artwork, in between bringing up twin boys under five. Elisabeth has had a rich and varied working life, starting out as an art teacher, then completing a postgraduate diploma in Gallery Management and Art Journalism. Her life abounds with creative expression: 'I've written poetry, a daily journal, articles and reviews; I've made art – drawing, painting and printmaking – and have had a couple of abortive attempts at learning to play musical instruments.' For Elisabeth, her creative impulses are 'proof to myself that I have existed, as I have the most appalling memory! They also help me to slow down and contemplate what is happening in my life. I also enjoy the act of creating something out of nothing. When I draw realistically, I love the way that drawing causes me to forget myself and focus on something external to me, to really see it and enjoy it'.

Running a gallery and being an artist have both enhanced Elisabeth's working life, because she has some idea what the people she is representing are feeling. For Elisabeth, the benefits of her own creative moments are many: 'I think that you gain a sense of confidence that you can actually think for yourself in a world that is constantly trying to reduce you to the lowest common denominator.' There are also philosophical benefits: 'Your creativity can help you make links between all the disparate elements in your life, so that you can create a sense of meaning in an otherwise apparently meaningless world – it's sort of like discovering the truth from within, rather than turning to other people to tell you what they think it is.' And to all those on the brink of their own creative journeys, she advises, 'Keep an eye out for what inspires you, and then simply enjoy playing – just go for it and let one thing lead to another, and don't let the voices in your head tell you that what you're doing is not as important as the other demands in your life. Everyone needs personal time out, and everyone around you will benefit from the joy and satisfaction you'll experience.'

The beauty of a creative life is that often one creative pursuit will lead to the next, until we are involved in a whole variety of activities beyond work. And because our lives are so full and because we feel alive, rarely will we be bored or unhappy, because we know there is always the next possibility awaiting us and the next. When we start out we will have no idea where our new enriched life will lead us but, as Jesse Martin notes, it will often be ten times better than we could have imagined.

TIME TO GET CREATIVE

The very fact you have been reading this chapter means that life is inviting you to enrich your own existence by allowing your creativity to blossom. This is an important moment. Why not make a list of all those things you have been promising yourself you'll do, and consider the following questions?

- If you no longer know what you'd like to do, what did you love doing as a child?
- What qualities might these pursuits bring to your life? Allow yourself to *feel* them.
- What difference would these pursuits make if they were present in your daily life?
- How might they enhance your time at work and beyond it?
- How can you get started?
- Do you need to enrol for some tutoring in this field?
- What materials might you need?
- How else might you support this activity?

Having got these basics together, take the plunge and see where this new journey takes you.

reinventing ourselves

Man's main task in life is to give birth to himself.
ERICH FROMM, *MAN FOR HIMSELF*

CHANGING CAREERS

There are many ways we can transform our working lives. With the increased access to training, and constant change in the workplace, many of us will end up finetuning or changing our profession a number of times during our working life. When we dare to go with the flow and continue to reinvent ourselves, we help ensure that life will deliver all we had hoped for. Sometimes the transitions we face will be obvious to us, sometimes they'll come out of left field – the important thing is to give them our full attention, because they are in our life for a reason.

Susie's story

From the moment Susie entered the workforce, her job came first. Susie was fortunate to have success early, and in no time she was a high-powered executive on the fast track. By Susie's own admission, her working life was driven. She had moved cities and let her marriage go to ensure she kept up the momentum she had worked so hard to achieve. Susie worked long hours, coping with an ever-increasing workload and escalating responsibilities, getting little or no sleep, and relying on alcohol and cigarettes to see her through. 'I knew the way I was working wasn't good for me, but I was hooked into the dream,' she admits. 'Every time I felt desperate, I kept telling myself that things would get easier when I got to the next level.' It was the healthy remuneration that came with her job that kept Susie going: 'I was earning serious money, and there was always the promise of an even bigger pay-rise just around the corner. My salary made me feel validated,' she reflects. Yet looking back, Susie likens her years in corporate life to the boiling frog syndrome: 'Little by little the pressure increases, but because it's so gradual, you don't realise what's happening. I knew I was stressed, but I had no idea I'd virtually reached boiling point.' In spite of the escalating pressure and fatigue, the enticements of Susie's salary package and status kept her going.

Over time, Susie became enslaved by the lifestyle that came with her job: 'The more money you earn, the more you need. When you've got plenty of cash, then whatever you want you can have, and so you just keep on spending.' Deep down, Susie knew her life lacked balance. She looked forward to having more time for herself, but did nothing about this in the short term, because there were always more projects and responsibilities.

Then came September 11, and Susie's world began to unravel. The combination of working so hard for so long, and having had almost no sleep for several nights before, left Susie less than equipped to deal with this disaster personally and professionally. This shocking episode had an additional resonance for Susie, because she had been scheduled to be in New York – at the Twin Towers – when the disaster took place. As she watched the massive buildings collapse, it was as if everything she believed in was being destroyed. As her company's assets were likely to suffer, Susie found herself having to handle the fallout with clients and staff. That momentous day at work proved gruelling – so gruelling that Susie collapsed. A couple of days later, she was on a plane when she began to hyperventilate. She had a seizure on board and ended up being hospitalised. This sudden breakdown in health meant that Susie was forced to take leave and her life became an endless round of doctors. Even though she wasn't well, Susie still kept moving. 'I was manic,' she admits.

Then, while she was sitting in her favourite café, she suddenly thought she wouldn't mind owning a café. 'I still planned to continue my corporate job, and thought I'd manage a café on the side,' she explains. While she was recuperating Susie bought that same café. She was still expecting to go back to work, but then she was diagnosed with manic depression. 'My doctor told me my condition had been brought on by work, and that I could no longer work under that level of pressure.' Susie was shattered – it had never occurred to her that she wouldn't be going back to corporate life. Her immediate reaction was one of shock: 'I felt I'd been ripped off – that my life had been taken from me.' Then came the anger, and so she decided to pursue litigation. But after many more appointments with doctors, psychologists and psychiatrists, Susie felt increasingly out of control. One specialist said she needed to be institutionalised and put on lithium, and the shock of this pronouncement catapulted Susie out of her downward spiral. 'My doctor assured me I was doing well, so I took stock. I realised that more than anything I wanted to get on with my life, so I dropped the litigation, and with professional help I came off the medication and haven't been on it since.'

The purchase of the café proved a lifesaver for Susie. 'If you had told me while I was still in corporate life that this is what I'd be doing, I'd have been horrified, because like so many I had been conditioned to think people who worked in such jobs were losers.' But then as the days and weeks passed, Susie began to appreciate what each working day brought. She had always loved being around people and food, and her café fulfilled these desires. It also gave her a community of people in whom she could take a genuine interest, and who in turn appreciated the good food and inviting space. 'I feel like I've got my life back,' Susie admits. 'I make my own choices and what I'm doing seems really worthwhile.' All the anxiety that plagued Susie is now gone. 'It's so liberating, because my future's not all mapped out. I'm not anxious about this, because even though I still have many other things I want to do with my life, I now know they'll happen at the right time.' Susie finally feels she is working at something that matters. Her message is not to leave work behind, so much as to live and work in a way that feeds us, rather than getting lost in the stereotypes presented to us, or in the expectations of others.

Karl's story

For years, Karl was immersed in the rich and colourful world of music, working with songwriters, recording artists and producers, where he managed emerging artists and big-name acts for a number of music companies and for an entertainment agency. Music was in Karl's blood, and so it was no surprise that he enjoyed great success in this career. He even had an opportunity to work in Hollywood as a record producer, but turned it down at the eleventh hour, because while it was an opportunity of a lifetime, it didn't feel right. Looking back, Karl is grateful he didn't take this route, because he could have been swallowed up by that world. As it was, Karl's life was already one of excess, with little thought of tomorrow – until eventually the long hours, the stress, and the constant round of liquid lunches and dinners began to take a serious toll on his health, leaving Karl feeling numb. Then Karl read Shirley MacLaine's *Out on a Limb* and suddenly realised life was a much bigger, more awesome experience than he'd imagined. He began to read widely and to attend courses on everything from macrobiotics and Ayurveda to tai chi. He continued to work in the music industry, but he no longer wanted to waste himself, and his many privileges no longer captivated him. Through each new course, he made new friends – people from all walks of life – who, like him, were looking for something more. With this new direction came a new language for life, which opened up even more possibilities. No longer was Karl totally concerned with himself and his own success – other people now mattered.

As his work became increasingly soulless and lacking in integrity, as the relationship with artists got lost in the preoccupation with the bottom line, Karl became increasingly disenchanted. Then an acquaintance in the industry collapsed and died at twenty-eight of a cerebral haemorrhage brought on by on-the-job stress. Karl decided it was time to move on. While he was more than ready to take the plunge, he still had to wrestle with how to support himself and pay child maintenance. He also wondered how he'd cope, leaving behind a world he knew intimately and all the kudos that came with it. Karl made the transition by playing several nights a week in a band, studying Reiki, and working in a health food shop. During this time, Karl was tempted to leave the city and join a spiritual community. Unsure of this direction, he asked for a sign and that same day he spotted a notice advertising the services of a Reiki practitioner. Karl went inside and asked whether there was an opening for another practitioner. Unbeknown to Karl, the practitioner whose notice he read had just decided to move on, and within a week Karl was finally practising Reiki.

This change in direction has given Karl a strong sense of gratitude for everything that comes his way, big and small. While there are occasional anxieties about money, Karl has more than managed to support himself. Further study has enabled him to teach Reiki as well as to practise it. He loves what he does, especially helping people with their own life choices. He cherishes his daughter and enjoys a sharing relationship with a loving partner, whose burgeoning career in alternative health has brought him additional joy. For those wishing to make a move, Karl suggests: 'Rediscover your passion and joy for living. Choose to engage with life, and see where it takes you. Be gentle on yourself. Set your own course, but then let go of how this might unfold and remember to speak positively about yourself and others.' He talks of reclaiming his life and his health, and moving from a merry-go-round kind of existence, to one that brings new and enlightening experiences each moment.

Helen's story

Sometimes we take a different route in our working life because we don't believe it's practical to work at what we love most. Helen's working life began in dentistry, but now she is an author and journalist. Reading and writing were always Helen's great-est passions, but when it came to her career, she didn't see writing as a viable choice, so she completed university studies and became a dentist instead. After eleven years of dentistry Helen's career change was sparked by a letter she wrote to the local newspaper. 'To my surprise and delight, it was published. I offered to write a few articles and my suggestion was accepted.'

Encouraged, Helen started to work towards her goal of becoming a full-time writer and, with training and support, what began as a pleasurable pastime became a rewarding career. 'I wrote in the evenings and at weekends over a few years until I reached the stage where I was working four days a week as a freelance journalist and only one day a week as a dentist.'

Helen's final transition to writing was made after working on an article about midlife career change for the *Reader's Digest* magazine. Although Helen was ready to take the plunge, the hardest step was giving up her one day's work as a dentist. As she faced this final change, she was forced to overcome her fears around her new life – fear of failure, fear of the change in her professional status, and fear of loss of income. Although Helen admits to feeling guilty about walking away from her former career, she continues to put her dental background to good use: 'I have trained health workers, written dental health education scripts and segments for broadcast on radio, as well as producing several magazine articles on dental health. My dental studies have also given me the background and knowledge to research and work on scientific and medical articles and present them in layman's terms. Working as a dentist even gave me the contacts – and inspiration – for the first of my five non-fiction books!'

Helen's new career has changed her whole outlook on life: 'Life is too short to be unhappy – do what you love or love what you do.' Her writing has enabled her to travel widely and to meet people from all walks of life. She also enjoys the feedback: 'I'm delighted my articles can help others. One individual contacted the *Reader's Digest* magazine requesting permission to make several thousand copies of an article I had written on strokes for an organisation with which he was involved.' Like all jobs,

Helen's work has its challenges: 'Professional and social isolation are constant issues. I address these by networking, attending conferences and, from time to time, taking on a project or contract work that enables me to work in a team.' Like so many who have changed course, Helen has also become involved in a number of community-based volunteer projects.

Iain's story

Iain's career change was sparked by an interest in the welfare of others that he couldn't fulfil in corporate life. He left his career in publishing, is now studying acupuncture, and will eventually set up his own practice. During his corporate years, Iain managed the production department of a national branch of one of the world's leading book publishers, where he supervised a busy team of staff and freelancers. His job entailed long days, frequent weekend work and a fair bit of stress. Now Iain is working from home as a freelancer while studying for a Bachelor of Health Sciences. This move wasn't easy for Iain, as he had worked hard for a decade to get to where he was, only to realise the office environment was not for him. 'Everything from the air-conditioning and fluorescent lights, through to the office politics went against the grain. I understood that making a profit was vital for the company and had the skills to help achieve it, but my heart wasn't in it.' Iain was also frequently ill with a debilitating back injury and endless recurrences of the flu. When he took a good look at himself, Iain realised he should be exploring other options, and after some consideration chose to study Chinese medicine. 'I wanted to help people live at their optimal level of health and wellbeing,' he explains.

Although Iain was excited about his change in vocation, his fear about financial security came to the fore. 'I was scared that I could be throwing away a level of financial security that I might never achieve again. I worried about the fact that I would have to pay fees and would have trouble affording to buy a house in the near future. I also feared that once I left my job I would feel worthless and unimportant.' Iain was also concerned about whether he would be suited to his new vocation: 'I feared that I might not have the skills and talents to make a good acupuncturist. What if I made the change, then realised it wasn't the right thing to do, quit university and looked like an idiot?' Iain was also concerned about his age: 'By the time I finish my degree I will be at least forty, so there were also moments when I feared that perhaps I had left my run too late.' Looking back, Iain is far more philosophical: 'There is an endless number of fears one can succumb to in darker moments!'

Now Iain has moved on, the fears that threatened to hold him back have evaporated. 'The world did not crumble and I did not lose my sense of identity when I gave up the job I had worked hard to get. Being able to break away from a familiar environment without falling apart has given me a more flexible view of the world. I have a greater sense of life's possibilities.' He has also noticed a dramatic improvement in his health and quality of life. Even though he is busy with study and work, Iain is far less stressed: 'I am no longer waking up in the middle of the night in a cold sweat thinking about something I should have done.' As he delves deeper into the intricacy of the human body Iain has discovered a new reverence for life. His fellow students come from all walks of life, including film, accounting and computing, and are a constant source of inspiration. Many have had major hurdles to overcome, often coming from difficult, if not violent homes, or struggling with depression, or their own ill health. 'It's almost as if these things have made them more compassionate, more open to life,' Iain reflects. His advice to anyone contemplating change is to 'listen to your inner voice over all the other voices competing for your attention. Your benchmark for success should be one *you* set yourself'. Having settled on what to do next, Iain stresses the importance of planning: 'Do plenty of research. Look closely at the financial, social and any other ramifications of making a change before you proceed.' Iain still has his challenges, but because he is in the right place at the right time, he feels better equipped to deal with them.

Jayne's story

By contrast, Jayne began working life as a kindergarten teacher and is now in corporate life. Jayne taught for a number of years, then resigned when she became pregnant with her first child. After being at home for a few years, she did some casual teaching, but soon realised she didn't want to spend all day with children, and then come home to her own children. Jayne is now a corporate training and development manager. It took courage for Jayne to re-enter the workforce and change direction. 'My fear was that I would never be good enough for anything but teaching,' she admits. 'This was not a fear, but a terror.' Moving on meant a return to university and less time with her children. However, looking back, Jayne feels her career change has enabled her to be a much better mother – by spending less time with her children, she is no longer living her life through them, which has enabled them to blossom as individuals.

Jayne's change of direction started when she enrolled in a creative writing course and then progressed to a postgraduate diploma in communications, which proved life-changing. 'One of the pieces I submitted, the lecturer wrote, "You are a star." This validation as something other than somebody's mother and wife was too much – I actually burst into tears. From that moment onwards, I was determined to try my hand at becoming a freelance writer. I got a million knock-backs, but I also got editors who were interested, paid me and asked for more work. With a little more confidence, I started applying for jobs teaching film and media. From there I received a position as a tutor in journalism. I loved it and I loved the students. At one lecture I even got a huge round of applause – I have no idea how I drove home that night. I had gone from being a kindergarten teacher, to a shy, stay-at-home mother, to someone who was applauded when she spoke.'

'I was then asked by a training company to do some corporate courses in communication. When I got there, I found out the training was about interpersonal skills, not mass communication. Undaunted, I said I could do it and then researched like crazy. I delivered my seminar and they asked me to do more. Before long, I found myself the preferred trainer for this company. I went on to work with high-profile multinationals who asked for me every time they needed training. I am now a training and development manager, and look after the training needs of 300 people. The job is completely autonomous and involves a lot of travel, as well as writing and training – I love it.' Jayne feels like a new person: 'I have been faced with all sorts of challenges and I feel strong and in control of my life for the first time in a very long time. People have no idea how old I am – they often ask me if I am forty yet. If they only knew I am forty-nine!' The benefits for Jayne have been numerous and include increased salary, increased confidence, more friends, and a level of understanding of herself and those around her that she never would have achieved otherwise. 'I have a closeness now with my children that I never had before, and I have incredible energy. I almost run to work every day, because I love it so much. I also love my lifestyle. My mix of friends is

incredible and I cherish them all.' For those seeking to make
changes, Jayne recalls a line from Mitch Albom's *Tuesdays with
Morrie*: 'To die is sad, but to live an unfulfilled life is tragic.' 'If
there is something wrong with your life, change it – simple as
that,' Jayne advises.

Monica's story

After over a decade as one of the most respected professionals
in publishing, Monica's life took an unexpected turn and she is
now living in Tashi Jong, a small Tibetan refugee community in
northern India, where she is project director for the building of
the Dongyu Gatsal Ling Nunnery, which will eventually house
and train Tibetan Buddhist nuns of the Drukpa Kagyu tradi-
tion. The nunnery has been established to preserve an important
Tibetan Buddhist female lineage, and to provide a full spiritual
education so often denied nuns. Even though the nunnery is
under construction, a number of young women from Tibet and
the Himalayan border regions of India and Nepal have already
been accepted for training. Some of these remarkable young
women have literally escaped Tibet with their lives to join the
nunnery. Monica works alongside the nunnery founder, London-
born Tenzin Palmo, one of the first westerners to be ordained
a Tibetan Buddhist nun.

Monica was attracted to Tibetan Buddhism while still running
a busy department, working to tight deadlines and overseeing the
many national tours of local and international authors. The list
of authors she has worked with reads like a literary who's who.
In among the many demands of her work, Monica made time
to attend a series of teachings given by the Dalai Lama. This
culminated in her embracing Tibetan Buddhism. Monica met
Tenzin Palmo the following year when in India with friend and

writer Vicki Mackenzie. Vicki was researching her book, *A Cave in the Snow*, Tenzin Palmo's life story. There was a distinct rapport between Monica and Tenzin Palmo, and during their subsequent conversations Tenzin mentioned the amount of work needed to get the nunnery built. Monica found herself offering to help with the project. It was two years before Monica joined Tenzin in Tashi Jong, about fifty-five kilometres from Dharamsala.

Monica's days remain full and start early. She liaises with Tenzin and her small team of staff, and the first twenty-four nuns, who live and study in temporary accommodation nearby. Monica also works with the architects, site manager and contractors building the nunnery; handles the funds raised for the project; deals with the project's international supporters; and has also accompanied Tenzin on some of her international teaching and fundraising tours.

While Monica's transition to this new working life might seem inevitable, given her commitment to Buddhism, she still had concerns: 'I guess my biggest worry was the long-term commitment to a project which would take me so far from family and close friends, plus the practical challenges of the project itself, and the learning curve required to work in a completely different culture and in construction.' Monica's life is so changed these days: 'I no longer take for granted things like reliable communication, regular water and electricity supply, let alone access to media and movies, conveniences like a washing machine, and luxuries like a massage, facial or pedicure. I now don't have the huge variety of choice in so many areas, and I often quite like that.'

One of the biggest challenges for Monica was the change of pace: 'I've tried to slow down – hard for me – and hopefully become a bit more patient and sensitive to doing things in the local way, and at the local pace.' Even though Monica's work places many demands on her, she is quick to recognise the benefits: 'I am constantly learning so much – from Tenzin Palmo who has undertaken to help these young women realise their spiritual potential; from the nuns whose devotion and commitment to their practice and their studies is really inspiring; and from the Tibetan and Indian people in whose cultures I'm now living and working. Without the distractions of Western life, I have more time to read and reflect, and I'm lucky to have some wonderful lamas nearby.'

Monica enjoys the very rich mix of cultural and spiritual experiences: 'I've been fortunate to attend some teachings by His Holiness the Dalai Lama, His Holiness the Karmapa, and also a very special yogi. I love life here – our occasional picnics with the nuns, the Tibetan festivities in our community at Losar (Tibetan New Year), the fascinating lama dancing at the monastery, the Indian festivals like Diwali, visits to the local Hindu temples, the beauty of the mountains behind our village, and the surrounding countryside with the rice and wheat crops, the tea plantations and pine forests.' Naturally, there are ongoing challenges: 'Sometimes it's hard not to be overwhelmed, and I'm sometimes lonely for my family and close friends. But there are triumphs and joys too, and I realise how lucky I am to be living in this quiet, beautiful place, learning so much, as a small part of Tenzin Palmo's team.'

It is the human dimension of Monica's work that gives her most fulfilment: 'When the first twenty-four young women came to be nuns, they were so very shy and they wouldn't look up to speak to us. It's now a very different story. They've grown so much in confidence and are full of life and laughter. As well as their present philosophical and general studies, soon they will begin training to take over the management of the nunnery. I am so proud of their achievements. If ever I'm a bit homesick, I go and see them and immediately feel better.' And to all those wanting to make a change, Monica urges us simply to do it: 'It's amazing how things fall into place once you've taken the plunge! It's not always comfortable, but it's not dull either! I've never regretted my decision.'

Alison's story

For most of her working life, Alison has managed to create enough flexibility around work to pursue her many passions. At first her work reflected the lives and aspirations of those around her: 'For a while I got caught up in wanting to buy and own things, but realised when I'd bought my first home and car, and some luxuries I'd always wanted, that they didn't make me feel any better about myself or life.' Alison started work as a secretary in a series of jobs, where she got totally involved in the businesses concerned. It was always the people she worked with who made the jobs come alive, but even this wasn't enough for her. 'I've enjoyed every job I've had, but then I started to feel dissatisfied by having to sit in an office all day doing the same thing over and over. So after a couple of years in a job, I would leave and more often than not put a pack on my back and travel until the money ran out. Then I would find another job and start again.' This pattern of work and travel has enabled Alison to travel widely and to experience many wonderful people and places.

Her last full-time job was as an agent. 'Starting as a temporary secretary, I moved into sales, and then became a director of the business, running a sales team, auditioning and recruiting new talent. I was responsible for major accounts. It was the job of my dreams in most ways – in addition to looking after people, I was drawing on my interests in business, the arts, sport and current affairs, and I found I had an unexpected talent for selling.' Then after a decade the job began to pall: 'As with many jobs in PR or entertainment it seemed glamorous, but it was hard work with long hours. I got to the stage where I dreaded having to dress up for yet another conference, breakfast or dinner. I started taking everything too seriously, felt angry, was depressed and was waking up at night worrying about not being on top of all the details, or feeling anxious without knowing why.' Before Alison could make any decisions about her future, she had a sudden personal crisis. 'I lost 80 per cent of the sight in one eye and had to face the possibility of losing the sight in the other eye.' While recuperating, Alison had time to contemplate where she was at: 'This made me think about how I wanted to live – not long-term, but day by day. I realised I was yearning for the freedom I'd felt on my travels, and that my sense of wellbeing often came from simple activities, including a long-cherished memory from childhood of the utter joy of dancing under trees.'

Again, Alison had the urge to move on, but her fears loomed large: 'I was worried about giving up my financial security and wasn't sure how I'd cope without a job title. I lost my sense of identity for a time – that's not an issue for me now.' In spite of a successful career and major health scare, Alison found the courage to take the plunge, and for the past six years she has been doing the administrative backup for a series of small businesses three days a week. While her current work isn't as interesting as some of her former roles, the many benefits of this new chapter of her working life more than compensate, because Alison is able to live more simply. Not feeling she has to be on the go all the time means many more delicious moments for reflection. 'I enjoy working part-time and the variety that moving around different offices brings.

I have more time at home, have got to know the neighbours and am involved with local issues. I love having time to do voluntary work and to have fun with friends. I'm reading again for the first time in years, as well as gardening, swimming and walking regularly. My health has improved enormously.' And to anyone contemplating a new start she says, 'Making a change requires courage and energy, but it's exciting and rewarding to take the step.'

Mira's story

Mira has moved from a high-stress role as the national events and publicity manager for a major retail chain with numerous and constant deadlines, to freelance work based in the country. Sixty-hour weeks were the norm for Mira, but eventually this lifestyle began to lose its appeal, as she and her partner dreamt of a rural life instead. When they finally made a pact to downsize their city home, they planned to buy a place in the country and let it for a while. However, once they found their new home, the city dirt, noise and congestion became intolerable, so they moved to the country within months. For Mira, the move was also prompted by work: 'I felt that the company for which I worked had become increasingly heartless, and placed little value on employee satisfaction and wellbeing.'

Even though Mira was ready for the change, still she felt anxious: 'I feared that leaving my position could cost me my friendships, and that the fact that I would no longer be a recognisable biggish fish in a smallish pond might impact negatively on my sense of self. I had also enjoyed a nice salary and knew that this would be sacrificed by making the geographical move.' There was also the question of how Mira would cope with a lot more time with her partner: 'I was scared that after long hours away from my partner through work commitments, more time in his company might be suffocating.' There were the anxieties of friends to deal with too. 'Some people assumed I would be bored and restless, and that because I had just turned fifty it would be impossible for me to find employment again should it turn out I had made the wrong decision – they echoed fears of my own.'

Looking back, Mira now has a different perspective: 'I think the reason some people were negative and worried about my decision to leave is that they felt it was a criticism of their own life choices and priorities.' Now she is settled in her new home Mira feels a deep sense of belonging: 'This is a place with the strongest sense of community. The bonuses include meeting a ragbag of wonderfully eccentric and warm-hearted people, and enjoying the company of witty and wonderful older women.' There are many nuances that warm Mira's day, from the tiny general store which is the heart of her local community, to 'greeting the owl on the back deck, driving to meetings with Cape Byron spread beneath me, and the absolute velvety stillness of night, with stars exploding like fireworks on New Year's Eve'.

Mira feels a massive sense of relief at being freed from working with and reporting to people for whom she had lost respect. She always knew she was more than her work or job title, and now she is living this reality as she builds a new working life for herself. 'I have nestled into a series of networks that have each offered me absorbing and challenging work. The work is of a voluntary nature, but I was expecting this and have confidence that eventually an income will result.' On making the change Mira reflects that 'sometimes your heart needs to give your head a push. I believe that the thought of change comes to you because you need it, because the time is right. If financial constraints are blocking your ability to make the change, make a commitment to transform the situation: give yourself a twelve-month project to get the money foundation, or see if you can implement part of the change, until the rest can be comfortably achieved'. Already Mira's change in direction has delivered far more than she could have imagined: 'This new life is a gift of love from me to me – I am living the miracle that our "if only" can become our everyday, and I am blessed.'

These and the stories of so many people who have dared to change the way they work inspire us to look at the countless ways there are to work. There are no formulas for the working life that will fulfil *us* – and so there need be no restrictions. Regardless of our age or present circumstances, there are opportunities out there for us. We mightn't be able to make a move tomorrow or next week, but with courage and foresight we can start to plan our new working life. Then when the time comes, we can make the transition to where we're meant to be next.

CONTEMPLATIONS ON MAKING YOUR MOVE

For most people, the change in occupation won't happen overnight. This gives us a chance to adjust to the possibilities ahead – to acquire the necessary skills and resources, to finetune our lifestyle – and means we can make the necessary changes a step at a time. Perhaps it is time for you to begin a new chapter of your working life. If so, then perhaps the following questions will help get you started.

- What is it you feel drawn to do?
- What appeals to you about this type of work?
- What might the disadvantages be?
- Can you deal with them?
- What other skills or resources do you need?
- How can you go about securing these?
- What is your time frame?
- Who else might you have to bring on board?

taking time out

I will arise and go now, for always night and day
I hear the lake water lapping with low sounds by the shore;
While I stand on the roadway, or on the pavements grey
I hear it in the deep heart's core.
W.B. YEATS, 'THE LAKE ISLE OF INNISFREE'

BREATHING SPACE

We can expand the possibilities for our working lives in so many ways. We might change direction at work or need some time out to replenish and refocus. This might mean a few days away from everything that's familiar, or we might need more serious space – a few months or so away to do our own thing. Most of us will come to the point where we yearn for an extended break, but because we tend to consider such possibilities as self-indulgent, we let go of what could be a life-changing experience. Or we fear that by leaving work for a while we might not get the kind of job we want when we return, or that by quitting our job we'll end up on the streets. Life rewards the courageous. This means daring to listen to the longings of our own soul, and believing that they will lead us where we're meant to be. Life prompts us to step out of our comfort zone for a reason – it's so we can travel to new places, literally and figuratively, places that often we can scarcely dream of.

333

James's story

James was a banker with a six-figure salary and all the other trappings, who had fulfilled the dreams of his Greek migrant parents by his mid-twenties. He worked and played hard, moving from relationship to relationship, but was feeling increasingly unhappy with his lot. He distracted himself with work and possessions, but they had little effect on the growing emptiness he felt inside. Then James received his superannuation statement. If he were to stay in the money market he would retire wealthy, but somehow this didn't seem enough. 'I found myself asking whether I wanted forty years of sacrifice for ten or so years of comfort.' As James took a closer look at his life, he realised he had become caught up in a ruthless game of winning at all costs: 'I'd become an empty vessel, as determined as the next guy to live fast and die young with as many toys as I could.'

With no clear idea of what else he might do, James decided to take a year out. He took off to New Zealand, then to South America. Previously when he had travelled, he had stayed in the world's best hotels, but now James wanted to travel more authentically. 'I bought myself a $400 pair of shoes and a Goretex jacket, and some other gear – hardly roughing it,' he recalls with a wry smile. It was South America that changed his whole view of life: 'I'd seen plenty of poor people and people with money, but not such extremes – not living side by side. As an economist, I'd believed in the trickle-down effect, but now I was forced to see this wasn't happening. There on the hillsides were shanty towns housing thousands upon thousands of people trapped in poverty.' During his travels, James ended up in the mining town of Potosi in Bolivia: 'It's not a place you'd choose to stop in but I was passing through, so I decided to check out the mines – they're hundreds of years old. It's mainly the indigenous people who work in the mines – they live in extreme poverty, and work in appalling conditions.

'For five or ten American dollars you can go on a tour of the mines. We went about 500 metres down the shaft, down a zigzag track, up and down which the workers pushed trolleys all day. The place was a nightmare – it was claustrophobic and unsafe. When we reached the bottom, workers were attacking the rock with their picks, while other workers were loading rocks into a trolley that was then pushed back up the track. As I watched the men working, I realised we were about the same age, and that this is what they did for twelve hours a day. Then I felt ashamed that the clothes I was wearing cost more than they could ever dream of. Then I discovered there was a second way into the mine – down a spiral staircase – used by kids of twelve with backpacks. They'd climb up and down these stairs all day carrying rocks. I was told that many of them died by twenty-seven or twenty-eight because of the dust in their lungs.

'When I asked where the metals extracted from the rocks were sent, I was told they went to a German car manufacturer. I felt sick then, because I had owned a German car. I do not know if this was true, but for me there was a clear connection made – that my decisions were affecting people all over the world.' On emerging from the mines, James sat on the mountainside staring out across the Andes. 'I realised that comparative advantage was about some countries winning, while poorer countries were forced to sacrifice whatever they could – their children, their environment – just to make ends meet.' Then a stocky kid appeared in front of James brandishing a stick of dynamite. His guide assured him it was nothing to worry about. James watched the kid crawl into a deep sandy crater and light the dynamite: 'Somehow the kid managed to crawl halfway up out of the crater and hide behind rocks before the stick exploded.' What kind of world was this, James wondered, when a kid had to risk his life daily just to survive? 'I suppose at that point I realised it was a world that exists every day – and because of my belief in the very system that caused these things to happen, I was contributing to it.'

When he returned home, James got himself contract work with credit unions. 'I had to work somewhere, and as community-based financial institutions, at least the credit unions were closer to my new values.' By James's own admission, he had 'screwed over' many people, and so he apologised to each of them. Some didn't want to know, but most cut him some slack. Over time he pared back his hours, until he was working part-time. As he considered what else he might do, he worried about how he would support himself. Six years down the track James can hardly recognise himself – he's in a stable, loving relationship, earns a fraction of what he once did, but is still able to enjoy the things he loves most. 'I've learnt to live differently,' he explains. His working life is now a rich blend of jobs. He tutors at university in various subjects focused on globalisation and the humanities, and is undertaking his PhD. James also does voluntary and semi-paid work for a number of aid organisations. He is now committed to a sustainable life that respects human and environmental resources, and that promotes dignity for everyone: 'I am privileged, and with privilege comes responsibility,' he reflects.

Judi's story

Our unhappiness about the way things are in our life is not to be feared – it's the door to new opportunities. We can only embrace these opportunities when we have the courage to reach out and make them our own. After a number of successful years as a senior sales executive in a leading multinational, Judi was in need of a change. 'I woke up one day and realised I was not that happy with my life – I was just working to pay a mortgage.' While Judi wanted to get away, her overriding concern was her security: 'I was in a good job. I had a nice apartment. I kept asking myself – did I really want to risk all that I had worked for?' Judi also had to deal with the misgivings of others: 'Lots of people thought I was crazy. Most were scared for me.' Fortunately for Judi, her closest friends and family were supportive.

The more Judi thought about the freedom travel would bring, the more she knew she had to get away. She decided on the Greek Islands. Her initial plan was to stay a few months and then move on, but as time passed she loved her new home so much, she stayed. The kindness she has received from strangers has at times been overwhelming: 'When I first arrived it was winter. I was staying in a beautiful little villa called Mimosa. One day I was sitting inside freezing. There was no heating. It was pouring with rain, so I couldn't go for a run. I was feeling a little lonely and wondering what the hell I was doing there, when I heard a tap at the kitchen window. A hand appeared from under a huge black umbrella, holding a plate full of wonderful hot Greek food – pork rolls stuffed with fetta and spinach and a huge pile of roast potatoes! Katarina, the lovely Greek lady next door, just smiled, said something in Greek, then left. After this, food would often appear through what I ended up calling the magic window.' As she settled in, Judi's new life began to emerge: 'I met people when I arrived and discovered they were looking for someone to help in the garden. I knew nothing about gardening, but was willing to learn, and so they gave me a go.'

Judi is now a gardener on an estate. She also has a small gift shop and is an increasing part of the local community. She still misses her home, friends and family, but she is deeply grateful for her new life, because it has transformed her outlook. 'I know now I can do anything I want to do – if I really want to do it.' She has enjoyed meeting many wonderful people and the chance to learn a new culture: 'Here the festivities are held down in the harbour, which is gorgeous. There is always loads of food and music. The best part is the dancing. It is wonderful to see whole families doing their traditional dancing – everybody, young and old, knows all the dances. They are proud to get up and do this. I remember the first time I saw the dancing – there were old men I had seen in the village sitting in the coffee shops with their walking sticks hardly moving, and now they were up dancing like teenagers. They were so light on their feet – it was fabulous!' Like so many who have dared to follow their heart, Judi is enjoying the day-to-day journey of her life. She advises those tempted to take time out to feel the fear and do it anyway: 'No matter what happens, you have moved the pieces and given yourself new options.'

Kristie's story

When we open ourselves up to all that awaits us in life, we need have no concerns about feeling fulfilled – our lives will have all the depth we could hope for and more besides. For as long as Kristie can remember, she has loved children and has had a passion for travel. While travelling through Vietnam in 1999 she visited Christina Noble's orphanage in Ho Chi Minh City. It was like being struck by lightning – Kristie just knew she would work with orphaned children. For the next couple of years she held on to her dream, then in 2001 she went to Thailand, hoping to find an orphanage to work in. She had virtually given up, when her taxi driver dropped her at a Buddhist orphanage by mistake.

Kristie stepped into a room full of babies – all reaching out their hands to her – and in that moment she knew this was where she was meant to be. The question was, how she was going to combine her career as a journalist with her volunteer work, given that she still had to support herself? 'I worried about whether I could afford to do it. Would it affect my career? Would I be lonely? What support would there be to fall back on? For so long it had felt like a nice dream that may or may not happen, but now I'd found the place I wondered whether or not I was being self-indulgent.'

All the magazine and newspaper editors Kristie worked with proved very supportive, so she hired a researcher and organised to file her stories by Internet. For two years, Kristie spent six months a year at the orphanage helping care for all kinds of children – from those abandoned at birth through to children aged seven – writing her articles in her spare time. Her days were spent changing nappies and feeding and playing with the children. Kristie regards this time out as a gift to herself: 'Like all volunteering you get far more than you give. For two years I was bathed in love.' Several journalist friends visited her while she was away. 'It was wonderful to see high-powered career girls sitting on the floor, playing with kids – they looked more beautiful then than I've ever seen them.' There were so many issues Kristie was passionate about, but being with the nuns gave her a new perspective: 'I learned to accept everything as it was, and to operate from there, instead of wasting my energy on things I can't change.'

Then Kristie was offered a magazine editorship back home. It was a tough choice to take on full-time work again, because of her commitment to the children. However, Kristie has worked out ways to spend time with the children in her holidays. 'Even though I'm not there at the moment, the children are always with me. They're now part of who I am. They're with me as I work – in how I deal with the staff and with deadlines.' This time away has made Kristie far more compassionate towards herself and others. She has learnt to be more honest both in her expectations and in her displeasure.

Kristie is passionate about her work, but being with the children has helped her put her work into perspective – she carries a fair amount of responsibility, but when she's feeling stressed she reminds herself that she's not saving lives. 'Work couldn't be everything to me any more,' she admits. 'Friends are an equal part of my life.' Kristie confesses to closing her eyes now and then, so she can be back in the garden at the orphanage with the nuns and the babies, enjoying the laughter and the warm breeze. Kristie knows that one day she'll be working with children again; in the meantime she's enjoying putting together her magazine. 'We can live the life we've imagined for ourselves, or we can live the life we've been told to – it's our choice,' she reflects.

When life is prompting us to take time out, it's time to get creative, to be inspired by the possibilities out there for us – and do something about them. While we might fear that it will look like we're running away, we are doing just the opposite. By creating space in our lives we allow ourselves to take a more panoramic view of things – of where we're at, of where we'd most like to be, and how we might make the transition. We all need space to breathe in life as well as space for intimacy. Time out gives us much-needed intimacy with ourselves, so that we can get to know ourselves again, and time to enter into a more intimate relationship with this tiny planet of ours. Then we can see where we have come from and how, with a little fine-tuning, we too can end up in the right place at the right time.

Jess's story

When we give ourselves the chance to get away, we are able not only to refocus and replenish, but to refine our values and direction. Jess's working life has taken her from broadcasting to a high-powered job in government, to working for a major multinational in just over a decade. In spite of all she has achieved, Jess has dared to step out of the workforce twice – first to travel through Europe for six months, then to travel the world for a year with her beloved, Eamon. This last trip happened on the spur of the moment: 'I knew that I was ready to leave my job, and exploring the world felt like a wonderful alternative. I felt liberated, brave and excited.' Like most, Jess still had to face her anxieties: 'I didn't want to let my boss or the people I was working with down. I worked hard in the last few weeks to finish things thoroughly, and can remember being completely exhausted by the time we got onto the plane.' When Jess looks back at this fear, she realises it was in part associated with her faith. 'I treasure my Catholic upbringing, but I definitely have a full quotient of Catholic guilt. I think I am quite prone to worrying about how my words or actions impact on others. This isn't always a bad thing, but I think I spent more energy than required in thinking about how to resign.'

Jess's fear about money also surfaced just before they left: 'It became apparent that our apartment wasn't going to be let easily, and that the rent we would get wasn't going to cover our mortgage. This was when a feeling of panic about running out of money began. The apartment wasn't rented until we had been away for over a month, but by then I had resigned myself to the fact that our trip was going to be more expensive than we had originally planned.' In part this fear was due to Jess's family background: 'I grew up in a household where my mother was sick and unable to work, and with a father who worked incredibly hard, but who was always worried about earning enough money to cover costs. I didn't realise I had the same tendency.' The trip proved liberating on so many levels. 'Three-and-a-half weeks of hiking through the Himalayan mountains helped me forget about the world back home and any fears associated with it.'

Jess was out of the workforce for just under a year. 'We had originally planned twelve months' travelling, but decided to spend a month's budget travelling to the Galapagos Islands for a week, so the trade-off was coming home a few weeks early.' They began their time away in Nepal, then travelled to Thailand, Cambodia, Vietnam and Laos. They had summer in Ireland with Eamon's family, then headed to Egypt. The next stop was New York, then on to Central and South America for several months. This time out has transformed Jess's perspective: 'I saw first-hand how the world is intricately interconnected, how one country's behaviour impacts another, typically in a very detrimental way. I was shocked to see the results of decades of interference by the West through Indochina and Latin America.'

Not only did Jess develop a deeper respect for other cultures, she and Eamon developed a love and appreciation for bird life during their travels. 'We surprised ourselves at how much time we spent watching birds, and the joy we experienced from them, whether they were eagles and buzzards circling above us as we hiked in Nepal, or the elusive condors gliding through a canyon in Chile. I am sure a great part of this discovery was that we actually had time to stop, watch and appreciate nature. Back in the city it is easy to rush through life without taking the time to appreciate the glory of birds, trees and the fresh air.'

Another great insight for Jess was how few material possessions were needed to survive: 'A guide book, a good pair of hiking boots, a pocket knife, a sleeping bag and medication for tummy ailments are the essentials. Any luxuries quickly became something else to carry and were discarded or given away. It was wonderful to be liberated from my clothes, make-up, shoes and other trappings that come with working and living in a city.' For Jess, perhaps the greatest lesson was one of relativities between life in the developed world and that of the Third World: 'In many towns where we slept, the average daily wage was less than $US1 per day. Children of four would never start school, as they were working by then, and people who grew vegetables couldn't afford to eat them.'

For Jess the context in which she will now work has been changed forever – so much of what she took for granted she now values, and so much of what seemed important has faded from view. 'I met so many people facing enormous obstacles to achieving a better life for their children, and yet they often seemed more content than we are. They are also more generous of spirit and obtain an almost sacred pleasure from their families.' When Jess and Eamon arrived home, they were both offered contract jobs within two weeks and have been working ever since. Determined not to end up in a rut, they are currently developing new plans for their working lives and for their lives beyond work.

Matthew's story

We can become so fixated on distant goals that we can get lost in the future. Part of the adventure of life is in setting our intent, then allowing each moment to unfold – that's the only way we can remain alive to life's wider possibilities and be inspired by them. Ever since he entered the workforce, Matthew had worked in the finance sector, but over the years the job began to pall. He wanted to make the break, but wasn't sure what to do next, so he decided he should take time out. This decision proved difficult – 'I struggled with the fact I was stepping away from the corporate world, where I felt a certain comfort in the security of a regular pay cheque. My girlfriend and I were leaving behind our apartment, the opportunity to build a career, and any hope of buying a place of our own – in the near future at least. This scared the hell out of me, as I was thirty-two at the time – I felt time was getting away.' Matthew's fears were based on how he'd assumed his life should unfold: 'When I was younger, I had all these notions of when I would achieve certain career goals – buy a place, get married and have a family.'

Matthew was away for nine months. He and Amy travelled through the United States and to Mexico. One of his most lasting memories of his time out is of a Mayan ruin near the Mexican town of Palenque: 'We had an awe-inspiring experience with howler monkeys swinging from branches one hundred feet above us. We sat there mesmerised in the intense jungle heat, surrounded by mountains and the thickest jungle I've ever seen.' These and many other experiences have enabled Matthew to take a much more inclusive view of his life and what he wants. 'An immensely liberating aspect of the trip has been the realisation that we all run to different schedules, and that I don't need to follow any set path.' He also learned 'not to judge success in terms of material possession or societal stature, but to appreciate the diversity and strength different people bring to this world'. This breathing space also gave him a great love of the natural world; he is now a passionate gardener and cook. Among other things, he and Amy enjoy finding ways to become more self-sufficient – in making their own pasta, and pesto from the basil they grow.

Family, friends and a more meaningful lifestyle are much more important to Matthew now. While he's returned to the finance sector, he has a very different perspective on work: 'I have an ability to look beyond whatever is happening and appreciate that there is a bigger, more important picture.' Back in the city, Matthew and Amy are saving and refocusing their life skills, so they can live in the country. Environmental concerns are now central, as is the ability to provide a genuinely nurturing climate for their future family. Matthew gets very frustrated by the complaints of friends who are clinging on to jobs they hate: 'We get too caught up in things. We don't allow ourselves to enjoy life. We keep promising ourselves it'll happen some time in the future.' Those around Matthew regard him as brave: 'I'm not brave. I just know it's what I have to do to be happy and fulfilled,' he admits.

Lena's story

Even though we might feel inspired to make a move, there are often factors that can test our resolve. Lena is an extremely competent sales executive who has worked in magazines for most of her professional life. Her progress at work had been impressive and her continued success was assured, but Lena began to feel increasingly restless, in spite of her many achievements. After an unsatisfying personal relationship, and having undergone the rigours of a takeover and emerged intact, she felt more than ready for some time out. Even though the economy was slowing down and the job market was shrinking, her impulse to travel remained strong. 'People said I was brave to go, but in all honesty it would have been cowardly to stay,' Lena admits. 'I still had to deal with issues around financial security and stepping into the unknown. I was also aware that what I planned to do wasn't considered conventional or smart in career terms, but underlying all this was a real sense of rightness in what I'd decided to do.'

Lena's travel plans were already well advanced when she met a wonderful man. Part of her wanted to stay and see where this new relationship might take her, but Lena knew she still needed time out. Unless she got away, she feared her life might end up being more of the same. 'I'd invested so much emotional energy in daring to make the break – I didn't want to sell myself short.'

Leaving her job, her friends, and the possibility of a fulfilling new relationship, Lena took off around the world for five-and-a-half months, catching up with a number of friends and seeing numerous countries, including Cuba, Mexico and Greece. While she was away, she kept in touch with her new man, and at the end of her travels he came to meet her on her final leg, so they could have a little time together before travelling home to their new life. Looking back, Lena believes that far from jeopardising their fledgling relationship, her time away gave them both the best possible start, because their relationship began honestly and was free of any baggage that a change in her travel plans might have created. This time away also gave Lena a much-needed perspective that is hard to find in a busy job. It gave her real space for herself, enabling her to immerse herself more fully in the world around her: 'When you're away for a while you're in a different space. You experience an expansiveness we don't tend to encounter in everyday life. It enables you to see every facet of life – your own life and the people and cultures you're experiencing – it's amazing.'

On her return home, Lena then landed an excellent job in a much sought-after magazine house. Not only has Lena's new job delivered a new level of career satisfaction, all the positive cultural aspects that were missing in her last job are present in her current role. She is convinced that although work is no longer her whole focus, her work is even better, and that her whole experience of work is far richer as a result: 'While I'd never compromise my professional standards, I don't have that same need to prove myself in that driven kind of way, which leaves me free to work with greater ease and to encourage others, and to gain the enjoyment of seeing them develop.' To all those who feel the need for time out, Lena advises us not to let our fears hold us back: 'Listen to your gut, then go for it, because once you make the decision, life will open up for you,' Lena smiles. Two years on from her travels Lena is married, still enjoying her work, and is about to embark on a new journey as she awaits the birth of her first child.

TAKING TIME OUT

Perhaps it is time for more space. Why not consider the following questions? Simply write down the first responses you get, so you can benefit from all your inner voice is trying to tell you.

- Where would you most like to be right now?
- What is holding you back from travelling there?
- What qualities about this place appeal to you?
- When you think of this place, how does it make you feel?
- How does this compare with how you feel at present?
- What are you going to do about this?

In this moment you are standing on the brink of something important – don't be afraid, be excited. Remember that even a journey of a thousand miles begins with one step.

on greatness

Life is no brief candle to me; it is a sort of splendid torch which I have got hold of for the moment, and I want to make it burn as brightly as possible before handing it on to future generations.
GEORGE BERNARD SHAW

We have an immense capacity for greatness, and so as we seek to enhance our experience of work, let us shed our indifference, helplessness and cynicism. Let us shift our focus beyond how work is right now to how it might be, and begin to embrace the many possibilities in each working moment to uplift the human spirit and meet our material goals. Then as our vision expands, we will start to feel alive again – to be courageous, to use our imagination, to sense opportunities where there seemed to be none. The more authentic we are, the more we cherish our freedom over the need to belong. And while we no longer need the approval of others, neither are we proud or self-seeking, because we see how soulless our lives become when we separate ourselves from those we work with. Instead, we seek ways to enable others to be a genuine part of our working life. We then see the wisdom of striving to achieve our personal best, rather than winning at all costs.

As our numbing sense of isolation dissolves, so too will our neediness. It is no difficulty then for us to be generous in victory and in defeat, to admit we are sometimes mistaken, because no-one is right all the time. The more meaningfully we work, the more we are able to take genuine pleasure in our achievements and to hold them lightly. Still there will be times when we wrestle with our demons, but we will never allow them to blight or restrict our lives, because no situation is beyond hope. Rather, we see our struggles at work as the means by which we can embrace our inherent greatness. As we take on these challenges, each working day becomes a profound gift, and each person we meet an opportunity to understand more of ourselves and others. As we get a growing sense of all we are capable of at work, we realise that it is not enough to dream the big dreams – we also need to make them a reality. And while we will not succeed with every project we undertake, we will be successful beyond our wildest dreams, and no moment of our working lives need be in vain.

What else should our lives be but a continual series of beginnings, of painful settings out into the unknown, pushing off from the edge of consciousness into the mystery of what we have not yet become?
DAVID MALOUF, *AN IMAGINARY LIFE*

resources

BOOKS

Anderson, Ray C., *Mid-Course Correction. Toward a Sustainable Enterprise: The Interface Model*, The Peregrinzilla Press, Atlanta, Georgia, 1998.

Ban Breathnach, Sarah, *Romancing the Ordinary: A Year of Simple Splendour*, Simple Abundance Press, New York, 2002.

Bek, Lilla with Philippa Pullar, *To the Light*, Unwin Paperbacks, London, 1985.

Bell, Derrick, *Ethical Ambition: Living a Life of Meaning and Worth*, Bloomsbury, London, 2002.

Brennan, Barbara Ann, *Light Emerging: The Journey of Personal Healing*, Bantam, New York, 1993.

——, *Hands of Light: A Guide to Healing Through the Human Energy Field*, Bantam, New York, 1987.

Cadzow, Jane, 'Kids? What Kids', *Good Weekend* Magazine, 17–18 August 2002.

Cameron, Julia with Mark Bryan, *The Artist's Way: A Spiritual Path to Higher Creativity*, Putnam, New York, 1995.

Coelho, Paulo, *The Manual of the Warrior of Light*, translated by Margaret Jull Costa, HarperCollins, London, 2002.

Cowan, James, *Journey to the Inner Mountain: In the Desert with St Antony*, Hodder Headline, Sydney, 2001.

Dalai Lama, His Holiness the, *Advice on Dying: And Living a Better Life*, translated and edited by Jeffrey Hopkins, Rider, London, 2002.

Elkington, John, *Cannibals With Forks: The Triple Bottom Line of 21st Century Business*, John Wiley and Sons, Hoboken, New Jersey, 1998. Reproduced with permission of John Wiley & Sons Ltd on behalf of Capstone Publishing Ltd.

Estès, Clarissa Pinkola, *Women Who Run With the Wolves: Contacting the Power of the Wild Woman*, Rider, London, 1992.

Goleman, Daniel, *Destructive Emotions and How We Can Overcome Them: A Dialogue with the Dalai Lama*, Bloomsbury, London, 2003.

Hamilton, Clive, *Growth Fetish*, Allen & Unwin, Sydney, 2003.

Hanh, Thich Nhat, *No Death, No Fear: Comforting Wisdom for Life*, Rider, London, 2002.

Hilton, Steve and Giles Gibbons, *Good Business: Your World Needs You*, Texere, New York, 2002.

Housden, Roger, *Chasing Rumi: A Fable About Finding the Heart's True Desire*, Harper, San Francisco, 2002.

Jung, C.G., *Memories, Dreams and Reflections*, recorded and edited by Aniela Jaffé, translated by Richard and Clara Winston, Fontana, London, 1963.

Kornfield, Jack, *A Path With Heart: A Guide Through the Perils and Promises of Spiritual Life*, Bantam, New York, 1993.

Linn, Denise, *Sacred Space: Clearing and Enhancing the Energy of Your Home*, Rider, London, 1995.

MacEowen, Frank, *The Mist-Filled Path: Celtic Wisdom for Exiles, Wanderers and Seekers*, New World Library, Novato, California, 2002. (extracts reproduced with kind permission New World Library, Novato, CA 94949, www.newworldlibrary.com)

Mackenzie, Vicki, *Why Buddhism?: Westerners in Search of Wisdom*, Allen & Unwin, Sydney, 2001.

Malouf, David, *An Imaginary Life: A Novel*, Chatto and Windus, London, 1978. Used by permission of The Random House Group Ltd.

Martin, Jesse with John Carnegie, *Dream On: The Journey of Kijana – Making it Happen*, Hardie Grant Books, Melbourne, 2002.

O'Donohue, John, *Anam Cara: Spiritual Wisdom from the Celtic World*, Bantam, London, 1997.

Rawles, Simon, 'The Killing Game', *Sunday Magazine, Sunday Telegraph*, 8 December 2002.

Roach, Michael, *The Diamond Cutter: The Buddha on Managing Your Life and Your Business*, Doubleday, New York, 2000.

Roberts, Josie, *The Wellington Women's Loan Fund Wahine Putea: A Ten Year Herstory*, Wellington Women's Loan Fund/Wahine Putea, Wellington, 2003.

Shan, Kwong Kuen, *The Cat and the Tao*, William Heinemann, London, 2002.

Sheldrake, Rupert, *Dogs That Know When Their Owners Are Coming Home: And Other Unexplained Powers of Animals*, Hutchinson, London, 1999.

White Eagle, *The Quiet Mind: Sayings of White Eagle*, White Eagle Publishing Trust, Liss, Hampshire, England, 1972.

Zukav, Gary, *The Seat of the Soul: An Inspiring Vision of Humanity's Spiritual Destiny*, Rider, London, 1990. Used by permission of The Random House Group Ltd.

WEBSITES

Associative Economics Network (www.associative-economics.com) promotes environmental sustainability and human rights in the workplace through its research, publications, and events, and through its *Journal of Associative Economics*.

Business for Social Responsibility (www.bsr.org) is a global network for business leaders interested in corporate social responsibility. It organises meetings, conferences and working groups, and provides training and education for executives, managers and employees.

Clean Clothes Campaign (www.cleanclothes.org) is an organisation devoted to raising awareness of and changing working conditions for those in the Third World.

Corporate Citizenship Company (www.corporate-citizenship.co.uk) provides research and consultancy services and publications, such as *Corporate Citizen Briefing*, to help companies succeed as good citizens in a changing global environment.

Corporate Social Responsibility Forum (www.csrforum.org) offers a wealth of global information for businesses wanting to be good corporate citizens, particularly in new and emerging-market economies.

Employers for Work-Life Balance (www.employersforwork-lifebalance.org.uk) provides case studies, and tools for problem-solving and benchmarking that are useful for employers, managers, human resources executives, and policy-makers.

Enlightened Business Institute (www.info@enlightenedbusiness.com) offers professional business coaching to help make businesses more profitable, creative and harmonious, based on the principles outlined in *The Diamond Cutter* by Geshe Michael Roach.

Ethical Corporation Magazine (www.ethicalcorp.com) is an excellent e-magazine covering global news, conferences,

jobs available in the corporate social responsibility area, and
conference materials.

Evolutionary Ventures (www.evolutionaryventures.com) is
devoted to healthy and sustainable lifestyles.

Institute for Management Excellence (www.itstime.com) is an
excellent website with links, events, a newsletter, products,
services, speakers and training.

Interface Sustainability Report (www.interfacesustainability.com)
gives full details of Interface Inc.'s environmental research
and initiatives.

Just Business (www.jusbiz.org) provides excellent information,
resources, forums and links on how different organisations
are tackling global and ethical issues.

Natural Step, The (www.naturalstep.org) is an international
organisation providing professional services to business and
governments, up-to-date advice and research on achieving
a sustainable environment.

World Business Academy (www.worldbusiness.org) produces
case studies, political, social and economic forecasts, articles
on global reconstruction and much more. It publishes
a weekly newsletter, *Connections*.

Zadek Net (www.zadek.net) is an excellent resource reporting
on global corporate social responsibility initiatives.

index